# Mainly the Truth

# Mainly the Truth

—ꟽ— INTERVIEWS WITH —ꟽ—

# MARK TWAIN

Edited by Gary Scharnhorst

The University of Alabama Press • Tuscaloosa

Copyright © 2009
The University of Alabama Press
Tuscaloosa, Alabama 35487-0380
All rights reserved
Manufactured in the United States of America
Designer: Michele Myatt Quinn
Typeface: ACaslon Pro

∞

The paper on which this book is printed meets the minimum
requirements of American National Standard for Information
Sciences-Permanence of Paper for Printed Library Materials,
ANSI Z39.48-1984.

Library of Congress Cataloging-in-Publication Data

Twain, Mark, 1835–1910.
    Mainly the truth: interviews with Mark Twain / edited by Gary
Scharnhorst.
    p.   cm.—(Studies in American literary realism and naturalism)
    ISBN 978-0-8173-5539-5 (pbk.: alk. paper)—ISBN 978-0-
8173-8237-7 (electronic) 1. Twain, Mark, 1835–1910—Interviews.
2. Authors, American—19th century—Interviews. I. Scharnhorst,
Gary. II. Title.
    PS1331.A2 2009
    818'.409—dc22                          2008025565

# Contents

# Introduction

Mark Twain was "the Lincoln of our literature," or so his friend W. D. Howells once called him. Like the sixteenth President, he was born into an impoverished family in a slave-holding state. Like Lincoln, he was an autodidact who succeeded against all odds as the result of ambition and native genius. He was a cornpone philosopher who spoke the language of the commoner and earned the confidence of kings. Like Lincoln, Mark Twain was an erudite raconteur *extraordinaire*, eloquent and quotable on topics from General Grant and the Civil War to the injustice of slavery and the promise of the American nation. And like Honest Abe, he understood intuitively the power of the press and when and how to talk with reporters.

Mark Twain usually tried to avoid them. "I have never yet met a man who attempted to interview me whose report of the process did not try very hard to make me out an idiot," he complained while in St. Louis in 1882. Sometimes he asked interviewers to paraphrase his comments rather than quote him directly because, as a writer by trade, he preferred to sell his words in books and magazines rather than give them away to newspapers. Still, he recognized the publicity value of interviews, particularly while he was on his lecture tours. More to the point, Twain was a pioneer in what we today call the "celebrity interview." At the home of a friend in Boston in November 1905, moreover, he held a "combination interview" or what was in effect an early press conference. According to Louis J. Budd, the dean of Mark Twain scholars, Twain "was probably interviewed more often" than any other author of his time. His conversations were often oral performances like those he delivered on stage. His interview with the *St. Louis Republic* shortly before his departure for Europe in 1894, with its ludicrous digressions, free associations, and evasions, for example, reads like another version of his sketch "Jim Blaine and His Grandfather's Old Ram" in *Roughing It* (1872). Twain frequently commented in interviews, too, on his own writings and on other writers (e.g., Howells, Henry James, Hawthorne, Lewis Carroll, Walter Scott, Dickens, George Washington Cable, and Bret Harte). His wife Olivia and his daughters Jean, Susy, and Clara make cameo appearances, as do several of his employees and domestic staff, including especially Katy Leary, Sherman Everett, and Isabel Lyon, as well as such friends and associates as Joseph Twichell, Rudyard Kipling, Harriet Beecher Stowe, Horace Bixby, Thomas Wentworth Higginson, Henry H. Rogers, George Bernard Shaw, and Albert Bigelow Paine.

In all, well over two hundred and fifty interviews with Mark Twain before his death in 1910 are known to exist. (I refer the curious reader to my annotated edition of *Mark Twain: The Complete Interviews*, published by the University of Alabama Press in 2006.) Neither private correspondence nor published writings, they represent another form of "autobiographical dictation" recorded over a period of nearly forty years. From that edition I have culled the complete texts of or excerpts from 128 interviews, nearly half of all those known to exist, for a more general audience. I have designed this edition to be something of a buffet, a variety of flavors to be tasted, a fair sampling of a full-course meal. The reader will discover here a syrupy Twain, a salty Twain, and an irascible Twain spewing bile. He was, after all, a much more complex and interesting figure than the white-suited humorist of the Mark Twain impersonators. In his most relaxed moments, Twain acknowledged his fondness for billiards, described his summers at Quarry Farm in the hills outside Elmira, New York, and joked about fashion, including his famous white serge suit. He reminisced about his years in Nevada and California and about his trip to Europe and the Holy Land in 1867. Though his interviews we follow him on his sentimental journeys in the spring of 1902 to Missouri, including his hometown of Hannibal, where he visited for the last time some of the playmates he had known as a child; and in June and July 1907 to England to receive an honorary Litt.D. from Oxford University. We find him at his first football game, the contest between the Princeton Tigers and Yale Elis in November 1900. And we learn about his work habits and writing methods, including his plans for an entirely new type of autobiography not to be published until at least a century after his death.

In his more serious moods, Twain defended woman's suffrage and the aborted Russian revolution of 1905. When Maxim Gorky came to the U. S. to raise money for the revolution, Mark Twain welcomed him. "I'm a revolutionist," he insisted, "by birth, breeding, principle, and everything else. I love all revolutions no matter where or when they start." His words echo those of Hank Morgan, the hero of his novel *A Connecticut Yankee in King Arthur's Court* (1889). He elsewhere ridiculed the failed attempts to ban *Adventures of Huckleberry Finn* (1885) in Denver in 1902 and *Eve's Diary* (1907) in Worcester, Massachusetts, in 1906. He scorned Mary Baker Eddy and the Church of Christ. Science no less in his interviews than in his essay *Christian Science* (1907). He satirized prohibition no less in them than in *Huck Finn,* where he has Pap take the pledge and then trade for a jug of forty-rod and he has the duke and king preach a temperance sermon which "didn't make enough for them both to get drunk on." Twain discussed such topics in these interviews as his failed investment in the Paige typesetting machine and his ensuing bankruptcy; and he was loquacious with reporters at virtually every stop on his 1895–96 round-the-world lecture tour, which enabled him to pay off his creditors.

In one of the most entertaining and vitriolic of these interviews, dated June 10, 1883, Twain excoriated C. C. Duncan, the captain of the *Quaker City,* the ship that carried him and the "pilgrims" to Europe and the Holy Land. This excursion became the basis of Twain's first important book, *The Innocents Abroad* (1869), and Duncan became the butt of Twain's jokes for years afterward. "Enough brains could not be found in a C. C. Duncan family to run the kitchen of a Sixth Ward restaurant respectably," he declared in the interview, before concluding that the captain was merely "an old piece of animated flatulence." Duncan was not amused. Less than a week later, the captain filed suit in U. S. District Court for criminal libel, claiming damages of $100,000. The case was brought to trial on March 3, 1884, and a decision rendered on May 12. The court awarded Duncan twelve cents in damages to his reputation.

Occasionally Twain voiced his well-known views about human nature and the "damned human race" in conversations with reporters. He joked that the pacifists who convened in New York in April 1907 may have warmed themselves in the illusion of their moral superiority, but they had not inaugurated "the millennium of universal peace" because "human nature hasn't changed in the past five thousand years." Nor did he trust any autobiography because it was "not in human nature to write the truth about itself." As for the faculty of conscience, it was "a nuisance," which may explain why in *Tom Sawyer* only Huck, unlike the other two boys, "slept the sleep of the conscience-free and the weary" on Jackson's Island, and why Twain once described *Huck Finn* as "a book of mine where a sound heart and a deformed conscience come into collision and conscience suffers defeat." After all, Huck rationalizes that he helps a slave to escape because he had been "brung up wicked" and couldn't help becoming an accessory to crime.

In his interviews, too, Twain delineated his theory of humor, one of the few sources of solace and consolation he believed was available in this vale of tears. "Against the assault of laughter, nothing can stand," as he wrote in one of his "Mysterious Stranger" manuscripts. According to Budd, in fact, Twain's interviews contain "his most detailed view of humor and humorists." Twain insisted that no one can be "properly funny" who is "not capable at times of being very serious. And more: the two are as often as not simultaneous." He explained that "humor is created by contrasts" and he illustrated the point by noting that a mourner at a funeral "is quite likely to be persecuted with humorous thoughts." This tenet of his theory accounts for the many hilarious funerals (or "fun'ls") in Twain's fiction, from Buck Fanshaw's "send-off" in *Roughing It*, to Tom, Huck, and Ben Rogers's appearance before a "sold" congregation in the midst of their funeral in *The Adventures of Tom Sawyer* (1876), to the "obsequies" for Peter Wilkes in *Huck Finn*, a scene "all full of tears and flapdoodle" as Huck tells it, when the town undertaker must quiet a dog howling in the cellar by whacking it with a stick. In the same interview, in fact, Twain narrated one of the many humorous stories in this collection which may be new to readers—a delightfully gruesome one about a funeral. In other interviews he reminisced about his "first vacation," when he stowed away aboard a packet at the age of seven, and the first time he stole a watermelon and then "saved" from perdition the farmer from whom he stole it. Sometimes, too, he expressed some of his familiar witticisms (e.g., "It is noble to be good; it is still nobler to show others how to be good, and much less trouble").

In several of these interviews, as in his essay "How to Tell a Story" (1895), Twain also distinguished among the various types of national humors. "The difference lies in the mode of expression," he asserted. The American brand of humor "is quieter, more modified, and more subtle" than others, such as the English or French. But make no mistake, he added elsewhere: types of humor may differ by nation, but the trait of humor is universal. "Every man in the world is a humorist" and "the quality of humor is not a personal or a national monopoly," he said. "It's as free as salvation, and, I am afraid, far more widely distributed." He had concluded after years of travel that humor is culturally determined, that every joke in a sense is an "inside" joke because "humor, to be comprehensible to anybody, must be built upon a foundation" that is "familiar." Every nation has a distinctive sense of humor, he averred, and all of them are fully developed. Twain illustrated the point by referring to a passage in Francis Parkman's *The Oregon Trail* about the domestic lives of Indians. Parkman describes a warrior "sitting at home in his wigwam with his squaw and papooses—not the stoical, icy Indian with whom we are familiar, who wouldn't make a jest for his life or notice one that anybody else made, but the real Indian that few white men ever saw—simply rocking with mirth at some tribal witticism that probably wouldn't have commended itself in the least to Parkman."

For one of the few times in his career, Mark Twain in this interview expressed an attitude other than condescension toward Indians. For all the talk in recent years about his racial progressivism, he had a racial blindspot on the subject of Native Americans as anyone would know who has read his derogatory remarks about "Digger Indians" in his early California sketches, his derision of idealized "Cooper Indians" in *Roughing It,* and his caricature of Injun Joe in *Tom Sawyer.* For one of the few times in the records of his life, Twain at least acknowledged their humanity while in Calcutta in February 1896. He allowed that the policies of the United States government had oppressed the Indians while the Canadian government had dealt with the tribes more humanely. "Look at the difference," he said. "In Canada the Indians are peaceful and contented enough. In the United States there are continual rows with the Government, which invariably end in the red man being shot down." He attributed the difference to "the greater humanity with which the Indians are treated in Canada. In the States we shut them off into a reservation, which we frequently encroached upon. Then ensued trouble. The red men killed settlers, and of course the Government had to order out troops and put them down. If an Indian kills a white man he is sure to lose his life, but if a white man kills a redskin he never suffers according to law." Twain's view of the problem here may be simple or even naïve, but compared to virtually all of his comments on Indians recorded elsewhere he seems positively enlightened.

Ironically, whereas Twain expressed surprising sympathy for Native Americans, he expressed a surprising failure of sympathy for the plight of African Americans in the same interview. The critical consensus in recent years has been exactly the opposite: ostensibly, Twain was virulently bigoted toward Indians but a champion of the rights of black Americans. Yet when asked if the "negro difficulty" was "allied to the Red Indian question" Twain agreed but, he added, he believed "in course of time that difficulty will settle itself. The negroes at present are merely freed slaves, and you can't get rid of the effects of slavery in one or even two generations." But he was confident "things will right themselves"—after all, as he observed in a patronizing air, "We have given the negro the vote, and he must keep it." Then he was asked a question he was never asked anywhere else in the records of his life: "Is there any likelihood of intermixture?" (The interviewer apparently meant "intermarriage." After all, blacks and whites had been "intermixing" for generations, especially in the South, as the author of *Pudd'nhead Wilson*

obviously knew.) Twain addressed the question not as a racial activist or
even as a nineteenth-century racial progressive but as a segregationist:
"Not the slightest," he answered. Then the coup d'etat: "The white and
the black population will in time learn to tolerate each other and work
harmoniously for the common good. They will co-exist very much as
the different races in India have done for centuries." As late as February
1896, over ten years after the publication of *Huck Finn,* at the nadir of
race relations in the United States, only three months before the Plessy
v. Ferguson decision of the Supreme Court sanctioned Jim Crow laws
in the South, Twain endorsed racial separation along the lines of the
caste system in India. He was, after all, more a creature of his time than
of ours, and any claim to the contrary is either wishful thinking or a
pleasant lie designed to fool the public.

He was rarely at a loss for words, nor did he pull his punches or duck
controversy when he wanted to make a point. Or as Howells reminisced,
"Upon most current events he had strong opinions, and he uttered them
strongly." Never was this observation more true than in his remarks
on military imperialism at the turn of the twentieth century. Twain's
opinions on this issue are well known to readers of such essays as "To
the Person Sitting in Darkness" (1901) and "King Leopold's Soliloquy"
(1905). But his anti-imperialist message reached far more readers of
his interviews printed in newspapers with circulations in the tens or
even hundreds of thousands than readers of his essays. That is, we have
a cropped and incomplete picture of Twain's opposition to military
imperialism unless his public statements recorded in interviews are also
included. In fact, he was critical of imperialism across the board—of
Germany in South Africa, of Russia in Japan, of Belguim in the Congo,
and especially of the United States in the Philippines.

When Twain returned to America in October 1900 after a five-year
absence, he was met by a bevy of reporters who literally interviewed
him on the gangplank. When he left on his round-the-world lecture
tour in 1895 to pay off his creditors, he told them, he had been a "red
hot imperialist. I wanted the American eagle to go screaming into the
Pacific. It seemed tiresome and tame for it to content itself with the

Rockies." But over the years, especially as he had traveled to countries such as India and South Africa, he had changed his mind. He approved of the U. S. withdrawal from China in the aftermath of the Boxer Rebellion. As for military intervention in the Philippines, he said,

> I thought it would be a real good thing to do. I said to myself, "Here are a people who have suffered for three centuries. We can make them as free as ourselves, give them a government and a country of their own, put a miniature of the American constitution afloat in the Pacific, start a brand new republic to take its place among the free nations of the world. It seemed to me a great task to which we had addressed ourselves.
>
> But I have thought some more, since then, and I have read carefully the treaty of Paris, and I have seen that we do not intend to free but to subjugate the people of the Philippines. We have gone there to conquer, not to redeem. We have also pledged the power of this country to maintain and protest the abominable system established in the Philippines by the Friars.
>
> It should, it seems to me, be our pleasure and duty to make those people free and let them deal with their own domestic questions in their own way. And so I am an anti-imperialist. I am opposed to having the eagle put its talons on any other land.

The war to liberate the Philippines had become instead an experiment in Manifest Destiny.

Nor was this the only occasion on which he expressed such views. In an interview with the *New York Herald* published on January 20, 1901, but conducted on January 5, Twain admitted that he had "said a thing last night in a speech that I didn't mean to say. It just slipped out because I had been writing an article on the subject. I didn't intend to say it there." The article was "To the Person Sitting in Darkness." The interviewer noted that the impromptu "thing" was "in reference to Presidential policy in the Philippines. I showed him the paragraph as reported in the daily papers." Twain had been invited to address the City Club of New York, a pro-civic reform, anti-Tammany Hall organization, the evening before. He had been expected to criticize corrupt local politics, but in a digression he had also criticized American foreign policy. Most of the ten or so city dailies had covered the event, and most had reported his remarks. Toward the close of his speech Twain commented on the recent presidential campaign and allowed that he had voted for neither William Jennings Bryan nor William McKinley. He abstained because he supported neither Bryan's "wildcat financial theories" about free silver (the "wildcat" metaphor refers originally to valueless silver mines on the Comstock) nor "the man who sends our boys as volunteers out into the Philippines to get shot down under a polluted flag." Most of the New York dailies quoted this line in their columns the next day—but only one paper, the New York *Sun,* included in its report its full context, specifically the response to it by the next speaker and most of the audience. According to the *Sun,* "The statement about the President, his Philippines policy and the polluted flag was not received with enthusiasm" and the applause when Mark Twain sat down was "in marked contrast to that which he received when he got up." The next speaker, the author and editor St. Clair McKelway, chided Twain for his words. "I cannot agree with him in his estimate of the able and dignified President of the United States and I cannot agree with him that our soldiers are fighting behind a dishonored musket and under a disgraced flag on the other side of the seas." McKelway's comment "was received with great applause" by the audience while Twain on the dais in full sight of the crowd "simply puffed away at a stub of his cigar."

Many Twain aficionados are familiar with his "Whittier Birthday Speech," when in December 1877 he failed miserably to entertain the audience assembled at the Brunswick Hotel in Boston with a comic story about three deadbeats named Ralph Waldo Emerson, Henry Wadsworth Longfellow, and Oliver Wendell Holmes—with these three dignitaries present. Instead of laughter, the silence in the room, as W. D. Howells remembered, "weighed many tons to the square inch." Twenty-four years later, Mark Twain suffered a similar response to his public criticism of President William McKinley and what he considered to be misguided U.S. policy in the Philippines, and he refused to retract or apologize for his statements. As late as 1907, in an interview with the *Brooklyn Eagle* Twain reiterated his belief that the occupation of the Philippines was "a stain upon our flag that can never be effaced." With good reason he repeatedly described himself as a "mugwump" or a political independent, damned the infection of the body politic by such robber barons as Jay Gould, and called for a third party alternative to the Democrats and Republicans.

No one these days presumes to impeach Mark Twain's patriotism. On the contrary, he set an example of patriotic dissent in his condemnation of the Philippines war and his criticism of the President. In the same interview with the *Brooklyn Eagle,* he elaborated on his notion of patriotism. He noted that Samuel Johnson well over a century earlier had said it was "the last refuge of the scoundrel—and I believe he was right." Rather than teach them to honor the professed values of a nation, he observed, "today in the public schools we teach our children to salute the flag, and this is our idea of instilling in them patriotism." The "true citizenship," the true patriotism, he insisted, "is to protect the flag from dishonor—to make it the emblem of a nation that is known to all nations as true and honest and honorable." In this spirit, he sued a New York cab driver for price gouging a month after his return to the U. S. in 1900 and successfully argued in court that he was simply "doing this just as any citizen who is worthy of the name of citizen should do. He has no choice. He has a distinct duty." Briefly put, more Americans learned about Mark Twain's politics and his ideas about citizenship from his interviews than from his political essays.

While these interviews do not disclose a "new" Mark Twain, they certainly reveal more than we had known before about the "old" one. His friend Howells reminisced shortly after Twain's death about the circumstances of his interview with reporters during Maxim Gorky's visit to the U. S. in the spring of 1906. Gorky was traveling with a woman not his wife and as a result he had been expelled from his New York hotel. Howells was visiting Twain at his home on Fifth Avenue at the time and remembered that a group of reporters came to the door for a comment on the controversy.

"What would you do?" he asked me.

"I wouldn't see them," I said, and then Clemens went directly down to them. How or by what means he appeased their voracity I cannot say, but I fancy it was by the confession of the exact truth, which was harmless enough. They went away joyfully, and he came back in radiant satisfaction with having seen them. Of course he was right and I wrong.

Deliberately or not, Howells in his memoir of Twain echoes ("the confession of the exact truth") what Huckleberry Finn says about the author at the beginning of his *Adventures* ("mainly he told the truth"). Just as the reporters left "joyfully," Twain returned to his parlor "in radiant satisfaction with having seen them." The experience was hardly a novel one. After more than thirty years, his encounters with interviewers had by then become routine.

Gary Scharnhorst
University of New Mexico

# Mainly the Truth

# 1

# Only Joking

## Nov 1874–June 1883

During the first flowering of his reputation as a humorist, Twain enjoyed many of his greatest literary successes, with the publication of *The Innocents Abroad* (1869), *Roughing It* (1872), "Old Times on the Mississippi" (1875), *The Adventures of Tom Sawyer* (1876), *A Tramp Abroad* (1880), *The Prince and the Pauper* (1881), and *Life on the Mississippi* (1883). In addition, he worked intermittently during this decade on *Adventures of Huckleberry Finn*.

### "Mark Twain / His Recent Walking Feat"
*Hartford Times*, 14 November 1874

As most readers of the *Times* are aware, Mark Twain, known to a select circle of relatives as Mr. Samuel L. Clemens, recently undertook, in company with his friend and pastor, Rev. J. H. Twichell, to achieve pedestrian fame. . . . Feeling certain that the public would like to know from the adventurous Twain's own lips the details of the journey, a *Times* reporter called on him at Young's Hotel last evening and enjoyed the following conversation with him:

Reporter—Mr. Clemens, the readers of our paper would like to learn the particulars of your journey from Hartford.

Mark Twain—Certainly, sir. We originally intended to leave Hartford on Monday morning and take a week to walk to Boston, just loafing along the road, and walking perhaps fifteen or eighteen miles a day, just for the sake of talking and swapping experiences, and inventing fresh ones, and simply enjoying ourselves in that way without caring whether we saw anything or found out anything on the road or not. We were to make this journey simply for the sake of talking. But then our plan was interrupted by Mr. Twichell having to go to a Congregational Conference of Ministers at Bridgeport, so we could not start till Thursday. We thought we would simply do two days, walking along comfortably all the time. . . . We got so ambitious, however, the first day, and felt so lively that we walked twenty-eight miles.

Reporter—Did you experience any fatigue at the end of that day's walk?

Twain—Well, at the end of that day when we stopped for the night I didn't feel fatigued, and I had no desire to go to bed, but I had a pain through my left knee which interrupted my conversation with lockjaw every now and then. The next day at twelve past five we started again, intending to do forty miles that day, believing we could still make Boston in three days. But we didn't make the forty miles. Finding it took me three or four hours to walk seven miles, as my knee was still so stiff that it was walking on stilts—or, if you can imagine such a thing, it was though I had wooden legs with pains in them—we just got a team and drove to the nearest railway station, hitched on, and came up here.

Reporter—You could doubtless have accomplished the journey on foot, sir?

Twain—Oh, our experience undoubtedly demonstrates the possibility of walking. By and by, when we get an entire week to make this pedestrian excursion, we mean to make it.

Reporter—When you renew the experiment, do you intend to follow any different plan?

Twain—No, I would just follow the old Hartford and Boston stage-road of old times. It takes you through a lot of quiet, pleasant villages, away from the railroads, over a road that now has so little travel that you don't have to be skipping out into the bushes every moment to let a wagon go by, because no wagon goes by. And then you see you can talk all you want, with nobody to listen to what you say; you can have it all to yourself, and express your opinions pretty freely.

Reporter—Were the opportunities for refreshment by the way good?

Twain—Well, I suppose pretty fair, especially if you are walking all day.

Reporter—Do you intend to lecture in Boston, now you are here?

Twain—No, not at all. I simply intend to go back home again. I shall lie over Sunday to rest, and let Mr. Twichell have a chance to preach at Newton. You may as well say that we expect hereafter to walk up to Boston, and after we get into the habit of this sort of thing, we may extend it perhaps to New Orleans or San Francisco.

## "Political Views of a Humorist"
### New York Herald, 28 August 1876, p. 3

After a rather dusty ride of five miles uphill from Elmira, the *Herald* representative met Samuel L. Clemens (Mark Twain), temporarily residing at Quarry Hill farm. . . . He took me to his studio, an octagonal structure, still further up hill, and commanding a romantic view of Elmira and its surroundings for miles. . . .

HERALD CORRESPONDENT—Well, Mark, now we are in your cozy and breezy studio, suppose I interview you in regard to your opinions respecting the present political situation?

MARK TWAIN—Politics are rather out of my line, yet not outside of my interest. I am not much of a party man, but I have opinions. I should never have pushed them before the public, but if you want to catechise me I will answer, but I want easy questions—questions which a plain answer will meet.

"You shall have them. First, which platform do you prefer?"

"That is easily answered. Platforms are of such secondary importance that I have not thought it necessary to build up a preference. In most essentials the creeds of both parties are good enough for me.

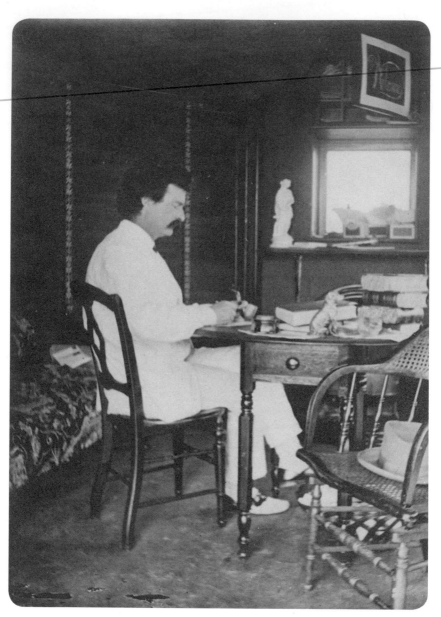

Quarry Farm study indoors.

Courtesy of the Center for Mark Twain Studies, Elmira College.

"But there is something back of the written creeds which is important. For instance, inflation and repudiation may be glossed over in a creed, but there are a good many erring people who want these things and would vote for them."

"What do you think is more important than platforms?"

"I think the men are. There used to be a party cry, 'Measures, not men.' That was in an honester day. We need to reverse that now. When you get below the politician scum—or above it, perhaps one ought to say—you will find that the solid men in both parties are equally good and equally well meaning. Both will furnish platforms which the country can survive and progress under. But of what use are these excellent platforms if the men elected upon them shamelessly ignore them and make them a dead letter? A sound and good democratic platform was powerless to save New York from the ravages of the Tweed gang; an excellent republican platform has no more been able to save the country from the ravages of the present administration's highwaymen than the pasting the four gospels on a bad man's back would be to save him from the tropical end of eternity. Platforms are not the essential things now—men are."

"Then how do you judge of your men?"

"Only by common report and their letters of acceptance."

"Which candidate do you prefer upon these grounds?"

"Hayes. He talks right out upon the important issues. You cannot mistake what he means concerning civil service, second term and the honest payment of the national debt. If you can understand what Mr. Tilden means it is only because you have got more brains than I have, but you don't look it. Mr. Tilden is a very able man; therefore I hold that he could have made himself understood. Why didn't he? Because one-half of his party believe in one thing and the other half in another, I suppose, and it was necessary to be a little vague. . . . I want to see an honest government established once more. I mean to vote for Hayes because I believe, from his own manner of talking and from all I can hear of his character and his history, that he will appoint none but honest and capable men to office. I don't care two cents what party they belong to,

I never tried to get a political office for but one man and I forgot to ask him what his politics were, but he was a clean man and mighty capable. Mr. Tilden is an old politician, dyed in the wool. History has tried hard to teach us that we can't have good government under politicians. Now, to go and stick one at the very head of the government couldn't be wise. You know that yourself."

"People speak well of both candidates, don't they?"

"I will tell you how it looks to me. I read a lot of newspapers of both creeds every day. The republicans tell me a great many things which Hayes has done; the democratic papers explain why Tilden didn't do a great many things. They keep on apologizing and apologizing all the time. I think that the woman or the candidate that has to be apologized for is a suspicious person. So do you. Now, let me urge you as an old friend to vote for Hayes—a man you don't have to apologize for."

"Well, but what do you think—"

"No, excuse me. You can't get any political elaborations out of me. I simply want to see the right man at the helm. I don't care what his party creed is. I want a man who isn't near sighted. . . . I want to see a man in the chief chair who can not only tell a buzzard when he sees it but will promptly wring its neck. I feel satisfied that Mr. Hayes is such a man; I am not satisfied that Mr. Tilden is. There, now, let us take a smoke. My opinions are important only to me. If they were important to others we would spread them all over the *Herald*. Here is your pipe. Now we will talk of things less harrowing."

## "Mark Twain's Tenets"
### *Boston Globe*, 19 March 1877, 3:2

While the well-known humorist Mark Twain was stopping at the Parker House recently, a reporter of the *Globe* called on him. . . . "You see for yourself," said Mr. Twain, puffing away at his cigar, "that I'm pretty near heaven—not theologically, of course, but by the hotel standard."

"Your room is rather high up, Mr. Twain, but it appears very cozy.

There is an elevator, I believe, is there not?"

Mr. T.—Doubtless there is; all first class hotels manage to have elevators. The fact is, I detest elevators, and I'm not ashamed to own it.

R.—Then you like walking?

Mr. T.—Much better. I do my own walking and talking and write my own books, which is more than every one can say.

R.—You don't believe in plagiarizing then?

Mr. T.—No, sir; I never plagiarize—unless I can do it successfully.

R.—Do I understand that you never have done it?

Mr. T.—No, sir; but that was probably because I wasn't successful at it.

R.—Do you believe everything that you related in *Innocents Abroad*?

Mr. T.—Absolutely everything.

R.—Do you think that the public in general do?

Mr. T.—Of course; why should they not? I related everything as I saw it.

R.—If I remember rightly you mention in *Innocents Abroad* that when you went into a hairdresser's in Paris to get shaved, he loosened your "hide" and lifted you out of the chair. Is that a correct statement, Mr. Twain?

Mr. T.—Certainly, correct to the chair; but you must remember that "statement" don't amount too much in any country—but particularly in this country.

R.—But you believe in them, nevertheless?

Mr. T.—Not even if they have the official mark. I have been trying to believe in the statements, which have been sent from Washington from time to time, but I can't make up my mind. I must tell you right here that my digestion is not so good as formerly.

R.—May I ask you what you think of President Hayes' Cabinet?

Mr. T.—It appears to me that he has made excellent selections; probably if I knew the men he has chosen immediately I might think right to the contrary.

R.—In that case I should think that you would eulogize them all the more.

Mr. T.—I never eulogize except when I don't know a person. It seems to me that the safest way is to eulogize a person you don't know.

R.—May I ask what are your politics, Mr. Twain?

Mr. T.—I am neither a Republican nor Democrat—for any length of time. Vacillation is my particular forte. During the last election, when the country thought Tilden would surely be elected President, I was a strong Tildenite; but as soon as I discovered that everything was against him, I was strong in my support for Hayes.

R.—Mr. Twain, do I infer from what you have just said, that you voted for both men?

Mr. T.—Why, of course; no one recognized me. I did all my voting in New York. I wasn't tolerated in Hartford; as soon as the people discovered that I was exerting all my strength for Hayes, they advised me kindly to leave the State. I went immediately to New York City and cast my vote for Tilden. And yet, people call this a republic!

R.—May I ask what you are now politically, Mr. Twain?

Mr. T.—Politics have completely died out within me. They don't take to me or I to them. Since I have come in possession of a conscience I begin to see through things.

R.—Then you have not had a conscience until lately?

Mr. T.—No, sir; it is only recently that I discovered it. It doesn't prove so great a blessing as I supposed it would. Only a day or two ago I exhausted my second deposit at the bank.

R.—I don't quite understand what you mean.

Mr. T.—Why, simply this: Everyone who knows that I have a conscience takes me now for a philanthropist.

R.—Do you refer to bad debts?

Mr. T.—Exactly; or, rather, I might say that they are hotel bills, which I thought were cancelled years ago. As I told you a few moments ago, since I discovered that I had a conscience I begin to see the right and wrong of things.

R.—Do you like Boston, Mr. Twain?

Mr. T.—Very well; but there seems to be a good many issues floating around here; but I suppose this is peculiar to the city. I am going to the Tabernacle this evening.

R.—Are you going merely out of curiosity, or are you going because your conscience says you must?

Mr. T.—I'm going for mere recreation. Religion often times soothes the mind and eases the conscience even if it doesn't penetrate deep into the memory."

## "Mark Twain's Opinion"

*Baltimore Gazette,* ca. 27 April 1877 rpt.
New York *World,* 28 April 1877, p. 5

Last evening a representative of the *Gazette* called to see his old friend Mark Twain at Guy's Hotel. Conversation turned on the war in Europe....

"Do you think Russia will move first on Silistria or Kalaiat?"

"Well, Nicholas is a long-headed man, but if he doesn't keep a sharp lookout all his fat will be in the fire. But I can't keep the run of the movements by the cable dispatches. Can't locate the places on Krackyourjawoff via Bullyboyyouknow onto Crushemailibet. Then I look on my European map and I don't find the places. A European map is like a blackboard with nothing on it. Leaving the industrious student of contemporaneous history to fill in the outlines. The hard part of it is that they'll go on fighting just as though good maps were to be had for the asking."

"Mr. Clemens, I think you are too severe on mapmakers. The *Evening Bugleblast,* of this city, today publishes a most carefully prepared and readable map of the seat of war. I have a copy of it here"—

"Well, I'm sorry for you, old fellow I didn't know that a strong cigar would affect you that way. You've got 'em on you bad. Why, that's a map of the St. Louis hotel in ruins."

From the war in Europe to the rumpus in the Black Hills was an easy turn.

"Having high times in the Hills, Mr. Clemens?"

"Yes; and I tell you my heart bleeds for the poor prospector. There may be gold there—I suppose there is—but there isn't the big money we hear of. The men who dig gold out of the Black Hills have got to work for it and earn it. The glitter gets into print; the tales of hardships and bitter disappointment don't. When a man comes in and tells about rich finds you must stop to consider what sort of a man he is. If he had been making a dollar or two a day, and hits on ten in the diggings, he thinks he's struck a fortune, and it isn't a bad thing; but a man with a good situation, a paying business or a thriving farm had better keep down to his work. The average man would do better to dig for clams than to go hunting for gold in the Hills. But speaking of mining and getting in big licks—in the best days of California mining, the best of it wasn't worth more than $200 a day to any digger. Now a man would have to hammer away for some time before he could make a fortune even at that and there were not many who struck it that rich." . . .

The reporter had something less than half a mile of questions wherewith to rack Mr. Clemens's brain, but he did all the talking, and the reporter had to give him respectful audience. Mr. Clemens saw a way out of the difficulty.

"Just say that you asked me the questions and I couldn't answer them."

## "The Start for Germany"
*New York Times,* 12 April 1878, p. 8

. . . Mark Twain, the innocent, who was soon to be abroad again, wore a small black silk cap, which, as one of the bystanders said, made him "look like a brakeman." Having checked of his family into the saloon, he came out upon the deck to shake hands with the new Minister.

"Where's Halstead?" said the innocent.

"I don't know," replied the Minister. "I haven't seen him today. I left him about 1 o'clock this morning."

"One o'clock!" echoed Mark Twain. "Why, you ought to have been in bed by that time."

"I know it," replied the Minister, "and I begged Reid not to keep it up the last night, but he insisted; and they were all so jolly, I couldn't get away. I've had a hard time of it the last two weeks."

"I've had just as hard a time," said Mark. "I've been railroading for two weeks and taking mixed drinks. I suppose you stick to one thing all the time—straight."

"Well, I don't know," said Bayard Taylor, "what do you call straight drinks?"

"Coffee," said Mark, "or whisky, if you drink it all the time." . . .

Mr. Samuel L. Clemens, while in one of the fits of sober earnest that strike him occasionally, said that he was going to Germany partly for the health of his family, and partly to give him the opportunity to write, which he finds he cannot do well at home.

"I am going to the most out-of-the-way place in Germany I can find," said he, "fifty miles away from any railroad, where I can sleep more than half the time. We have not rented our house in Hartford so, if we get tired soon, there is nothing to prevent us from coming back at any time; but, if we like it, we may stay for two or three years."

On being asked whether he had more *Innocents Abroad* in mind, he replied: "I am going to do some writing. I have been contemplating it for a long time, and now I'm in for it. But it will not be any more *Innocents Abroad*. That is done up and done for."

"You'd better travel this time as the Sage of Hartford," suggested Minister Taylor.

"I will," said Mark, "or the Thyme, or any other herb."

## "Mark Twain Interviewed"
### Richard Whiteing, New York *World*, 11 May 1879, p. 1

The sojourn of a certain distinguished American in Paris ought to receive more notice than I have lately given it. . . . I first asked him about the book he is now writing and he gave me the following answer:

"It is a gossipy volume of travel, and will be similar to *The Innocents Abroad* in size, and similarly illustrated. I shall draw some of the pictures for it myself. However, that need not frighten anybody, for I shall draw only a few. I think the book will not be finished in time for the summer season, but will appear in the fall. I call it a gossipy volume, and that is what it is. It talks about anything and everything, and always drops a subject the moment my interest in it begins to slacken. It is as discursive as a conversation; it has no more restraints or limitations than a fireside talk has. I have been drifting around on an idle, easy-going tramp—so to speak—for a year, stopping when I pleased, moving on when I got ready. My book has caught the complexion of the trip. In a word, it is a book written by one loafer for a brother loafer to read."

The mention of the book naturally led to the question of international copyright, of which he said:

"I think we can't tell much about the matter yet. I hope the convention of authors, which is to hold its second annual meeting in June, in London, will be able to give it a start. No doubt the authors could have achieved international copyright before this if the publishers had kept their fingers out of the pie. But they wouldn't." . . .

Finally came the inevitable question, "Why have you never written a book about England?"

"I have spent a great deal of time in England (your question is not a new one to me) and I made a world of notes, but it was of no use. I couldn't get any fun out of England. It is too grave a country. And its gravity soaks into the stranger and makes him as serious as everybody else. When I was there I couldn't seem to think of anything but deep problems of government, taxes, free trade, finance—and every night I went to bed drunk with statistics. I could have written a million books, but my publisher would have hired the common hangman to burn them. One is bound to respect England—she is one of the three great republics of the world—in some respects she is the most real republic of the three, too, and in other respects she isn't, but she is not a good text for hilarious literature. No, there wasn't anything to satirize—what I mean is, you couldn't satirize any given thing in England in any but a half-hearted way, because your conscience told you to look nearer home and you would find that very thing at your own door. A man with a humpbacked uncle mustn't make fun of another man's cross-eyed aunt."

"The English love for the lord, for instance? I don't mean the Lord of the prayer-book, but the lord of peerage."

"I couldn't gird at the English love for titles while our own love for titles was still more open to sarcasm. Take our 'Honorable,' for instance. Unless my memory has gone wholly astray, no man in America has any right to stick that word before his name; to do it is a shame, and a very poor shame at that. At the beginning of this century members of the two houses of Congress were referred to simply as 'Mr.' So-and-So. But this sham 'Honorable' has since crept in, and now it is unlawfully conferred upon members of State legislatures and even upon the mayors and city counselors of the paltriest back settlements."

## "Mr. Twain Again With Us"
### New York *World*, 3 September 1879, p. 1

On the eleventh day of April 1878, Mr. Mark Twain . . . set out for Europe on the steamer *Holsatia*. The following day he did the same thing over again, the steamship, for reasons which were explained at the time, having been obliged to come back and take a fresh start. Yesterday Mr. Twain returned. He was one of the passengers on the *Gallia*.

"There," said he, as the ship left quarantine and began her journey up the bay, "the danger is finally passed."

"To what danger do you refer, Mr. Twain?" asked a reporter for *The World*, who had been trying for ten minutes without success to lift the great humorist from a deep and silent melancholy.

"Why, you see," replied the returning wanderer, whose voice has lost none of its querulous plaintiveness by dealing with foreign tongues, "I haven't been at all certain but what we'd have to go back and begin this voyage all over again. I said to my friend Mrs. Clemens the other day, 'If they had to try twice to get us started, what reason have we to hope that they won't find it necessary to try several times before they are able to get back?' It's one of the peculiarities of sea life that, given the same circumstances, you always look for the same results. When the ship begins to roll sideways and kick up behind at the same time, I always know that I am expected to perform a certain duty. I learned it years ago on the *Quaker City*. You might suppose that I would have forgotten my part after so long a residence on shore. But there it is again. It's habit; everything connected with the sea comes down to a matter of habit. You might confine me for forty years in a Rhode Island corn patch, and at the end of that time I'd know just as well what to do when a ship begins to kick up as I do at the moment. The darkest night never confuses me in the least. It's a little singular when you look at it, ain't it? But I presume it's attributable to the solemn steadfastness of the great deep. By the way, how is *Pinafore?*"

"Beg pardon, how is what?"

"*Pinafore;* I understand you have had *Pinafore* in America. I told Sullivan and Gilbert *Pinafore* was sure to be a great success."

"Indeed! Why did you think so?"

"I didn't; that was the reason it was sure to succeed."

It was pleasant to hear Mr. Twain run on in this easy way, but the reporter, realizing that there was much that the public was burning to know, felt compelled to conduct the rest of the interview in a systematic, business-like manner.

"You sailed in the same ship with Bayard Taylor and Mr. Murat Halstead, of Cincinnati, did you not, Mr. Twain?"

"The same craft, all honor to her (Mr. Twain lifted his hat reverently), carried all three of us."

"It was said at the time that you inveighed Mr. Halstead into making the voyage by promising him free use of your linen?"

"Well"—Mr. Twain spoke leisurely—"I did tell Murat that I'd lend him a clean shirt. You see, he didn't expect to go. His wife was going and he'd sort of come down to see her safely launched. You remember the ship ran away with a party of excursionists who had got aboard to bid poor Mr. Taylor goodbye and was obliged to anchor off the Hook all night. During the evening Murat sort of got his sea-legs on and says he, 'Clemens' (he always calls me Clemens), says he, 'Clemens, if you'll lend me a shirt I believe I'll go across.' 'All right,' says I, 'I'll do it.' So Murat he fixed things with the captain and stayed aboard. We got along pretty well with winds a-middling, about nor-nor-west by sou', till we came to latitude 36, longitude 49½, and then Murat wanted his clean shirt—that is, he wanted mine. It was about three bells from noon when I took that garment to the door of Murat's stateroom. 'Here,' says I, 'clothe yourself like a prince of the realm' At eight bells Mr. Halstead came out of his apartment with his coat buttoned up to his chin and his face as red as a red, red rose. He wore his coat buttoned up to his chin all the rest of the voyage, and I never so much as got a glimpse of my shirt. There was a kind of rumor on the ship that Murat never wore that shirt or any other shirt. I don't know how true it was, but when I came to study the thing it did look to me as if I'd put a rather tough problem to the editor of the *Cincinnati Commercial,* for his neck measures eighteen inches, while mine never footed up more than fifteen, even when I had the mumps."

## "Mark Twain Back Again"
### New York *Sun,* 3 September 1879, p. 1

. . . "When I sailed in the *Batavia,*" said Mr. Clemens to the seafaring man, "I had a different opinion of the Cunard line from that which I now entertain. I objected to the prunes. I suppose you know that when the Cunarders changed from sailing to steam power, they maintained some of their old sailing ideas on the new steam propelled ships. Prunes was one of these old ideas. Why, they had regular days for things—'duff day' was Thursday, and I guess Sunday was a duff day too—that was when they served out puddings, the same as they do to sailors aboard a sailing ship. Then there were Tuesday beans, and Saturday beans, and prunes twenty-one times a week for dessert. They hunted the world for cooks and got the worst there were. Why, you could make up your bill of fare a week ahead—yes, for the return trip—but that's all done now."

## "Mark Twain Home Again"
*New York Times*, 3 September 1879, p. 8

Mr. Samuel L. Clemens . . . reached this City in the steamship *Gallia* yesterday, after an absence of a year and a half in Europe. . . .

"Yes," said he, in response to questions asked by a group of reporters who surrounded him on all sides, except that occupied by the saloon table, so thickly that he could not fill out his Custom house declaration, "I have been writing a new book, and have it nearly finished, all but the last two or three chapters. The first half of it, I guess, is finished, but the last half has not been revised yet; and when I get at it I will do a good deal of rewriting and a great deal of tearing up. I may possibly tear up the first part of it, too, and rewrite that." With all this tearing up in prospect, the book seemed in such danger of being entirely destroyed that one of the reporters suggested the production of a few chapters in advance in the newspapers, as samples; but Mr. Twain said that the manuscript was in the bottom of one of his trunks, where it could not possibly be reached. He added, however, that the book was descriptive of his latest trip and the places he visited, entirely solemn in character, like *The Innocents Abroad* and very much after the general plan of that work; and that it has not yet been named. It is to be published by the same company that brought out his other books, and is to be ready in November. "They want me to stay in New York and revise it," he continued, "but I cannot possibly do that. I am going to start tomorrow morning for Elmira, where we will stay for some time." . . .

He was particularly well pleased with the steamer. . . . "We could leave a mirror lying on the washstand, and it would not fall off. If we stood a goblet loose on the shelf at night, it would be there in the morning." Mr. Twain declined positively, however, to say whether a cocktail, left standing on the shelf at night, would be there all safe in the morning.

## "An 'Innocent' Interviewed: Mark Twain Pays a Visit to St. Louis"

*St. Louis Post-Dispatch,* 12 May 1882, p. 2

Samuel L. Clemens, Hartford, Conn., registered at the Southern this morning. . . . A *Post-Dispatch* reporter met him in the rotunda of the hotel and was received very cordially. It was only when the possibility of an interview was broached that Mr. Clemens grew slightly restive.

"I guess I haven't got time," he said. "The fact is you can say anything you like if you put it in your own words, but don't quote me saying anything. No man can get me right unless he takes it down in shorthand, very particularly, too."

"You don't love the interviewer, I see, Mr. Clemens."

"No; I don't. I have never yet met a man who attempted to interview me whose report of the process did not try very hard to make me out an idiot, and did not amply succeed, in my mind, in making him a thorough one. They try to imitate my manner of speech, and not being artists, they never succeed, you see. No, I want to fight shy of that class of people."

The reader can imagine the position of a reporter whose fate was fixed that he should write himself down as an idiot, but Twain was assured that no attempt would be made to exhibit his style of conversation. . . . Mr. Clemens melted a little and said:

"I have not been out here since 1864, I think, and I had intended on remaining some time in the city. But I waited too long at New Orleans to catch the *Baton Rouge,* the commander of which was my old master, and in consequence will have to leave tonight."

"You ought not to be in such a hurry. The newspapers represent you as being fabulously wealthy and in living in great splendor at Hartford."

"Oh, there is quite an amount of fiction in that statement. Of course I'm living at Hartford, and I had a house when I left there, but I have not gone into competition with Vanderbilt yet, and I don't think that I'll do so."

"What about the statement that humorous writing is not paying now as it did formerly?"

"That is fictional, too, I think. Is the writing that does not pay really humorous? I'm not talking about myself, but in my opinion good writing of any kind pays always."

"How is it in your case?"

"Well, I don't think that any kind of books will ever yield quite as well as the Bible and indecent works—I might say other indecent works, but that might get the church people down on me. Don't put that in, now."

"No; but, really, is there not a rich harvest in your line?"

"Now, I don't want to make an assignment, and why should I prepare a statement of my assets? I am preparing to try the public again, and my shorthand secretary accompanies me on this trip."

"What is the nature of the new work?"

"I have been writing a series of articles in the *Atlantic Monthly* on subjects connected with the Mississippi, and I found that I had got my distances a little mixed. I took this trip for the purpose of making observations on this subject. I was getting a little rusty about it."

"The new book will treat of your early life on the river?"

"Yes; altogether of that subject."

"When will it be finished?"

"In about nine months."

"And what will you call it?"

"Oh, that is the last thing to be thought about. I never write a title until I finish a book, and then I frequently don't know what to call it. I usually write out anywhere from a half dozen to dozen and a half titles, and the publisher casts his experienced eye over them and guides me largely in the selection. That's what I did in the case of *Roughing It*, and, in fact, it has always been my practice."

"You have come a little late," said the reporter, changing the conversation. "You should have been here in time for the banquet of the Army of the Tennessee."

"I came very near to jumping on the cars at Cairo yesterday and slipping in on that occasion. As a general thing I dislike banquets, if I am down for a speech. The sense of responsibility weighs me down and destroys all the enjoyment until I have gotten the confounded speech out of my system. But I really had something that I would like to have said last night—a matter that I am really interested in."

"What was that?" asked the reporter. "Why can't you say it now? General Sherman and all the members of the Army of the Tennessee are regular subscribers to the *Post-Dispatch*. Make your speech to them through its columns."

"I wanted to talk to them about Arctic expeditions. I wished to say that, in my humble judgment, we have spent too much money on these trips. Too many valuable lives have been immolated in this search. Even if it is finally successful, what is the good result of it? We could not borrow any money in the North Pole, and I don't think it would become fashionable as a summer resort. Now, I am full of an expedition of another kind. I want the next set of explorers sent in another direction. We have got some doubts to the exact location of hell, and I was very desirous to suggest to the assembled warriors last night, and through them to the government and the American people, that the next expedition go in search of the place I have mentioned. If we ever locate that region, we can make some practical use of it. I had sketched a plan, which is shadowy yet, but I thought it might grow real and practical under the potent influence of champagne." . . .

"Would it be strictly in accordance with the fitness of things if the expedition, like those to the Arctic regions, should get stranded and lost, and those who sailed in it should never reach their destination?"

Mr. Clemens smiled broadly and declared that he was not being interviewed and that he really would not answer leading questions.

## "A Day with Mark Twain"
[Commodore] R[ollingpin], (12 May 1882),
*Rollingpen's Humorous Illustrated Annual* (New York, 1883)

The boat that was to convey Mr. S. L. Clemens—Mark Twain—

northward was to leave St. Louis at four o'clock in the afternoon. It was now ten in the morning.... [R]unning his hand over his face, he suggested the propriety of visiting a barber shop before entering upon the day's program. During the tonsorial performance we carried on a rambling conversation about this trip south, which Mark declared had proved a dismal failure, resulting in nothing but some social interchanges.

"I expected," he went on, "to travel incognito and return east loaded to the guards with solid information about the late flood and other matters of interest concerning the people of the Mississippi river and the valley, but I was discovered the first day I arrived here from the east, and again when I took passage on the boat for New Orleans, and undertook to interview the boatmen. This confounded speech of mine betrayed me to the enemy; and just when the pilot on watch began to 'scape out' in the most beautiful fashion. No, it's all up. I'd have given worlds to have been permitted to pass unrecognized, and stand around and listen to those matchless lies by the hour. But I'm in the hands of Providence, and I suppose Providence does not propose to suffer my morals to be corrupted in that way." ...

By and by we called a carriage.... During the drive the conversation ran on books, authors, and literary topics generally. I suggested that his last book, *The Prince and the Pauper*, was his best, and would outlive any of the others that he had written, notwithstanding some of the critics had been rather severe on it as a work of art. Any minor errors or anachronisms that might have unconsciously slipped into the first edition, I urged could readily be eliminated or corrected in a second.

"Not a word will I ever change," was the prompt response. "I never undertake a piece of work until I have thoroughly prepared myself for the task, and when it issues from the press, it is done as well as I can do it, and that's the end of the matter."

We then talked of *The Innocents Abroad* and *A Tramp Abroad,* I maintaining that the latter was equally as good a book as the former, though coming after it, could never hope to be so popular.

"A much better book," said Mr. Clemens. "Twelve years ago I could not have written such a book from the same material." ...

On the trip south on the steamer *Gold Dust,* Mark went up into the pilot house and entered into conversation with the pilot, for the purpose, as he himself expressed it, of enjoying some good, old-fashioned, unadulterated Mississippi river lying. . . . At length the conversation turned to piloting, when Mark ventured to inquire of the man at the wheel if he knew Sam Clemens, who at one time was reported to be a pilot. "What! Mark Twain?" said the other. "Yes, that's what they call him," was the rejoinder. "Well, I should say I did! Sam left here 'bout twenty years ago, an' has been writin' books ever since. He's better at that'n he was steerin', for he wasn't much of a pilot. He'd just as like as not go to sleep on watch and run the boat into the bank, head on, if you didn't keep a watch on him. If thar was a snap in the river he'd go miles out of his way to get a whack at it, and was never happy unless he was bouncin' somethin'. Why, you'd think he was gettin' the biggest kind of money from the government to clear the river of snags if you'd seed how he hustled 'em out of the way." "Do you remember his personal appearance?" "Who? Sam Clemens? Yes, I should say so." "What was it?" "Wall, sir, to tell you the truth, to look at Sam Clemens, he wasn't worth sweepin' up!"

## "Mr. Mark Twain Excited on Seeing the Name of Capt. C. C. Duncan in Print"
*New York Times,* 10 June 1883, p. 1

Mark Twain sat upon the portico of his handsome home this morning and made merry. He had chanced upon an item concerning an old acquaintance, Capt. C. C. Duncan, New York's Shipping Commissioner and the father of the three illustrious young men whose powers of absorbing the funds of the United States Government are, as far as is now known, illimitable. "Well, well, well! So the old man's in hot water," says the author of *Roughing It* and *Tom Sawyer,* with a mock expression of pity on his face. . . . "Poor devil! I should think that after a while he'd conclude to put a little genius into his rascality, and try to hoodwink the public as his little game of robbery goes on. It don't become a scoundrel to be an ass. The combination always makes a mix of things, and if Duncan will persist in his wicked ways somebody ought to have a guardian appointed for him—a guardian with sense enough to throw a little gauze over the work of the gouge. He is still Shipping Commissioner, is he? And his dear noble boys surround him in his old age, supporting his steps, lightening his cares, and helping him to bankrupt the Government. . . .

"I see *The Times* says that just about $2,000 has been turned over to the Government's Treasury by Captain C. C. Duncan during the 10 years he has been Shipping Commissioner. There must be some mistake here. If a single penny in any year, or by any means, has fallen into the Treasury, a doleful error has occurred. Old Duncan never intended it, and I'll wager this new white duck suit I put on this morning that when the old man read the *Times* this morning and saw that a little cash had glided out of his grip, he hurried down town to cook up some job by which he could make the hoggish Government hand that cash back again.

"So he and his three sons appropriated to themselves $15,944.90 of the Government's funds for the work they profess to have done last year. That's monstrous. There's no joke in that. It's scoundrely, it's nauseating, bald, barefaced robbery: but it's Duncan, through and through. Why, my boy, if I wanted to get rich rapidly the one contract I'd most delight in making would be to hire 150 Duncan families by the year, and get just half of this $15,944.90 which Captain C. C. and his noble offspring take and, as I calculate it, my profits would be precisely the whole amount the Government gave me if I hired them at their true value, for a Duncan of the C. C. stripe is worthless absolutely. Multiply him by 150, or 150 times 150. It will make no difference.

"Enough brains could not be found in a C. C. Duncan family to run the kitchen of a Sixth Ward restaurant respectably. Brains never were there; brains could not be induced to enter there; it is the old story of water declining to climb up hill. As to the matter of honesty, that always was an absent quality with the old man. Where the honesty ought to have been in his make-up an inscrutable Providence provided a vacuum, walled in by hypocrisy and the meanest of meanness.

"It has been my honor to know the old man for a number of years— longer, much longer, than has been to my profit, perhaps. The honor fell to me away back in 1867, when I got my text for *Innocents Abroad* in his gorgeous scheme of an 'excursion to the Holy Land, Egypt, the Crimea, Greece, and intermediate points of interest.' People who have read my tract will remember that I was one of the victims of that excursion. And they may remember, too, how I endeavored to immortalize the fair name of Duncan, though through reverence to truth I was obliged faithfully to note some things which a narrow-minded world chose to set not down to the glory and honor of the man who left New York Harbor a Captain and developed within 24 hours into the ship's head waiter. Queer things happened on that excursion. I performed but my duty to the world and coming generations when I narrated those happenings in words of soberness and truth . . .

"I don't think Captain C. C. Duncan was any happier when I got through with him than he was before I began. I put on parade one or two of his little frauds that had not been seen hitherto. I called attention to his advertisements that on his big excursion Henry Ward Beecher, General Sherman, Maggie Mitchell, and other celebrities were to be among the passengers; how none of them appeared: how none of them, I guess, ever had any thought of making the trip. I showed up a few other of his thinly disguised frauds and exposed him pretty thoroughly as an old piece of animated flatulence."

# The "Twins of Genius" Tour

## Nov 1884–Feb 1885

Mark Twain and his friend George Washington Cable traveled across the country between 5 November 1884 and 28 February 1885 on what their promoter called the "Twins of Genius" lecture tour. Together they performed 103 times in some eighty cities, from St. Paul in the west, Louisville in the south, Montreal in the north, and Boston in the east. He often read excerpts from the unpublished *Adventures of Huckleberry Finn* to his audiences. Attendance averaged slightly over five hundred per date, and Twain earned about sixteen thousand dollars from the tour. During this period he also founded his own publishing firm, best known for issuing the memoirs of the Civil War general and president Ulysses S. Grant.

### "Mark Twain as Lecturer"
New York *World*, 20 November 1884, p. 5

Mark Twain, in dress suit, received the correspondent of *The World* yesterday in a waiting room at Chickering Hall. Mr. George W. Cable was giving his recital of Creole life.

"Ah, you are cruel," he said, with an air of utter sadness, "to attempt to interview a man just at the moment when he needs to feel good. You've got to feel good, you know, in order to make the audience feel the same way, but to try to be funny after you've been interviewed"—the thought seemed to overpower him.

"I did not know it was such a physical strain to deliver a humorous lecture."

"Ah, you have never attempted it; you don't know. On a day like this, when we give two performances, I feel like I'm all burnt out after the first performance. As soon as I get back to the hotel, I go to bed. I must get some sleep, somehow. If I don't, I will not be able to go through with the evening performance the way I want to. It's the same thing when you're traveling. The audiences, intelligent newspaper-reading audiences, are responsive enough. They quickly catch the point you are trying to make; often times they anticipate it. Then you are put on your mettle to give a sudden turn to the story so as to bring out a new and unexpected point. If these things don't happen, don't blame the audience; it is yourself who is at fault. The traveling has exhausted you, and, as I said before, you're not feeling good."

"All this you can judge of by the effect you produce on the audience?"

"Oh, yes. If you hear a rustle here or there, or see a particularly stolid face, you can tell that there is something wrong with yourself. The effect, of course, is not general. Heaven forbid! You would then have to stop right off. Audiences have their peculiarities, you know. It is a great inspiration to find a particular individual fairly respond to you as if you were in telegraphic communication with him. You are tempted to address yourself solely to him. I've tried that experiment. Sometimes it is dangerous. Laughter is very infectious, and when you see a man give one great big guffaw, you begin to laugh with him in spite of yourself. Now, it would not do for the lecturer to laugh. His is a grave and serious business, however it might strike the audience. His demeanor should be grave and serious. He should not ever smile."

"You have had ample opportunity to average your audiences on their respective faculties for fun."

"Audiences are much the same everywhere. I have been delighted with all before whom I have had the honor of appearing. In Boston,

Mark Twain and George Washington Cable, 26 September 1884. Publicity photograph for the "Twins of Genius" tour.

From J. B. Pond's *Eccentricities of Genius* (NY: Dillingham, 1900).

where Mr. Cable and I appeared before coming *here*, the audiences were delighted with our efforts to please them. You should have witnessed the enthusiasm last evening. Oh, I have nothing to complain of my audiences; perhaps they cannot say the same of me. Our entertainment lasts one hour and three quarters. The fact that Mr. Cable and I alternate makes us able to extend it to that length. Were I lecturing alone, one hour and five minutes is as much as I would dare impose on the audience. The strain on them in the humorous direction would be too much. But now Mr. Cable gently soothes them, then I excite them to laughter, or try to, at least. Then Mr. Cable has his turn and so the change is very healthful and beneficial."

"Your tour will be an extended one?"

"Our agent has booked us to the end of January. I should like to go to California, if I can manage it. You know this is my farewell performance.

I so intimated to the audience last evening. I told them that I had not practically appeared on the platform for nine years, and that when this term was over I would not appear again—at least, not for nine years. It will do me good; it will do my hearers good. Yet I've known people to give farewell performances for 50 years in succession."

## "Mark Twain's Ideas / A Talk with the Humorist"
### *Baltimore American,* 29 November 1884, p. 4

"Yes, we have stood the test very well," said Mark Twain last night, as he sat behind the scenes in the Academy of Music concert hall. . . .

Mr. Twain speaks in a slow, deliberate manner, almost with a drawl. . . . "I don't like traveling. I would, mind, if I could take my family with me; but there are those blessed darlings—the children—and what a trouble children are when they travel! And the average American child when he travels generally makes himself known. Therefore, this is my last appearance on the platform."

The *American* representative smiled, as he thought of the numerous stars now making their farewell tours, and the smile faded away to almost tears, as he thought Mark Twain was to be added to this list. Mr. Clemens noticed the look, and quickly—well, as quickly as Mr. Twain ever allows his voice to be accelerated, said: "Yes; I mean it, I was forty-nine years of age yesterday; and if I remain off the platform seventeen years, put that to forty-nine, and by that time nobody will want to hear me. I love the platform, and I would like to live on it, but I cannot be traveling about all the time. There is my family at home doing the lonesome. If I could settle down in New York, they could come in and stay there while I talked. Why, look how long a play runs in New York. I don't want such a big hall. I could talk in a small one, and I am sure there would be one man in it to hear me. . . .

"Yes, the platform has a great fascination. In regard to the way the audiences take the jokes. They say English people are slow to perceive a joke; but you get a large audience before you—why, they catch on to the joke before you have half told it. Yet, you talk to four or five Englishmen and tell them a funny story. When you get through they'll never smile. But next day they'll laugh. Fact. What is the difference between the crowd and the select party? Oh, I think it is a sort of sympathy with the crowd. One laughs, the others laugh with him, not with the fear they have to digest the fun. I was sitting one night in the Savage Club in London with Tom Hood, editor of *Fun*, and one or two others. I told them a funny story, and not one laughed. Next day I met Hood in the club, and he came up to me and said, 'Twain, tell that funny story you told last night to my friends here.' I told it. Hood laughed loud and long. The other men near smiled. Will you believe it, I told Hood that story five times, and each time he laughed heartier than the preceding time, and the last time I thought he would die. Yet, those who heard it for the first time never smiled. They wanted it to soak in." . . .

Mr. Cable, who reads with Mr. Twain, had been exploring the wings, and when it was time for Mr. Twain to go on Mr. Cable remarked: "Look out for the wall as you go in, and don't brush against it, or you'll get whitewash all over you."

"They will have to look out for their whitewash," replied Mr. Twain in his droll manner. "I will take care of myself." . . . His *Adventures of Huckleberry Finn*, from his latest work, was his first "reading." It was a happy selection, and made him at home at once with the audience. To those who had read his *Tramp Abroad*, the tragic tale of "The Fishwife and a Trying Situation," taken from it, hardly recognized them, for Mr. Twain told them in his inimitable manner, and gave almost a new reading to them. He was in the midst of "a trying situation," when there was a rustle in the gallery. It grew louder and louder, until the sounds of hustling feet and women's dresses were heard coming down the stairway.

Mr. Twain stopped, and taking out his watch said: "Time to catch a train, I expect."

Just then the form of the principal of a female college near the city appeared at the south doorway and led the troop of thirty or forty girls across the hall, right in front of the stage. The aisle divides the audience equally, and the people applauded terrifically. Mr. Twain looked bored. He was bored, and as the form of the female assistant disappeared Mr. Twain resumed: "You can't always tell the customs of the country. In Boston once it was customary for the people to catch the train at 9:05 o'clock. One night I was reading there, and at that hour everybody in the hall got up and left. I did not know of this tonight. How can one tell of these things?"

## "Mark Twain Gets Shaved"
*Pittsburgh Penny Press*, 29 December 1884, p. 4

Mark Twain . . . underwent the operation of shaving in his private apartment at the Monongahela House this morning, when a *Press* reporter was ushered in. . . . "How long since you were in Pittsburgh before, Mr. Twain?" asked the scribe.

"About fifty years," was the answer, in a deep, sepulchral voice, that seemed to proceed from the soles of the funny man's boots.

"And how do you like it?"

"As well as I did then," again came the sepulchral reply. At this point a bill boy entered, bearing an autograph album. . . . "Now, let me see; where shall I write in this thing? I can't find a blank page, and it takes a whole page for me. Hullo, here's an outlaw like myself," and, turning the book towards the scribe the latter read, *Bob Ford, the Slayer of Jesse James.* "Bob and I are both outlaws and murderers," Twain continued. "He killed Jesse James, and I am constantly murdering the North American English, so Bob shall be my *vis-à-vis*," and down went the name of Mark Twain opposite that of Bob Ford. . . .

"How do you like the idea of reading in a church?" asked the *Press* man, referring to the fact that Twain and Cable are to appear in the Cumberland Presbyterian Church tonight.

"I don't mind it, but I have always found going to church so conducive to slumber that I am afraid I may go to sleep. Perhaps by the time I have done so the audience, also realizing the fact that they are in church, will be asleep also, and if Cable doesn't disturb us we may spend a very pleasant evening together.

"Can you be funny in church?"

"I guess so, for I shall feel very funny there."

At this juncture Mr. George W. Cable entered the room.

"Here is my partner in crime. Why don't you bore him now?"

## "Talk with Twain"
### *Pittsburgh Chronicle*, 29 December 1884, p. 1

Mark Twain is in town. . . . He was sitting in an easy chair in his room, having his hair cut, when the writer called on him today.

"Take off your overcoat and sit down," said he with the air of a man who in his time has overcome many impediments to happiness by courtesy and perseverance.

"Thank you, but I have not time. I merely called to have a five minutes' talk about cosmos."

"Oh, indeed!" he retorted gravely. "Well, I am sorry I cannot oblige you but that is a subject I never speak of except at home after a week's preparation. I always treat light subjects in that way; however, sit down and let us talk. You would not care for a discourse on American art, would you, in place of cosmos?"

"Not just at this time."

"Well, I thought you might. I don't know anything about the subject, but of course that would enable me to be more graphic and entertaining. I met a drummer on a train a short time ago who asked me for my opinion on that matter. I knew he was a humbug in asking it, but I was also a humbug, for I proceeded to tell him what I did not know, but what I pretended to know."

"Suppose you tell me something of what you think about recent American magazine literature?"

"I have not an opinion which would be worth having on that subject. It seems to me, however, that there has been a wonderful advance of

late years in the general tone of the magazines. . . . The trouble is that
the two or three magazines which are a good market for a writer, and
which can aid him in his work for fame, are overcrowded. The *Century*
has perhaps $100,000 worth of accepted articles in its vault which may
not appear for years. They are pushed aside by articles on timely topics
which cannot be delayed. There are other magazines, it is true, but
when you send them an article you send a burial permit with it, for you
know that it will entombed even if it is printed. These combinations of
newspapers which print stories and sketches once a week will, it seems
to me, give rising and capable writers the field they desire as well as the
market. . . . I admit I am not a careful reader of novels. I read portions
of them, but do not read them through with the care some of them
deserve. Much of my opinion is based upon what I hear from men and
women of sound judgment whom I know intimately and whom I can
rely upon. Take Hawthorne as an example of my peculiar literary bent of
thought. It has become quite the custom to speak of him as the greatest
of all American romanticists. I read him now and then for his style, the
exquisite manner in which he writes, but I do not care for his stories, for
I do not think that they are as great as many others by American writers.
. . . I was in Europe when Henry James' 'Daisy Miller' reached there. I
chanced to be where there were a great many American ladies, and I
must confess I never heard a literary production so roundly denounced
as was 'Daisy Miller.' It was called an absurd exaggeration, a gross libel
on the American girl, and all sorts of things. Nothing was too bad to
say of it. And yet within a few hours I heard these same ladies allude
to young American girls who just fitted into the description of that
irrepressible young lady. The work has been caviled at and found fault
with, but it is true and just and close to the truth in spite of all that. The
blemishes complained of in recent American books are to be found just
as readily in English works or those of other countries. The trouble with
many authors of books as well as of plays is that they let their work run
too long. The interest dies before the story ends. That is the only fault
to be found, for instance, with such an admirable book as *Lorna Doone*.
I read two-thirds of it with keen relish and interest and then stopped. I

felt that there was a disposition to—using a New England phrase—'run emptyings' at the close. I have re-read the first of the book many times, but never have gone through it, yet I suppose this book now has as many people who read it over again annually as *Jane Eyre,* which in many households finds a place between a Bible and the prayer book."

## "The Humorists Interviewed"
### *Cincinnati Enquirer,* 3 January 1885, p. 4

The lecturers, Mark Twain and George W. Cable, with their managers Messrs. J. B. and Ozias W. Pond, were seated at a table in the St. Nicholas dining-room . . . when an *Enquirer* reporter was ushered in. . . . Mr. Clemens had before him a half emptied bottle of Bass' pale ale.

"Glad to see you, *Enquirer,*" he said, as he extended a hand and introduced the caller to his associates.

"Thought you might be able to say something interesting. You have been both interviewed probably on every conceivable subject, so if you will just rattle away and talk about any thing it will answer. You know how it is yourself."

"You should not expect a fellow to be very interesting after two hours on the platform," said Mr. Clemens.

"You are not expected to say much."

"Do you give a fellow a fair show?"

"Always."

"What I mean by that is, when a man talks to you, do you, in publishing it, eliminate all that he has said that is stupid and retain all that is bright?"

"Well, that is a question of judgment generally. The 'guying reporter' of the paper thought it would be better to interview you without seeing you. How did you used to work it?"

"Well, it's a pretty good scheme. If you know your man pretty well you can size him up about right. . . . I used to make reports of speeches in long hand that I could not begin to get the bulk of. I would take the merest skeleton, jot down a word here and there, and then fill it out at the office, using the speaker's ideas and my own language. It made me feel good when they complimented me and said it was better than the original."

"You were what we call a common reporter at one time, then?"

"Oh, yes, in 1862 and '63 I was on the Virginia City *Enterprise,* and in 1864 and '65 on the San Francisco *Call,* besides many other minor journals in my earlier days."

"Were you ever associated with Bret Harte?"

"Not in business. We were neighbors once in San Francisco. Harte was Secretary of the Mint. His office was in the same building with the *Call.* I often met him there, and we became well acquainted. He was editing the *Weekly Californian,* a literary paper, at the same time."

"What is Harte's best work, or at least has brought him the most fame?"

"'The Luck of Roaring Camp' and 'The Heathen Chinee.' 'The Heathen Chinee' nearly ruined him in his own estimation. He was ambitious to shine as a prose writer, and when he found that 'The Heathen Chinee' had caught on and was in everybody's mouth he was disgusted. He did not relish being known as a writer of funny doggerel. It did not do him any real harm, though. Some like 'Tennessee's Partner,' but I don't. Harte could not write dialect."

"I differ from you," said Mr. Cable. "I thought the speech of Tennessee was a grand thing. It was all there. The sentiment is superb."

"There you go again on an argument," returned Mark Twain. "But I tell you when Harte tried to write frontier dialect it was idiocy. Do you mean to tell me there was any literary merit in an effort that contained five or six kinds of dialect? Why, he could have taken it to any miner and had it remedied; but he did not."

Mr. Cable responded by grasping an empty ale bottle and threatening to break it over his companion's head.

"What do you consider your best work?" continued the reporter, addressing Mr. Clemens.

"I play no favorites. I am like the woman with her offspring."

"I think a sirloin steak is his best work. You would have thought so had you seen him this morning," said J. B. Pond.

"No puns," cried Clemens, as he also grabbed his bottle and made a gesture toward his manager. Turning to his inquisitor again he remarked, "*Innocents Abroad* paid in the greatest royalty." . . .

"Who got up that story about yourself and Bret Harte removing a newspaper outfit from one town to another long ago, being attacked by Indians, and firing your articles at them?"

"That was a clever story. It originated in the *Carson Appeal*. It said we ran out of ammunition, and began to throw in matter already in type. A half-column leader of mine scattered the Indians, and one of Harte's poems knocked them silly." . . .

Mr. Twain looked at his bottle. It was empty. He then gazed sorrowfully upon it for a moment, held out his hand and said: "Excuse me, I must go to bed," and he ambled away toward the stairway.

## "A Great Humorist"
### *Louisville Post*, 5 January 1885, p. 1

Messrs. Mark Twain and George W. Cable arrived in the city at 12:30 and registered at the Galt House. . . . A *Post* reporter sent up a prayer to be allowed a five-minute talk, and Mr. Twain relented. . . . "This is Mr. Twain, I presume," said the reporter.

"I guess it is," replied Twain. "I haven't any reason to the contrary. You may call me Twain."

"Have you and Mr. Cable been successful with your readings?"

"Well, now, we haven't any reason to complain. We have been drawing the people anyhow. I don't know whether we deserve it, but that doesn't make very much difference."

"Have you appeared in Southern cities yet, and have you been well appreciated there?"

"We have only visited one or two places south of the Ohio yet," replied Mr. Twain, with his peculiar drawl, "and we have gotten along all right. They take to us kindly. People of the South can laugh just as loud and as long as anybody, and that's what I'm here to do. I don't want to make them cry."

"But your partner, Mr. Cable, does."

"Oh, well, that is his affair. If he can't do it he is left, not I; but after all our tour has been all that I could wish, and we have had good houses wherever we have gone."

The reporter alluded to the fact that Mr. Twain had brought suit against the house of Estes & Lauriat for advertising his new book, *Huckleberry Finn,* at less than the price.

"I only protect myself," said the author. "That firm doesn't publish my book. It isn't even out yet. Therefore they have no copies, and they can't sell them at what they advertise. It is interfering with my legitimate business, and is a piece of impudence sure to damage me. Therefore I intend to stop it."...

"Mr. Twain, I see another statement—that you and your wife are worth $1,000,000. How about that?"

The author of *Tom Sawyer* opened wide his eyes, gazed at the reporter for a few minutes, and with a perceptible lengthening of his drawl, said: "Mr. Cable, did you hear the question the young man asked?"

"I did," replied the latter. "I am awaiting your answer with anxiety."

"I suppose," said the Missourian, "I must acknowledge that I am not a millionaire. It is worse than pulling a tooth, young man, but it must come. No, I and Mrs. Twain don't possess a million dollars that I ever heard of, but I wish we did."

## "Cable and Twain: The Author and the Humorist Arrive in the City Today"
### St. Louis *Post-Dispatch,* 9 January 1885, p. 7

... After the tableau vivant had signed their names in the hotel register they were accompanied by the *Post-Dispatch* reporter to Mr. Clemens' room, where the conversation at once turned upon an accident which had happened to the train they were on just as it entered upon the first of the arches coming from the Illinois shore. Mr. Clemens undertook to supply the descriptive work:

"We had," he said, "just reached that portion of the bridge which overhangs the crystal waters of the Mississippi River when a misunderstanding arose between the forward and rear portions of the train. The engine conceived the intention of leaving the track upon which the rest of the train was and moving upon another one, while the remainder of the train decided to remain where it was. The result was that one of the forward passenger cars was switched diagonally across the track. If we had not been going very slowly at the time the whole train would have left the track."

"Personally, I suppose, you had no fears, being familiar with the river currents?"

"Not in the slightest. It would not have discommoded me in the least to have been tossed into the Mississippi. I know the river thoroughly. It was the other people I was thinking of."

"I noticed that you seemed very anxious about the other people," Mr. Cable remarked with a quiet smile.

"It's no wonder," Mr. Clemens resumed. "There was a continuous kind of jolting which became more and more ominous and suggestive as the train advanced. A sense of crumbling—something crumbling beneath us, where stability was of the highest importance to us all personally— became very prominent. I fully expected the bridge to break down—I have always done so when I crossed it—and my anxiety for the safety of the other passengers led me to leap quite hastily from my seat and make a rush for the nearest exit. I wanted to get out and see what was the matter so I could intelligently supply the required relief."

"And you got there?" the reporter asked.

"Yes, but unfortunately, too late to be of any service. The train had stopped of its own accord. There were not many people hurt in the accident."

"How were they injured?"

"They happened to be in the front when I was going out. I went out in a great deal of a hurry and they were in the way. I'm sorry that I cannot furnish you with a list of the wounded and a statement of where they came from and the nature of the injuries. I did think of getting up such a list and giving the name of prominent men, but it don't do, after all, to play a practical joke on a newspaper. There are so many people who don't understand a joke, however plain it may be, that the possibility of serious results stands in the way of their perpetration."

## "Talk with Mark Twain"
### Milwaukee *Evening Wisconsin*, 29 January 1885, p. 2

. . . "How do you like your present business?" asked the reporter, after he had shaken hands with Mr. Clemens and had accepted an invitation to a seat. The question referred to the reading tour of the Twain-Cable combination.

"Very well, indeed," answered the humorist, rubbing his chin. "When we first started out," he continued, "I didn't think I should like the business. I had been off the platform for about fifteen years. But I've got into it now and enjoy it, although the present weather is not calculated to promote one's comfort."

"I understand that you have been doing a very good business."

"Oh, yes. We started out the day after the presidential election and have appeared before the public six times a week ever since. Our houses have, as a rule, been very good. In fact, we have seldom been greeted with any other kind of house. The only fault I find is that the trip blocked out for us is too long. It will take a month yet to complete it." Mr. Clemens rubbed his chin while he was speaking.

"Mr. Clemens, what was the true cause of the public not getting your latest book—I mean *Adventures of Huckleberry Finn*—sooner?"

"Well, you see, the delay was caused by a man employed in the stereotyping department of the New York printing house where the

Uncle Silas.

Original defaced illustration from first edition of *Adventures of Huckleberry Finn.*

book is being published. This man, with one slight gouge of a graver, made an indelicate addition to a cut of one of my characters. The fact that the picture had been ruined was not discovered until several thousand copies of the work had been printed. When discovery was made, the edition was suppressed and a new one is being printed and will be ready shortly."

"How are your older books selling now?"

"The sale, I believe, ranges from 15,000 to 25,000 every year, in the aggregate. On a rough guess, I should say that 170,000 copies of *The Innocents Abroad* have been sold since it was first published. *Roughing It* is not far behind, with a sale of say 150,000 copies. The sale of *A Tramp Abroad,* a comparatively new book, reached between 80,000 and 90,000."

## "Mark Twain Interviewed"
### Lafayette, Ind., *Courier,* 6 February 1885, p. 1

A *Courier* representative corralled Mark Twain in the rotunda of the Lahr House shortly after the noon hour today and put the screws to him. . . . "Would you believe it, young man, Cable and I never fail to make a hit. If the audience fail to materialize to any alarming extent, Cable kicks, and I strike the treasurer for all he has in his box. It's a hit every time; if it's not one kind, it's another. You have a very fine city here. I particularly admire the grand canal. I was attracted to it by some invisible influence the moment I arrived. In fact, before I had left the train I knew there was one here. It reminds me forcibly of Venice. Anyhow, there is something familiar like about it. Perhaps it's the odor.

"I thought I saw a gondola fast in the lee, but it proved to be only some misguided animal that had found its way into the water. . . . I think the canal is even more attractive than the artesian well, though that is powerful, too. There is a something, however, indescribable about the canal that the artesian well don't have—but you know all that, both speak for themselves—the canal a trifle the loudest perhaps. As a steady intoxicant, I should prefer the well, but in case of sickness where a powerful emetic is wasted, I should recommend the canal—to the other fellow." . . .

The reporter caught on. Twain got his beer and continued: "Well, Cable is just *splendid.* But you must ask him about it. He is even more enthusiastic on that subject than I am. I only know he is a powerful card. Would you believe it?—when I, even, fail to exert that soothing influence on the audience, necessary to the real comfortable enjoyment of a lecture or a sermon, Cable can actually close every eye in the hall in exactly five minutes by the watch. I have timed him frequently and always with the same result. But you must come and hear him. We charge members of the press two prices to make them feel independent. We like to encourage free speech on the part of the press. We hope to catch one of them some day for libel, and that would be $5,000 apiece, at least, in our pockets. Good scheme, eh?"

# The Best and the Worst of Times

## July 1886–Jan 1895

Never an astute businessman, Twain parlayed a series of disastrous investments into financial ruin. After the publication of *A Connecticut Yankee in King Arthur's Court* (1889), which betrays his growing disillusionment with "the damned human race," Twain and his family closed their Hartford house and lived in Europe most of the time between June 1891 and May 1895 to save on expenses. He also rushed his last major novel, *Pudd'nhead Wilson* (1894), into print in a vain attempt to stave off personal bankruptcy. His publishing firm, Charles L. Webster & Co., failed in April 1894.

### "Amusing the Children"
*Chicago Tribune*, 9 July 1886, p. 1

Mark Twain, traveling incognito under the name of "S. L. Clemens, one wife, three children, one maid," was at the Richelieu Hotel yesterday.... "We came in last night," he said, pulling at the left side of his mustache. "Mrs. Clemens is not very well; neither am I. I have been amusing the children. I have taken them to a panorama. I understand there are three others near here. I will take them there, too. I want to satiate them with battles—it may amuse them." Three little girls, composed of three red gowns, three red parasols, and six blue stockings stood on the steps and grinned.

"Run up and tell mamma what a jolly time you've had and I'll think of something else to amuse you."

When the three little girls had disappeared Mr. Clemens sighed. "Did you ever try to amuse three little girls at the same time?" he asked, after a pause; "it requires genius. I wonder whether they would like to bathe in the lake?" he continued, with sudden animation, hardly pausing five minutes between each word; "it might amuse them."

"Are you on your vacation trip, Mr. Clemens?"

"No; I have just returned from a visit to my mother in Keokuk, Iowa. She is 83 years old and I had not been home for over a year. We came from Buffalo to Duluth by a lake steamer and then from St. Paul down the river to Keokuk. Neither in this country nor in any other have I seen such interesting scenery as that along the Upper Mississippi. One finds all that the Hudson affords—bluffs and wooded highlands—and a great deal in addition. Between St. Paul and the mouth of the Illinois River there are over 400 islands, strung out in every possible shape. A river without islands is like a woman without hair. She may be good and pure, but one doesn't fall in love with her very often. Did you ever fall in love with a bald-headed woman?" The reporter admitted that he had drawn the line there.

"I never did, either," continued Mr. Clemens meditatively. "At least I think I never did. There is no place for loafing more satisfactory than the pilot-house of a Mississippi steamboat. It amuses the children to see the pilot monkey with the wheel. Traveling by boat is the best way to travel unless one can stay at home. On a lake or river boat one is as thoroughly cut off from letters and papers and the tax-collector as though he were amid sea. Moreover, one doesn't have the discomforts of seafaring. It is very unpleasant to look at sea-sick people—at least so my friends said the last time I crossed."

"It might amuse the children, though," suggested the reporter.

"I hadn't thought of that," replied Mr. Clemens; "but perhaps it might."

# "A Day with Mark Twain"

Edwin J. Park, *Chicago Tribune*, 19 September 1886, p. 12

. . . Yesterday Mr. Clemens bade me a hearty welcome [at Quarry Farm]. . . . At the suggestion of Mr. Clemens we walked to his study, an octagonal structure of dark brown color, situated right on top of a high pile of refuse stone. It is reached from the residence by a winding walk, and rough, uneven stone steps without lead to its doors, from which a magnificent view of the city and valley may be obtained. The floor was covered with papers and letters, while on the table and mantel reposed a half-dozen pipes, some tobacco and cigars, of which the owner is an inveterate user. He says that his constitution is such that tobacco does not injure him, and, as he enjoys it, he keeps a choice stock on hand.

On the very top of the quarry is a summer house fitted with rustic chairs, hammocks, etc., where, if a breeze is not to be found at the house, the entire family retire to sleep and enjoy the invigorating atmosphere. We climbed up to this delightful spot, and while the stiff breeze blew the humorist's bushy hair into tangled confusion we talked on subjects of mutual interest. . . . Our rough surroundings recalled to me the striking similarity to those of Virginia City, which place is so well described in Mr. Clemens' book, *Roughing It.*

"The comparison," said he, "is very timely and apt. At the time I was on the staff of the Virginia City paper the place was similar to this, although on a much larger scale."

Continuing the conversation, I asked Mr. Clemens if he was doing any work this summer.

With a tired expression in his large eyes, he gazed down into the valley for a few moments, and then, as though he had arrived at a very difficult conclusion and felt relieved, said: "No, I am not at work; not doing a single thing; just loafing; that's all. I made up my mind that I would loaf all summer, and I intend to do it. I left all the books I have started on at my home in Hartford, so that I couldn't get at them, and I'm just lying around and resting, and trying to get tired at that. I have started some new books, but I am in no hurry to finish them. I'm not anxious about them. As it is now I am 'at home' to any of my friends, although before this summer I have had to refuse them during office hours, which were from 9 until 4 in the afternoon. But then in the summer, while I am here, you know that there is a good deal of daylight between 4 and 8 o'clock, and I could get around some then. The three summer months which I spend here are usually my working months. I am free here and can work uninterruptedly, but in Hartford I don't try to do any literary work. Yes, as you say," he continued, in answer to my interruption, "this may be called the home of *Huckleberry Finn* and other books of mine, for they were written here."

## "Mark Twain Chatty: He Tells of His Former Life as a Reporter"
St. Louis *Post-Dispatch*, 19 May 1889, p. 20

I met Mark Twain the other day wandering around the Capitol. . . .

"A good deal changed," he said, glancing at the life-size photographs of Whitelaw Reid and younger editors which now decorate the walls, "and it seems a hundred years ago. . . . I was here last," he went on, "in 1868. I had been on that lark to the Mediterranean and had written a few letters to the San Francisco *Alta* that had been copied past all calculation and to my utter astonishment, a publisher wanted a book. I came back here to write it. . . .

"A pretty good place to write," I remarked as we took seats.

"Some things," he said, "but an awfully bad place for a newspaper man to write a book as the publisher demanded. I tried it hard, but my chum was a storyteller, and both he and the stove smoked incessantly. And as we were located handy for the boys to run in, the room was always full of the boys who leaned back in my chairs, put their feet complacent on my manuscript, and smoked till I could not breathe."

"Is that the way you wrote *Innocents Abroad?*" I asked.

"No; that is the way I didn't write it. My publisher prodded me for copy which I couldn't produce till at last I arose and kicked Washington behind me and ran off to San Francisco. There I got elbow room and quiet."

"It was apparently a wise move," I concurred, "but you could write here now, and this is exactly the place for a man like you. More intellectual society is attainable here than in any other city in the world. The only big mistake of your successful life, Clemens"—for only his intimate friends address him as "Mark"—"is not coming to Washington to live. Why, all over the United States people of leisure and culture are"—

"Yes, I know, I know," broke in Clemens, "but don't tantalize me. Do you take a fiendish enjoyment in making me suffer? I know perfectly well what I am about, and I appreciate what I am losing. Washington is no doubt the boss town in the country for a man to live in who wants to get all the pleasure he can in a given number of months. But I wasn't built that way. I don't want the earth at one gulp. All of us are always losing some pleasure that we might have if we could be everywhere at once." . . .

"I suppose you have been pirated a good deal," I said to Mr. Clemens. "I do not mean by illegal publication of your works, but by private individuals claiming to write your writings?"

"Oh, yes," he said, "considerably—some scores of cases, I suppose. One ambitious individual in the West still claims to have written the 'Jumping Frog of Calaveras County,' and another is sure that he produced that classic work known as 'Jim Wolfe and the Cats.' I suppose either would face me down with it; and their conduct has led me to conjecture that a man may possibly claim a piece of property so long and persistently that he at last comes honestly to believe it is his own. . . . But I haven't been bothered that way so much as I have been by personators. In a good many places men have appeared, represented that they were Mark Twain and have corroborated the claim by borrowing money and immediately disappearing. Such personators do not always borrow money. Sometimes they seem to be actuated by a sort of idiotic vanity.

"Why, a fellow stopped at a hotel in an English city, registered as Mark Twain, struck up an acquaintance with the landlord and guests,

recited for them and was about to accept a public dinner of welcome
to the city when some mere accident exposed him. Yet I myself had
stopped for weeks at that same inn and was well known to the landlord
and citizens. His effrontery was amazing."

"Did he resemble you?"

"I do not know. I hope and believe that he did not. Parties whom I
have since been inclined to regard as my enemies had the indecency to
say that he did.

"The same thing happened in Boston and several other cities.
It was not pleasant to have bills coming in for money lent me in
Albany, Charleston, Mexico, Honolulu, and other places, and my calm
explanation that I was not there bringing sarcastic letters in reply with
'Oh, of course not! I didn't see you with my own eyes, did I?,' etc., and
I resolved that I would follow up the next swindle I heard of. I had not
long to wait. A dispatch came from Des Moines, Iowa:

"'Is Mark Twain at home?'

"'Yes, I am here and have not been away,' I answered.

"'Man personated you—got $250 from audience—shall I catch him?'
came back, bearing the signature of a lawyer.

"'Yes,' I telegraphed in reply, 'have sent you check for expenses.'

"He was a good while catching him—some weeks—perhaps months,
and then he made me an elaborate report, giving the route of his
labyrinthine and serpentine chase of the swindler, the money he had
expended, and the information that he did not entirely and completely
catch him, though he 'got near him several times.' I was out some
hundreds of dollars.

"I was disgusted; and when I got another dispatch—from New
Orleans, I think it was—

"'Man swindled audience with pretended lecture here last night,
claiming to be you. What shall I do?' I telegraphed back unanimously,
'Let him go! Let him go!'

"I'd give $100, though, to see one of these doppelgangers who
personate me before an audience, just to see what they look like."

# "Mark Twain and His Book,"

R[obert] D[onald], *New York Times,* 10 December 1889, p. 5

... Mr. Clemens soon appeared. ... He was to start for Canada in the course of the week to register at a hotel and to obtain copyright for his new book [*A Connecticut Yankee in King's Arthur's Court*] there and in England. He had a good deal to say about that book and the modifications which he had to make to suit the English market. ... Mr. Clemens was one of the first to agitate the question of international copyright, and started on it as a knight-errant many years ago, but the heroic crusade collapsed for want of support [in Congress] ....

"They are more likely," he said, "to clap on some more protection where it isn't needed, rather than give us a little protection which will do good."

"What," I asked, "do you think of Mr. Stedman's opinion that American literature doesn't now require protection, that it has survived and overcome pirated editions, and is now on its legs?"

"That," said Mr. Clemens, "is true, so far as it goes, but it doesn't go far enough. Publishers are constructed out of the same material as other men, and they are not likely to pay a royalty on the work of an unknown author when they can get works of established writers for nothing. But the protection of American authors is not the main thing. The great question is the preservation in this country of a national literature, the spread of national sentiments, national thought, and national morals. What becomes of a few chuckle-headed authors who can go and saw wood, or live or die just as they like, is a mere trifle compared with the colossal national question involved, which is whether our people are going to continue to imbibe foreign ideas, and to take their opinions of American institutions from foreign writers. If I were going to England and delivering myself conscientiously on your royalties—pour out my contempt for your pitiful lords and dukes—no one would publish my book. But an Englishman comes along here, and after looking around for a few minutes, goes home and writes a book in which he abuses our

President, jeers and ridicules our institutions, and that book is gobbled up by our American publishers and scattered throughout the country at twenty cents a copy. After that we are told that the Americans are thin-skinned! We are also told that our newspapers are irreverent—coarse, vulgar, and ribald. I hope that this irreverence will last for ever; that we shall always show irreverence for royalties and titled creatures born into privilege, and all that class which take their title from anything but merit. Merit alone should be the only thing that should give a man a title to eminence. I am sorry that some of our newspapers are losing that irreverence which I wish to see preserved. They talk too much about that miserable puppet, the German Emperor; and the spread of foreign ideas is having its effect on our people. . . ."

After this he told me something about his new book, and how he had changed it to suit the English market.

"I want to get at the Englishman," he said, "but to do that I must go through the English publisher; and your publishers and your newspapers are cowards. I have modified and modified my book until I really couldn't cut it any more; and now Mr. Chatto, who is the most courageous of them, will have to cut it more. I am anxious to see my fate. I have got the preface, and as only the first part remains I presume he has cut it. Yes, cut off more than half my preface," said Mr. Clemens, in sorrowful tones; "and all because of a little playful reference of mine to the divine right of kings." . . .

The question as to whether there is such a thing as divine right of kings is not settled in this book. . . . Mr. Clemens also fears that some of the illustrations tell their tale too plainly for the English people. He is delighted with the way the artist has entered into the spirit of the book in executing the illustrations, and pointed to what he considers a very fine portrait of Jay Gould in the capacity of the "slave driver."

"It is four years," he said, in answer to another question, "since I projected this book, and three years since I wrote it. When I write a book I put the manuscript in pigeon-holes for a year or two. I take it out and look at it now and then to see how it is getting on. I began to think some months ago that the time was about ripe for this one.

The Slave Driver

Jay Gould by Dan Beard. Original illustration from first edition of
*A Connecticut Yankee in King Arthur's Court.*

And sure enough it is, for there is Brazil getting rid of its Emperor in twenty-four hours, there is talk of a republic in Portugal and federation in Australia; and, curiously enough, the short proclamation in which my hero abolishes the monarchy is similar—I don't mean the language, but the ideas—to the proclamation establishing the Brazilian Republic."

## "'Mark Twain' at Home"
### New York *World*, 12 January 1890, p. 14

. . . "I'm glad to see you," says he, "and somewhat ashamed to be so late. But we had a little theatre here last night and I find I'm growing old. I don't get up so early as I used to after a night's fun." So saying Mr. Clemens led the way up to his workshop with as springy a gait as a youngster of twenty-five. This room is a treat. A big billiard table with black and gold legs stands in the middle of it. . . . "I'd rather play you a game of billiards," said he, picking up a cue, "than try to instruct *The World*'s readers about myself. I know mighty little about the game, but less about the things you want to know." So many people have spoken about Mark Twain's sleepy drawl that it isn't worth while to say much about it here. . . . "When do you write?" asked the visitor, with visions of the humorist grappling at midnight with a large idea and slamming around on paper in the old conventional way.

"From 11 o'clock in the morning until 3 in the afternoon," said Mr. Clemens. "I work only three months in the year, when we all go up to Elmira, in New York, where my wife's folks live. I have a little octagonal house made chiefly of glass. It stands on the top of a high hill about three miles from the city. I think it is one of the quietest spots on the face of this globe. Still I have had tribulations in it. Shortly after it was finished and I had begun work on a drowsy summer day, with nothing to break the stillness but the peaceful birr of humble insects, quieter than solitude, I was aroused by a tremendous snorting and squealing and grunting. I looked down the hill and found that our nearest neighbor, a farmer, had established a hog orchard where I could get all the benefit of it. The sounds those hogs made when they quarreled and the smells that floated from them on the soft southern breeze drove me wild. Work was impossible. I went over to the farmer's house and bought all those hogs and his right to keep hogs forever. A few weeks after that another chorus aroused me, and there were six guinea hens squawking to one another in the place where the hogs had been. Well, the farmer said he had paid a quarter apiece for ten hens. . . . I offered him a dollar a head for the lot and reserved the privilege of never seeing or hearing them again. He agreed. Three days later I was disturbed by the same cackling and clattering, but much more of it, and on looking down the hill I found that the farmer had invested my money in four times as many hens. In the haste of my bargain I had overlooked specification as to all future hens. 'Time for a new trade,' said I, and I made it. The farmer, a well-meaning man, next indulged in a flock of sheep that skipped as near my workshop as possible and ate grass and bleated loudly at regular intervals. I bought mutton. The quiet has been preserved around that hill now for some time, but one by one nearly all of that farmer's rights have been extinguished.

"I don't know how much copy I write each day in those three summer months. The amount varies. 'Do a little every day' is my rule. Stick to it and you find the pile of manuscript growing rapidly. If on reading it over I find things I don't like I simply tear up twenty or thirty pages and there is no harm done. Don't be in a hurry to do too much, but work regularly."

"Then you don't wait for inspiration?"

"I don't think the prose writer needs to. If he were to depend upon that support he'd have an inspiration—say once in three months; it would last forty-eight hours, and what would he have accomplished? The poet is a man who works by what is called inspiration, but if he had to sit around and wait for it month after month he wouldn't be much of a poet."

"Well, I work four hours a day five days a week, for three months every year. That is half as much a day as I worked ten years ago. I wrote *Innocents Abroad* in sixty days, working from noon until midnight every day. I wouldn't dare do it now. I'm an old man. It would break me down." . . .

"I never charge any one with plagiarism, for to do so would prove me incapable of gratitude for the highest compliment a man can pay me. I remember that when *The Innocents Abroad* was published a man asked me—he was an old friend and had the privilege of asking such a question—'Why did you steal the dedication of your book from Dr. Holmes?' We stopped at the first bookstore we came to in Broadway and got a copy of one of the earliest editions of Dr. Holmes' poems, a little blue book. There was my dedication not changed so much as one word. Well, I didn't like to make a charge of plagiarism against Dr. Holmes, for he was a much older man than I and I respected him greatly, and besides his book had been published about twenty years before mine. I carried myself back to the time when I had written that dedication, and further. At last I remembered that in 1867 I had been sick for two weeks in a hotel in Honolulu. A copy of Dr. Holmes' little blue book was the only volume in that hotel. You can imagine how I had read it. I knew every poem, I knew the title page, the dedication, the imprint, the first page, the last, the covers even. The dedication had remained. I had absorbed it more thoroughly than anything else. I wrote a letter to Dr. Holmes explaining things, and there was no bloodshed between us."

## "Rudyard Kipling on Mark Twain"
### New York *Herald*, 17 August 1890, p. 5

. . . It was in the pause that followed between ringing the brother-in-law's bell and getting an answer that it occurred to me for the first time Mark Twain might possibly have other engagements than the entertainment of escaped lunatics from India, be they ever so full of admiration. And in another man's house—anyhow what had I come to do or say? Suppose the drawing room should be full of people, a levee of crowned heads; suppose a baby were sick anywhere, how was I to explain I only wanted to shake hands with him?

Then things happened somewhat in this order. A big, darkened drawing room, a huge chair, a man with eyes, a mane of grizzled hair, a brown mustache covering a mouth as delicate as a woman's, a strong, square hand shaking mine, and the slowest, calmest, levellest voice in all the world saying: "Well, you think you owe me something and you've come to tell me so. That's what I call squaring a debt handsomely."

"Piff!" from a cob pipe (I always said a Missouri meerschaum was the best smoking in the world) and behold Mark Twain had curled himself up in the big arm chair and I was smoking reverently, as befits one in the presence of his superior.

The thing that struck me first was that he was an elderly man, yet, after a minute's thought, I perceived that it was otherwise, and in five minutes, the eyes looking at me, I saw that the gray hair was an accident of the most trivial kind. He was quite young. I had shaken his hand. I was smoking his cigar, and I was hearing him talk—this man I had learned to love and admire fourteen thousand miles away.

Reading his books I had striven to get an idea of his personality and all my preconceived notions were wrong and beneath the reality. Blessed is the man who finds no disillusion when he is brought face to face with a revered writer. That was a moment to be remembered, the land of a twelve pound salmon was nothing to it. I had hooked Mark Twain and he was treating me as though under certain circumstances I might be an equal.

About this time I became aware that he was discussing the copyright question. Here, as far as I remember, is what he said. Attend to the words of the oracle through this unworthy medium transmitted. . . . "I remember an unprincipled and formidable publisher. Perhaps he's dead now. He used to take my short stories—I can't call it steal or pirate them. It was beyond these things altogether. He took my stories one at a time and made a book of it. If I wrote an essay on dentistry or theology or any little thing of that kind—just an essay that long (he indicated half an inch on his finger), any sort of essay—that publisher would amend and improve my essay.

"He would get another man to write some more to it or cut it about exactly as his needs required. Then he would publish a book called 'Dentistry by Mark Twain,' that little essay and some other things not mine added. Theology would make another book and so on. I do not consider that fair. It's an insult. But he's dead now, I think. I didn't kill him. . . .

"The proper way to treat a copyright is to make it exactly like real estate in every way." . . . What I saw with the greatest clearness was Mark Twain being forced to fight for the simple proposition that a man has as much right in the work of his brains (think of the heresy of it) as in the labor of his hands. When the old lion roars the young whelps growl. I growled assentingly, and the talk ran on from books in general to his own in particular.

Growing bold, and feeling that I had a few hundred thousand folk at my back, I demanded whether Tom Sawyer married Judge Thatcher's daughter and whether we were ever going to hear of Tom Sawyer as a man.

"I haven't decided," quoth Mark Twain, getting up, filling his pipe and walking up and down the room in his slippers. "I have had a notion of writing the sequel to *Tom Sawyer* in two ways. In one I would make him rise to great honor and go to Congress, and in the other I should hang him. Then the friends and enemies of the book could take their choice."

Here I lost my reverence completely and protested against any theory of the sort, because, to me at least, Tom Sawyer was real.

"Oh, he is real," said Mark Twain. "He's all the boy that I have known or recollect; but that would be a good way of ending the book"; then, turning round, "because, when you come to think of it, neither religion, training nor education avails anything against the force of circumstances that drive a man. Suppose we took the next four-and-twenty years of Tom Sawyer's life and gave a little joggle to the circumstances that controlled him. He would logically and according to the joggle turn out a rip or an angel."

"Do you believe that, then?"

"I think so. Isn't it what you call kismet?"

"Yes, but don't give him two joggles and show the result, because he isn't your property any more. He belongs to us."

Thereat he laughed—a large, wholesome laugh—and this began a dissertation on the rights of a man to do what he liked with his own creations, which being a matter of purely professional interest, I will mercifully omit.

Returning to the big chair he, speaking of truth and the like in literature, said that an autobiography was the one work in which a man against his own will and in spite of his utmost striving to the contrary, revealed himself in his true light to the world.

"A good deal of your life on the Mississippi is autobiographical, isn't it?" I asked.

"As near as it can be—when a man is writing a book, and about himself. But in genuine autobiography, I believe it is impossible for a man to tell the truth about himself or to avoid impressing the reader with the truth about himself.

"I made an experiment once. I got a friend of mine—a man painfully given to speaking the truth on all occasions—a man who wouldn't dream of telling a lie—and I made him write his autobiography for his own amusement and mine. He did it. The manuscript would have made an octavo volume, but, good honest man though he was, in every single detail of his life that I knew about he turned out, on paper, a formidable liar. He could not help himself.

"It is not in human nature to write the truth about itself. Nonetheless the reader gets a general impression from an autobiography whether the man is a fraud or a good man. The reader can't give his reasons any more than a man can explain why a woman struck him as being lovely when he doesn't remember her hair, eyes, teeth or figure. And the impression that the reader gets is a correct one."

"Do you ever intend writing an autobiography?"

"If I do, it will be as other men have done—with the most earnest desire to make myself out to be the better man in every little business that has been to my discredit, and I shall fail, like the others, to make the readers believe anything except the truth."

This naturally led to a discussion on conscience. Then said Mark Twain, and his words are mighty and to be remembered: "Your conscience is a nuisance. A conscience is like a child. If you pet it and play with it and let it have everything it wants, it becomes spoiled and intrudes on all your amusements and most of your griefs. Treat your conscience as you would treat anything else. When it is rebellious spank it—be severe with it, argue with it, prevent it from coming to play with you at all hours and you will secure a good conscience. That is to say, a properly trained one. A spoiled conscience simply destroys all the pleasure in life. I think I have reduced mine to order. At least I haven't heard from it for some time. Perhaps I've killed it through over severity. It's wrong to kill a child, but in spite of all I have said a conscience differs from a child in many ways. Perhaps it is best when it's dead."...

Once indeed he put his hand on my shoulder. It was an investiture of the Star of India, blue silk, trumpets and diamond studded jewel, all complete. If hereafter among the changes and chances of this mortal life I fall to cureless ruin I will tell the superintendent of the workhouse that Mark Twain once put his hand on my shoulder, and he shall give me a room to myself and a double allowance of paupers' tobacco.

"I never read novels myself," said he, "except when the popular persecution forces me to—when people plague me to know what I think of the last book that everyone is reading."...

"You see," he went on, "every man has his private opinion about a book. But that is my private opinion. If I had lived in the beginning of things I should have looked around the township to see what popular opinion thought of the murder of Abel before I openly condemned Cain. I should have had my private opinion, of course, but I shouldn't have expressed it until I had felt the way. You have my private opinion about that book. I don't know what my public ones are exactly. They won't upset the earth."

He recurled himself into the chair and talked of other things.

"I spend nine months of the year at Hartford. I have long ago satisfied myself that there is no hope of doing much work during those nine months. People come in and call. They call at all hours, about everything in the world. One day I thought I would keep a list of interruptions. It began this way: "A man came and would see no one but Mister Clemens. He was an agent for photogravure reproductions of Salon pictures. I very seldom use Salon pictures in my books.

"After that man another man, who refused to see any one but Mister Clemens, came to make me write to Washington about something. I saw him. I saw a third man, then a fourth. By this time it was noon. I had grown tired of keeping the list. I wished to rest.

"But the fifth man was the only one of the crowd with a card of his own. He sent it up—this card of his own. 'Ben Koontz, Hannibal, Mo.' I was raised in Hannibal. Ben was an old schoolmate of mine. Consequently I threw the house wide open and rushed with both hands out at a big, fat, heavy man, who was not the Ben I had ever known— nor anything of him.

"'But is it you, Ben,' I said. 'You've altered in the last thousand years.'

"The fat man said: 'Well, I'm not Koontz exactly, but I met him down in Missouri and he told me to be sure and call on you, and he gave me his card and'"—here he acted the little scene for my benefit—"'if you'll wait a minute till I can get out the circulars—I'm not Koontz exactly, but I'm traveling with the fullest line of rods you ever saw.'"

"And what happened?" I asked breathlessly.

"I shut the door. He was not Ben Koontz—exactly—not my old schoolfellow, but I had shaken him by both hands in love and I had been bearded by a lightning rod man in my own house. As I was saying, I do very little work in Hartford. I come here for three months every year, and I work four or five hours a day in a study down the garden of that little house on the hill. Of course I do not object to two or three interruptions. When a man is in the full swing of his work these little things do not affect him. Eight or ten or twenty interruptions retard composition."

I was burning to ask him all manner of impertinent questions as to which of his works he himself preferred, and so forth, but standing in awe of his eyes I dared not. He spoke on and I listened groveling. . . .

"Personally I never care for fiction or story books. What I like to read about are facts and statistics of any kind. If they are only facts about the raising of radishes they interest me. Just now, for instance, before you came in"—he pointed to an encyclopaedia on the shelves—"I was reading an article about 'Mathematics.' Perfectly pure mathematics.

"My own knowledge of mathematics stops at 'twelve times twelve,' but I enjoyed that article immensely. I didn't understand a word of it, but facts, or what a man believes to be facts, are always delightful. That mathematical fellow believed in his facts. So do I. Get your facts first, and," the voice died away to an almost inaudible drone, "then you can distort 'em as much as you please."

## "Mark Twain on Kipling"
### New York *World*, 24 August 1890, p. 18

Most people know by this time what Rudyard Kipling thinks of Mark Twain. . . . It is natural for them to wonder what Mark Twain thinks of Rudyard Kipling. . . . Mr. Clemens was asked what he thought of Rudyard Kipling's story of his quest for him.

"Why," said he, with the artless frankness of a man too busy to read the Sunday newspapers, "I haven't seen it! I haven't read a line of it, nor even heard, as yet, about it. Tell me what it is. Is it blame or otherwise?. . . Yes, I was at my wife's mother's when he found me, and that accounts for a singular, almost unaccountable lack of hospitality on my part. It was just about the luncheon hour when he arrived, and while he and I were sitting talking and smoking the rest of the family were eating. Now, I have a habit of never eating in the middle of the day. As I didn't get hungry the idea of luncheon didn't occur to me, for we were pleasantly engaged, and as I was not in the habit of going to lunch none of the family came to me to announce it. I never once thought of Mr. Kipling's views on the luncheon question; it didn't occur to me that he could have an appetite after his drive!

"Well, when he had gone and I was talking to my wife about his visit she at once recurred to this luncheon business and said: 'Why, do you mean to tell me that after this young man had come all this way to see you and had made such a search to find you, you didn't offer him any refreshments!' And thereupon she berated me for not being 'natural, like other men,' in my habits of eating!" Here Mr. Clemens' eyebrows laughed briskly.

"I thought," he continued, "that was the difference between a natural sense of hospitality and the absence of it.

"The next morning I went down to the hotel to call on Mr. Kipling without taking the precaution to telephone and see if he were still there. He was gone, and I, of course, haven't seen him since. Shall I see him in London soon? No, I don't expect to go to London in the near future; but when I do go I shall call upon him. I shan't wait to have him hunt me up, as you suggest the likelihood of his doing. I shall assuredly hunt him up!" . . .

It was not necessary to ask Mr. Clemens what he thinks of Kipling's tales.

"It would be a good thing," said he, "to read Mr. Kipling's writings for their style alone, if there were no story back of it. But, as you say, there always is a story there and a powerfully interesting one generally. How people have gotten to read and talk about his stories! Why, when a young man, not yet twenty-four years of age, succeeds in the way Kipling has succeeded, it simply shows, doesn't it, that the general public has a strong appreciation of a good thing when it gets hold of one?

"His great charm to me is the way he swings nervous English! It is wonderful. That it seems to me is one great secret of the hold he takes on his readers. They can understand what he is at. He is simple and direct."

"Have you any book of your own in hand at present?" Mr. Clemens was asked.

"No, nothing in particular," he replied; "but I have unfinished books on hand nearly all the time, if that is what you mean. I have one book begun seventeen—let me see, seventy-three, eighty-three—yes, just seventeen years ago. And it isn't more than half finished yet!"

"Haven't you abandoned it, or do you still take an interest in it and expect to finish it?"

"I shall certainly finish it, that is—(with a smile)—if I live seventeen years longer! I reckon I am good for that! How old am I now? About fifty-four and a half."

"I began 'The Diary of Shem in the Ark,'" continued Mr. Clemens, and at the drollery of the title and the seriousness with which it was announced the auditors burst into laughter. "Just seventeen years ago," he went on, "I wrote the first six chapters in Edinburgh, when the idea of it occurred to me. I was much interested in it then and am now. But I have laid it down and taken it up perhaps a half dozen times in those seventeen years. You ask if it be more akin to my early or my more recent writings in its conception and style? Well, the plan of the book has changed greatly since I began it in Edinburgh. I have acquired different ideas about it since then and they have expanded and grown and changed."

This led naturally to Mr. Clemens' declaration of his highly original method of evolving a story out of his brain.

"That is a curious thing about stories," he went on. "You have your ideas, your facts, your plot, and you go to work and write yourself up. You use up all the material you have in your brain and then you stop, naturally. Well, lay the book aside, as I do, and think of or go at something else.

"After a while, three or four months, maybe, or perhaps three or four or five years, something suggests your story or your book to you and you feel a sudden awakening of interest in it and desire to go to work at it; and then, lo and behold, to your surprise, maybe, but not to my surprise now—for I am used to it by this time—you find that your stock of ideas and facts and concepts has been replenished and your mind is full of your subject again and you must write, your brain is overflowing, your thoughts are beginning to burn to be put down on paper.

"Is this unconscious cerebration? I suppose so. A most interesting illustration of it, you may well say. The form of the concept of the original purpose may have greatly changed, but the root of it is there in the mind unchanged, and from it, without our being conscious of it at all, has grown a tree, with fresh, new foliage and spreading branches.

"Or, suppose the brain is like a cistern from which you draw off the ideas on the subject in hand as you write, until the cistern goes dry and you have to stop. You busy yourself about something else and put the other behind you and away. By and by from the imperceptible seeping in of ideas, thoughts, facts, fancies, as you have worked or slept or thought of something else, lo, the cistern is once more full to overflowing, and with fresh relish and a wonderful appreciation of the new material you have been acquiring in spite of yourself, you draw off the ideas again and add them to your former stock already committed to writing.

"The field that you reaped and garnered has grown up again and there is another harvest there to reap. The 'think-tank' of your brain overflows once more. The snowball has been rolling all this time without your knowing it and gathering more snow."

## "Mark Twain on Humor"
### Raymond Blathwait, New York *World*, 31 May 1891, p. 26

. . . Introduced to the presence of the genial and gifted humorist, I found him knocking about the balls upon an old-fashioned billiard table. As I entered, he at once stepped forward and gave me his hand and a very hearty welcome. . . .

"Come and sit down and have a cigar. I myself smoke all the time."

I sat down in a comfortable armchair, lit the cigar he gave me, and it was a very good one, for, as he said, "I always buy my cigars in America, a special brand. I want to take some to Europe with me, for I never can buy a cigar fit to smoke in England, nor, indeed, anywhere in Europe, and there I am going to live for the next two or three years to educate my little girls.

"Yes, it is a great break up, but I do not see how I can avoid it. However, I am reconciled to it now. You see we are in great confusion, as we are more than half packed up. You have just come in time to catch me, and I am very glad to have a chat with you. You shall lead and direct the conversation. That, you know, is the interviewer's business. He must bear the lion's share, or, at all events, his very full half. A good interviewer has in him the makings of a perfect novelist."

I said: "Very well then, Mr. Twain, I should much like you to give me your opinion as to the comparative merits of American and English humor."

The great humorist ran his hands through his mass of fast graying hair, eyed me quizzingly, and then slowly drawled: "That is a question I am particularly and specially unqualified to answer. I might go out into the road there," pointing as he spoke to the pretty, sun-flecked, shadow-stricken pathway, a glimpse of which I gained through the open window, "and with a brickbat I would knock down three or four men in an hour who would know more than I about humor and its merits and its varieties. I have only a limited appreciation of humor. I haven't nearly as catholic and comprehensive an idea of humor as you have, for instance." I demurred loudly to this: "Oh, Mr. Twain, and you who wrote the dialogue in *Huck Finn* between Huck and the runaway Negro about kings and queens."...

"Exactly, and that book, perhaps, reveals the very thing of which I speak. Within certain rather narrow lines, I have an accurate, trustworthy appreciation of humor. It is not guesswork, this estimate of mine as regards the limits of my humor and my power of appreciating humor generally, because with my bookshelf full of books before me I should certainly read all the biography and history first, then all the diaries and personal memoirs and then the dictionaries and the encyclopedias. Then, if still alive, I should read what humorous books might be there. That is an absolutely perfect test and proof that I have no great taste for humor. I have friends to whom you cannot mention a humorous book they have not read. I was asked several years ago to write such a paper as that you suggest on 'Humor,' and the comparative merits of different national humor, and I began it, but I got tired of it very soon. I have written humorous books by pure accident in the beginning, and but for that accident I should not have written anything."

I very heartily remarked that it was an accident by which nations had profited. "The gaiety of nations, Mr. Twain, will be eclipsed when your humor ceases."

Mark Twain bowed slowly and gravely, and went on in a voice that would have made his fortune as an undertaker: "At the same time that leaning towards the humorous, for I do not deny that I have a certain tendency towards humor, would have manifested itself in the pulpit or on the platform, but it would have been only the embroidery, it would not have been the staple of the work. My theory is that you tumble by accident into anything. The public then puts a trademark onto your work, and after that you can't introduce anything into commerce without that trademark. I never have wanted to write literature; it is not my calling.". . .

"To all of which, Mr. Mark Twain," said I, "I can only say in reply that we are all heartily glad that you succumbed to your trademark. And now, in connection with this philosophical chat on humor, I want to ask you why it is that great humor is always found in very solemn people and nations. The Presbyterian Scotchman or the Puritan New Englander are really the most humorous people on earth."

"Ah, now," replied Mark Twain, "You have put your finger on a great verity. It is, after all, quite natural. I answer in one word that it is reaction. It is a law that humor is created by contrasts. It is the legitimate child of contrast. Therefore, when you shall have found the very gravest people in the world, you shall also be able to say without further inquiry, 'I have found the garden of humor, the very paradise of humor.' You may not know it, but it is true, if a man is at a funeral and broken-hearted, he is quite likely to be persecuted with humorous thoughts. The grotesque things that happen at funerals depend on their solemn background. They would not be funny but for contrast. Take an instance in which you look in vain for fun if it were not intimately connected with a very ghastly occasion.

"Here is the story: A clergyman in New York was requested by a man to come over to Brooklyn to officiate at his wife's funeral. The clergyman assented, only stipulating that there must be no delay, as he had an important engagement the same day. At the appointed hour they all met in the parlor, and the room was crowded with mourning people, no sounds but those of sighs and sobbings. The clergyman stood up over the coffin and began to read the service, when he felt a tug at his coattails, and bending down he heard the widower whisper in his ear: 'We ain't ready yet.' Rather awkwardly he sat down in a dead silence. Rose again and the same thing took place. A third time he rose and the same thing occurred. 'But what is the delay?' he whispered back. 'Why are you not ready?' 'She ain't all here yet,' was the very ghastly and unexpected reply. 'Her stomachs at the apothecary's.'

"You see it is the horizon-wide contrast between the deep solemnity on the one hand and that triviality on the other which makes a thing funny which could not otherwise be so. But in all cases, in individuals, in peoples, in occurrences such as that I have just described, it is not the humorous but the solemn and grave element that predominates, and that affords the strongest background." . . .

After my luncheon I resumed the conversation with a remark that *Huckleberry Finn* was my favorite of his books, and I specially commented on the wonderful knowledge of dialect which he displays in that book.

"Yes," he replied, "I was born in one of those States and I lived a great deal of my boyhood on a plantation of my uncle's, where forty or fifty Negroes lived belonging to him, and who had been drawn from two or three States and so I gradually absorbed their different dialects which they had brought with them. It must be exceedingly difficult to acquire a dialect by study and observation. In the vast majority of cases it probably can be done, as in my case, only by absorption. So a child might pick up the differences in dialect by means of that unconscious absorption when a practiced writer could not do it twenty years later by closest observation. But a dialect can be acquired. . . . The cunningest things have been said in dialect. It has got to be a mighty poor Scotch story that dialect cannot save. Look at the dialect in *Uncle Remus.* Why, the dialect there is absolutely scholarly. The only one of my own books that I can ever read with pleasure is the one you are good enough to say is your favorite, *Huck Finn,* and partly because I know the dialect is true and good. I didn't know I could read even that till I read it aloud last summer to one of my little ones who was sick. My children all read *The Prince and the Pauper*, but none of the others."...

"One more remark and I have done, Mr. Twain. How far, in your opinion, does culture, education, what you will, enter into the making of books?"

"My dear sir, they speak of book culture as being the end of all things. That is applied in criticism upon novels of all kinds, whereas I say it is only applicable to certain classes of novels. Nine out of ten of the qualities required for the writing of a good novel are summed up in the one thing—a knowledge of men and life, not books or university education. If I could write novels I shouldn't lack capital, because I have had intimate acquaintanceship with many groups of men, many occupations, many varieties of life in widely separated regions. It would be impossible for me to use that capital, that culture, for that is really what it is, because I should never be able to acquire the novel-writing art. But it makes me impatient to see that requirement constantly made by the critics that a novelist shall have book culture...."

"My *Innocents Abroad* was my first book. I am sure it was not the outcome of book culture. Oh, yes, it was true enough. They really existed. They were only a kind of Cooks' excursionists; only Cook, as Cook, had not then been heard of."

## "Mark Twain Gone Abroad"
### *St. Louis Republic*, 1 April 1894, p. 28

Mark Twain sailed for Europe on the steamer *New York* on March 7. At 11:30 o'clock on the night previous to the vessel's leaving he stood on the deck near the gangplank smoking a cigar.... He was chuckling with the thought that he was stealing quietly off to Europe without undergoing the cross-questioning of a parting newspaper interview, when a soft and plaintive voice sighed into his right ear the words:

"Pardon me, but isn't this Mr. Clemens?"

He turned his head slowly—he never turns anything quickly, not even a sentence—and saw standing by his side the writer. He shifted his cigar to the other corner of his lips and answered:

"Is that a bug, or what is it on your shoulder?"

It was a bug, and the reporter brushed it off. Then he said:

"Mr. Clemens, I was sent to interview you and to inquire about your European trip."

"One of those bugs got on my shoulder a little while ago," drawled the author. "At first I thought it was a spider; then I thought it was an ant, but I didn't find out."

"Do you expect to remain abroad long?" asked the reporter.

"If I had a light here I could very quickly find out what it was. If you will kindly stand still a moment I will ask the ship's steward to bring a lantern and we can discover whether it was an ant or a spider."

"But Mr. Clemens, if you will excuse me, it's getting late and—"

"If it was an ant," continued Mark Twain in a musing tone, "he is different from any ant I ever saw. I knew an ant once in Nevada who used to come out every evening in clear weather and roll a little pebble along for about—"

"Excuse me, Mr. Clemens, but how long did you say you intended to remain abroad?"

"Five weeks. Exactly why he was continually rolling that pebble or where I never could find out. He was the biggest fool of an ant I ever knew, and I have watched a good many fool ants. Once in the Sandwich Islands—"

"Are you going to write another book of travels?"

"No; there is no use in writing a book unless one puts hard work into it, and no book can be successful or worth reading unless the author puts his heart and soul into it. I can't do that in a book of travels any more. It is depriving me of a big source of income, too—a big source of income. I think I'll just keep on lying quietly and systematically hereafter. A good lie is always worth writing. A man who can lie well ought never to do anything else."

"Where do you propose to go?"

"Well, I think I shall visit some points in Europe which I have never seen more than once or twice."

"Do you go on business or pleasure?"

"Exactly. I always visit Europe with that idea in view. You see, Europe is a capital place for that sort of thing—much more so than this country."

"Business or pleasure?"

"I haven't thought much about it, to tell the truth, although it opens up an interesting train of thought. Thought is, after all, only an ascription of a mathematical reason for a coexistent plurality, and if we eliminate its cogency we will get right back to the starting place every time, and that reminds me of that bug. What has become of him?"

"Will you do any writing while you are away?"

"That depends upon circumstances. You see, I never write when I am reading, and I never read anything while I write. I find that if I read a book for a while and then begin to write, I can't help borrowing that author's style. Just read Shakespeare for 15 minutes and try to write afterwards and you'll find yourself embarrassed. You'll be trying to describe an ordinary everyday incident in his high and mighty style and you'll be thinking in blank verse." . . .

"Pardon me, but won't you tell me, Mr. Clemens, what part of Europe you will visit?"

"Certainly," said he. "I am always glad to oblige a newspaper man. They have invariably misquoted me in the pleasantest and most charming manner and I owe much of my success as a moral instructor to their efforts. If it were not for the newspaper men of America much of the valuable information which I have acquired in the study of—"

"Where did you say you were going?" inquired the reporter in a falsetto voice, to attract Mr. Clemens' attention.

The author reflected for a moment. Then he drew a little book from his overcoat pocket. Opening it, he said:

"I have been thinking of taking a shy at the Holy Land again. Here is a fascinating place where I have longed for years to visit. It has a quaint suggestive name which of itself has always pleased me. I refer, as you may have guessed, to Kibrothhattaavah. I shall probably remain there for a few days for rest, if I go there at all, and then will slide over to Hazaroth. Then I may go to Rithmah and, if the traveling is good, may go on to Rimmon-parez. From there to Libuah, thence to Kehelathath, thence to Mount Shapher, thence to Haradah, thence to Makheloth—"

"But—"

"Thence to Tahath, thence to Tarah, thence to Mitchcah, thence to Hashmonah, thence to Moseroth, thence to Benejaakan—"

"Mr. Clemens, if you—"

"Thence to Hor-hagidgad, thence to Jothathath, thence to Ebrozth, thence to Ezlongaber (that's easy), thence to the wilderness of Zin, then I shall skip a number of unimportant places and go straight to Ije-abarim. From there I will take little excursions to Almondiblathaim, Oboth, and other near points.

"However, I have not yet fully decided upon this route, but may instead begin at Zalmonah and go thence to Punon, thence to—excuse me, but have you a match?"

Mr. Clemens paused to relight his cigar, which had gone out, and the reporter said: "I am afraid I haven't time to get another route before the steamer goes. How long did you say you intended to stay abroad?"

"I had originally made up my mind to remain about five weeks, but my memory is so wretched that I find it difficult to remember how long I had intended to stay. That recalls the wonderful memory that old black cat of ours had. She did have the most remarkable memory of any cat almost I ever knew. Why, once she came into the kitchen and sat down on a hot stove lid, and do you know that ever after that, as long as we had her, she never sat down on a hot stove lid again? She wouldn't even sit down on a cold stove lid. At one time I thought it was her sagacity, but now I know it was her memory. She was like the bull pup that belongs to Miss Appleby's old uncle, Ezra Pilkins. He was a wonderful old fellow. Had a bald head all his life from his babyhood. He never did have a single hair on his head, so old Marm Wilson said. Marm Wilson lived in the family, you know, for years and years, and I don't believe she would have left them if it hadn't been for the accident to young Jabel

Endicott. That was the most peculiar accident I ever heard of. You see, Jabel was acquainted with Miss Appleby, and he used to visit her house a good deal and people said he was going to marry her. Well, her uncle's bull pup had one of his eyes put out when he was very young, and Jabel bought a glass eye and fitted it into the socket.

"It was not exactly a match to the other eye because the oculist that Jabel got it from only kept human glass eyes. Said he had never kept a stock of bull pup's glass eyes, anyhow. So Elihu Vedder—that was the name of the pup—used to wear the light blue glass eye, and he did have the strongest expression of most any dog I ever saw on the left side of his head—that was the side the glass eye was on. He was mightly proud of that glass eye, though. He used to kind of sidle up with his left side turned to strangers just so that they'd notice the eye and they always did notice it, too. Well, one day—"

"Excuse me, Mr. Clemens, but really about this European trip. If you—"...

"I was coming to that. As I said, one day, while Elihu Vedder was feeling so cocky about this glass eye of his and poking it under everybody's nose, so to speak, a strange bull dog came along. He walked up to Elihu in the friendliest kind of way and there wouldn't have been any trouble at all if Elihu hadn't tried to show that eye of his. He turned it suddenly on the other dog and kind of lifted his nose in the air in a superior, supercilious sort of way. That made the other dog mad clean through and he made a jump for Elihu and grabbed him by the throat. Just then Jabel came along to call on Miss Appleby and when he saw her uncle's bull pup being choked by a strange dog he sailed in to separate them. In doing this he jabbed his finger into Elihu Vedder's glass eye and cut it most off. Of course he pulled his finger out again right away, but—"

"Mr. Clemens, I don't like to interrupt you, but if you will tell me just a little about your plans I would be greatly obliged."

"Plans," said Mr. Clemens, "are things that always appealed strongly to me. There is a certain mystery to my mind about plans that is very captivating. I was always a great fellow for making plans. It is a little hobby of mine. . . . Now I knew a man once in California, who had a second cousin named Zachias M. Botts. This man Botts had a trained horn frog—"

"Mr. Clemens, if you will pardon me, I should like to be able to write only a few lines about this trip of yours. It is getting la—"

"My dear fellow, you may. Just write everything I have told you and submit it to me before the steamer sails. Use all of the information— every bit of it. I don't want the public as a general rule to know too much about my intentions, but in this case I'll make an exception. Give it all without reserve and let me see it before I go. Go into the smoking-room now and write it out."

Mark Twain turned away to speak to the purser and the reporter went into the smoking-room and wrote what he had said. Then he hunted up Mr. Clemens and showed him what appears above. The author read it over carefully and said:

"That's all right. It is all right. It is what I call a perfect interview. Just as incorrect as any interview I ever read. Young man, you understand your business. Keep at it and someday you will be one of us—one of the perfect liars of the world."

## "Personal Reminiscence"
### William T. Stead, London *Review of Reviews,*
### 16 (August 1897), 123–33

It was my good fortune some four years ago to cross the Atlantic in the *New York* as a fellow passenger with Mark Twain. It was in the early months of 1894. I was returning from Chicago. Mark Twain was hastening from New York to rejoin his family at Paris. We had a capital passage, and, as we were neither of us inconvenienced by *mal de mer,* we used to have long and pleasant conversations every day on deck. . . .

We had much talk about his books, and I was delighted to have the opportunity of saying to him in person how much I felt indebted to him for many a laughter-lifted hour. He said that laughter was a very good thing, but for himself he scarcely got two laughs a month, and this was natural, because every humorist dwelt upon the serious side of life. All true humor was based on seriousness, and hence the humorist, who often made other people laugh, laughed least himself. He said it was so in his own case anyhow.

On my saying that I thought I had laughed more over his description of the German language in *A Tramp Abroad* than over anything else, he said that probably appealed very much to those who were struggling with German. As for himself, he had never been able to master the mysteries of a foreign language to his own satisfaction. He had done his best, but it had been no use. For seven years he used to put himself to sleep by constructing German sentences. He got on fairly well on those occasions, when there was no one to listen, but he had never been able to stand up and face a human being and air his German more than two words at a time without coming to a dead stop.

A short time before he came on board he had made a speech on George Washington. He said that the Washington joke had always been one from which he had made a great deal of fun. The usual way he got it off was by remarking that there were many points of difference between himself and Washington, only one of which he need specify. He used to say, "Washington could not tell a lie, I can" then he would pause until they took in the joke, and then would add, "but I won't." . . .

He said that *A Tramp Abroad* was the greatest favorite of his books, then *Roughing It*, and after them *The Innocents Abroad*. At one time *The Innocents Abroad* was the most popular, but now his works stood in the above order. In England *A Tramp Abroad, Huckleberry Finn*, and *Tom Sawyer* were the most popular. He could not say whether *Roughing It* was as popular in England as in America. Humor, he remarked, could not be served up alone, it needed something with it. It was like embroidery, very good as an ornament, but one could not dress in embroidery; you needed something else to keep the cold out. . . .

When he was asked to sign his name on the back of a steamer-ticket, I said they could keep it as an autograph. He said, "Yes, it ought to be worth 25 cents." He said that Aldrich had come in one time with a

catalogue of autographs to Howells and said with great glee, "Here is
fame indeed! I find that my signature is valued in this catalogue at 25
cents. There is glory!" Howells turned over the pages, and then said, "Yes,
I see. Here is Habberton who wrote *Helen's Babies*—his autograph is
worth 75 cents, three times as much as yours."

The color of the sea being green led him to remark that we were
in shoal water. He did not know why the water should be green in
shoal water, but it was so. Certainly after we got out of sight of land it
became deeply and beautifully blue. I asked him about the Mississippi.
He said that the color of the Mississippi was the color of coffee when
made up with a very great deal of cream; that it was a varying shade of
brown, changing according to the quantity of rain. I asked him if they
drank it. He said, "Yes, and people who drink it never like to drink any
other." If he went back to the Mississippi, he would as soon drink that
as any other water. It was very strange the taste people acquired for
drinking Mississippi water. To a person accustomed to drink it, clear
water is positively distasteful. If you took a glass of Mississippi water
and allowed it to stand for a little time, there formed a sediment of about
an inch deep at the bottom. If you are accustomed to Mississippi water,
you stir it up before drinking in order that you may have the sediment
in solution. Was it not very unhealthy? No, he said, it was good alluvial
loam, and the utmost that it would do would be to line you inside with
more aluminum than would otherwise be the case. I asked him about
the river. He said you could always see both sides of it, and that both
banks were flat, with the exception of the Chicasaw Bluff and the Bluffs
before Memphis; but they were very small. The only impression that he
got from the river was one of immense solemnity, such as you got from
the desert or any other immense wild place. . . .

Speaking of Chicago, he said he thought there was a greater mixture
of all nationalities there than in any other place excepting Hell. Speaking
of Chicago, he laughed heartily over the story of the contest between
the Chicago liar and the St. Louis liar, which was won by the St. Louis
man, who began by saying, "There was once upon a time a gentleman
in St. Louis—" whereupon the Chicago man gave up and declared

that no one could possibly tell a greater lie than that. Twain said: "A Chicago man was once in St. Louis and sent a telegram to some place in Missouri. He was charged so heavily for it that he protested. "Great Scott," he exclaimed, "Why in Chicago it does not cost so much to telegraph to Hell!" "No," said the operator quickly, "that's in the city limits"—an unpremeditated and unconscious sarcasm, which is always worth much more than a premeditated one. . . .

Mark Twain himself was then contemplating no less a monopoly than the exclusive contract for the typesetting of the world. For many years past he said he has been engaged on a typesetting machine. I asked him how he was getting on. He said they were about to place the machine upon the market. Two machines had already been built, nine were almost finished, while forty were in process of construction, when the cyclone of the financial disaster struck the country last year and compelled them to postpone everything. He said he was very glad it was so, for by his old arrangement there were two companies, one of which had granted a concession to another. The second company was a business-like concern, but the other was of moonshine and water. When the crisis came last year the moonshine one had to disappear, and the two companies were amalgamated into one. He said that he had struck oil. The two companies amalgamated into one had a capital of five thousand dollars instead of seven and a half millions, and were then ready to go ahead.

I asked him what kind of machine his was. He said it was a perfect machine. "It is made of blue steel, polished, graceful, and beautiful; a thing of beauty and a joy to the eye. You could place it upon the finest carpet in the house without fear of any dirt or broken type. It is a machine which to know is to love; a machine which the men who were making it were so fascinated by that they said that if I had not money to pay their wages, they would go on working at it as long as they had anything left to pawn in order to keep them alive. They are now being gathered together from where they have been working. They will come back any distance in order to work at the machine. It is a fascination," he said. "To be allowed to work on that machine is enough for them.

When that machine is in the market all other machines will disappear; 65,000 compositors in the United States will be thrown out of work, or will have to find other work to do."...

In his domestic life Mark Twain has been almost ideally fortunate. He told me that during the twenty-four years of his married life whenever his wife had been absent she had written to him with the punctuality of a planet, every day of the week. He had written to her every mail with one exception, which caused him great grief. Some mutton-headed idiot, he said, had told him that the quickest steamer sailed on Thursday, whereas it sailed on Wednesday. He wanted to add some more to his letter, and so missed the mail. She was greatly grieved, and he has been getting letters full of despair ever since. When she first left he wrote once, twice, or thrice a day, until he discovered that the mail only went once or twice a week. He still wrote every day, but he kept them till mail day. He put everything into the letters that came into his life, writing with a freedom which was utterly impossible when he was writing for a magazine or a book. "From a literary point of view," he said, "these letters to my wife in the last six months satisfy me much better than anything I have ever written; there is a lightness of touch and a vividness of description, and altogether a lightness which I try for in vain when I am writing for magazines or books."

He said on an average his letters were twenty-five pages, each containing from four to five thousand words. These were sent twice a week, so that in the six months he must have written some 200,000 words to her. "I was telling Walker, of the *Cosmopolitan*," he said, "the other day what I had been doing. He said, 'What a waste, what a waste to send all those letters to your wife, when you know I would give you a thousand dollars apiece for them.' So I wrote to my wife, and told her I was afraid I had been guilty of much waste, and that I must ask her to send me my letters back, inasmuch as Walker of the *Cosmopolitan* would give me one thousand dollars apiece. She replied she would not give them up for one thousand five hundred dollars apiece." I suggested he might get that from Walker. "No," he replied, "she would go up again." I said it would be well if in a few years he published these letters, altering the names and places. He objected that it would make them unreal. They were a picture of New York as it is today. "There is nothing that I have written or read compared in value to these letters to my wife."

## "Mark Twain in Paris"
### New York *Sun*, 27 January 1895, III, 4

Mark Twain and his family are installed for the winter in one of the most charming houses in Paris. . . . "Yes," he said, with his long, peculiar drawl, "it is rather pleasant. It was built by a French artist. That's the reason for this," with a slow wave of the hand. "Studio, you see. Well," putting the pipe back and taking a long puff, "he went away. One day Mr. Pomeroy, New York artist, nice man, came along. He looked around a little, then in his quick [puff] American [puff] way [puff] he said, "I want that house!" And before the fellow knew what [puff, puff, puff] he was about, Mr. Pomeroy had the lease signed for three years. . . . Mr. Pomeroy had to leave Paris for the winter, so we took the house. I was obliged to be here five or six months, any way."

The distinguished humorist made these few remarks with an air of pathetic resignation which said plainly that such explanations were a weariness of the flesh.

"You read and speak French, do you not?" The question was addressed to the back of the famous crop of curls, as Mr. Clemens still wandered uneasily up and down.

"I read it. I don't speak it," he said.

"What do you think about French humor? Is there such a thing among modern French writers as humor?"

His eye brightened. He was interested. He took his pipe from his lips and punctuated his remarks with short, decisive waves.

"Ah! now you ask me something about which I dare not express an opinion. I have thought about that a hundred times, but I have never been able to arrive at a concrete opinion which I would feel I had a right to express. I have even tried to put my thoughts on paper, to see if in that way I could come to a more definite conclusion. But I don't know. We hear so much about 'French wit,' as if it were a particular kind of wit, different from that of other countries. And 'French polish,' too. Now a nation may claim to be the politest nation in the world. And that proves nothing. And it may claim to be the wittiest nation in the world. Only, by advertising the statement sufficiently, the nation makes everybody, including its own people, believe that it has told the truth.". . .

"How about the modern French writers? Do any of them pose as humorists?"

"I believe there are one or two who do, but I don't remember their names."

"And evidently you do not know their work?"

"No."

"Are your books translated into French?"

"*Tom Sawyer* and *Huckleberry Finn* have been translated, but I think that is all."

"Do you know whether French people find your books amusing?"

"I don't think they do," said Mr. Clemens, at last sitting down and treating himself and his visitor to a quizzical smile. "A friend of mine told me of a little conversation he had with a Frenchman, and I feel pretty sure, since then, of the way I strike the French mind. This Frenchman is a great critic and is an authority on all literary matters. I don't remember his name, because I never remember names, but he is an authority. That is what makes it so hopeless.

"'I myself,' he said, 'have read a great many American books, and I have heard the opinions of others who are familiar with your literature. This being the case, and knowing the French mind as I do, I think I may claim to speak for the nation itself in what I say. In the first place, then, we regard Edgar Allan Poe as your greatest poet. The French who know his writings look upon him as a great genius. Bret Harte we think your greatest novelist. He is an artist, a great artist. Emerson—well.' Mr. Clemens supplied a beautiful French shrug and lifted his heavy eyebrows, 'we don't understand what you can find in Emerson to admire. I believe you Americans think him great, but we cannot understand why. And lastly, there is Mark Twain, but when it comes to him we are in despair, because no intelligent Frenchman can make out your reasons for thinking Mark Twain funny!'"

The pipe had gone out in the course of this recital, and Mr. Clemens tapped it regretfully and laid it down as he got up to resume his pacing back and forth.

"Perhaps we lose the quality of the French humor as completely as they lose the quality of yours."

"Oh, unquestionably," interrupted Mr. Clemens as he lighted his cigar. "That is the reason why I say I am not competent to express an opinion on the subject. A man may study a language for years and years and yet he is never inside of the holy of holies. He must get into the man himself, the man of another country, and he cannot do that.

"But as for French wit being different from any other wit, I do not know about it. To decide a point like that a man would have to gather hundreds of instances and compare them as a naturalist compares his specimens. He would be obliged to sift them, assay them, and find out the real essence of each. Then, if he could say, 'I have among the specimens from this country 500 where the wit turns upon a certain point, while I find no more than fifty similar examples from the specimens from any other country, and those I regard as accidental,' he would be justified in describing that particular form of wit as specially belonging to that one country. But no one has done that to prove that 'French wit' is a unique product of the French brain.". . .

"Do you find American tourists over here any different from what they were the first time you came to Europe?"

"Well, now, you've asked me something I don't like to answer," was the reply, and Mr. Clemens relapsed into his most pronounced drawl. "If I said anything it might be misinterpreted as applying to the American colony at Paris, and I'd rather blaspheme something of—er—even more holy, you know, than accept people's hospitality and then criticize them."

# Across North America

## July 1895–Sept 4 1895

In order to pay his debts, Twain contracted with the lecture agent J. B. Pond to speak across North America with a world tour to follow. Under Pond's management, he left Elmira, New York, in July 1895 and over the next five weeks he performed twenty-four times in twenty-two cities, from Cleveland to Victoria, B.C.

### "Very Much Abroad / Mr. Clemens on Tour"
Unidentified Cleveland newspaper, 16 July 1895; rpt. in Melbourne *Australian Star*, 14 September 1895, p. 7

Stopping on the way at Cleveland (Ohio) the noted humorist, who was suffering from what he termed a Pullman carbuncle, was bailed up and interviewed. "I understand," said Mr. Clemens in the course of some interesting biographical details, "that Artemus Ward once lived in Cleveland and worked on a newspaper here. I met him in Virginia City. He was delivering a lecture at the time. That was in—let me see. Well, I can't remember exactly, but I left Virginia City by request, and it was previous to that time. Virginia City, you know, was situated directly over the great Comstock silver lode. I was a reporter on the Virginia City *Territorial Enterprise* at the time, and I used to sit up in the office after midnight. Then I could hear a long, low boom, and then I knew that some fellow was blasting quartz right under me. Parts of the town caved in from time to time, and when I heard that boom I used to feel uncomfortable.

"You have heard it said, I suppose, that I was not a success in newspaper work. What more success could have I had? I was a reporter and then city editor of a paper in Virginia City, and I gave satisfaction. That I was not a success in San Francisco was due to circumstances, or I might say to a circumstance. I was on the *Call,* which had but the one reporter. There was not too much for a man to do, but it required constant exercise and a gift of industry. I won't say that I didn't have the gift of industry, but anyhow it was leaky. My job was a good steady job. It kept me working from 9 o'clock one morning until 2 o'clock the next morning. Finally I intimated to the proprietor of the paper how pleasant it would be if I could have an assistant. He gave me one—a patient, cheerful lad whom the printers nicknamed Smiggy McGlural. I used to tell Smiggy to do the police court, and then a fire or two, and it was Smiggy this and Smiggy that, until it became noticeable that Smiggy was doing all the work. I never was so lazy in my life and never enjoyed it so. Finally the proprietor—well, he asked me to hand in my resignation. The facts were all against me. The case admitted of no argument, and I resigned.

"How did I happen to leave Virginia City? Well, I wonder if I ought to tell. Sill, anyone would have left under the circumstances. I was in the full side of my editorial popularity when the editor-in-chief went down to San Francisco to visit some friends and left the paper in my charge. I wrote a very satisfactory editorial about Shakespeare, thinking that it would be news to most of the boys and right away after that I got down to level business, arguments supported by epithets. Every day or two the editor of the rival paper took exception to my epithets, and he answered back.

"It was the custom of the country to call a man out to the field of honor and kill him when he answered back. I didn't want to call the other editor out, but custom made it necessary. I challenged him, naming Colt's navy revolvers the weapons, each to walk 15 steps, turn, fire, and advance firing. That was the way they always had in those days.

Duels weren't picnics or Sunday school excursions. 'Twas business. Well, I challenged my man, Sandy Baldwin, the son of the author of *Flush Times in Alabama,* and a prominent lawyer came and routed me out of bed and said to me that the news of the challenge had got to the Governor's ears at Carson City, and that I would be arrested for sending it. The law was new and they wanted to try it on. Of course, I was the first victim. But I preferred that to the duel. Sandy said that he had heard the Governor say that the trial would see that I stayed there until my term expired.

"'Now,' said Sandy Baldwin, 'as you know, the stagecoach leaves at 4 o'clock this morning, and you have just time to catch it. If you have any delicacy about running away like this you can say that you did it at my request.' So my second, Major Gillis, and I took the stagecoach. Governor North was a man whose word was at par all the time. If he said he'd give me two years and let me keep them it was not open to dispute." . . .

The assertion having been made frequently of late that Mr. Clemens is the author of *Personal Reminiscences of Joan of Arc,* which is being published in serial form in *Harper's Magazine,* the reporter asked Mr. Clemens if he had either affirmed or denied the truth of the rumor. He paused for a moment and then drawled out: "That question has been asked me several times, and I have always said that I considered it wise to leave an unclaimed piece of literary property alone until time has shown that nobody is going to claim it. Then it's safe to acknowledge that you wrote that thing whether you did or not."

## "Twain"

*Minneapolis Penny Press,* 23 July 1895, p. 1

. . . A group were gathered about the bedside of the author who was resting after a fatiguing journey.

"Mr. Clemens," said one, "there was published a short time ago an article which stated that one of your daughters had never read your works."

A smile flitted over the features for a moment, then the reply: "That must be another of those fairy fictions that start from nothing. My children have edited my manuscript since they were seven years of age; that is, they have had it read to them for criticism. They always sided with their father," with a tender but humorous smile, "and the sentence which mother would say should be stricken out, they would assert should remain. But," with the corners of the mouth curling into half a smile again, and the tone growing delightfully dry, "we did not stand on these little things. Madam was really the best editor of the lot. Before I used my flock of editors at home I sent my manuscript to Howells, but now we don't." . . .

"I will tell you, though, where the story regarding my daughter might have arisen," he continued. "When one of my daughters was nine years of age, Elsie Leslie, the child actress, who was of the same age, visited her. At the dinner table my little daughter Jean sat and listened to her extravagant conversation, the subject of which was entirely too abstract for her to grasp. She sat there, gazing with admiration, and very likely, envy, too, to hear Elsie taking part in such conversation with such ease. And she waited until something should be introduced about which she knew. In the course of the conversation the book entitled *Tom Sawyer* was mentioned and Jean saw her chance. 'I know who wrote that book,' she exclaimed; 'It was Harriet Beecher Stowe.' You see that this might have been used as a foundation for that story," and the great author laughed noiselessly at the recollection.

Turning to other things, one of those present asked Mr. Clemens if he had ever visited Minneapolis before. He had years before.

"Why," put in Major Pond, the manager of the lecturing tour, a jolly fellow: "I was in Minneapolis when there were no saloons here."

"Well, you didn't stay long," flashed back Mr. Clemens, and the group laughed at the major's expense.

## "Mark Twain in Winnipeg"
*Winnipeg Tribune,* 27 July 1895, p. 5

On Friday afternoon a reporter of *The Tribune* called on Mark Twain at his rooms in the Manitoba. . . . After talking in a general way about his trips in Europe and the Holy Land, the reporter drew his attention to the very funny incidents which occurred when the Innocents Abroad refused to be astonished or to show any emotion at the stories of European guides.

"Yes," said Mr. Clemens, "they are very amusing when considered in a certain light. When you interrupt a guide in the middle of his harangue, back he flies to the beginning and starts to tell it all over again. And this is not to be wondered at. The repetition of a certain statement a number of times makes it automatic, so at last it tells itself. I know in my own experience, when lecturing fifteen years ago, I told some stories so often that at last they told themselves. Sometimes when I have been very tired, my mind wandered all over; wasn't in the lecture room at all, but my mouth went right along tending to business."

"However excellent these European incidents may be," remarked the scribe, "you doubtless consider the Mississippi your real field of work? You are, so to speak, the prophet of the Mississippi."

"Yes, and the reason is plain. By a series of events—accidents—I was the only one who wrote about old times on the Mississippi. Wherever else I have been some better have been before, and will cover after, but the Mississippi was a virgin field. No one could write that life but a pilot entered into the spirit of it. But the pilots were the last men in the world to write its history. As a class they did not naturally run to literature, and this was made more unlikely by another reason. Every pilot had to carry in his head thousands of details of that great river. Details, moreover, that were always changing, and in order to have nothing to confuse those details they entered into a compact never to read anything. Thus if they had thought of writing, they would have had no connected style, no power of describing anything; and, moreover, they were so engrossed in the river that there was nothing in the life unusual to them. Here then was my chance, and I used it."

In speaking about the spirit of adventure which led people to discover new countries and try new processes, Mr. Clemens suddenly came out with the sentence that the fools in the world were not half appreciated. Going on to explain his meaning, he pointed out that those who discovered new lands or new inventions were always considered fools. The people who put their money into the telegraph, the telephone, and other revolutionizing inventions were always the fools of the age. "Behind every advance you will find your patient and underestimated fool."

## "Mark Twain Talks"
[Lute Pease,] *Portland Oregonian*, 11 August 1895, p. 10

At the Portland yesterday morning, Mark Twain stood surrounded by a medley of handbags waiting for a carriage to the train. . . . That genial, courteous gentleman, Major J. B. Pond, was busy with introductions and other matters, but the carriage didn't come, so Mark and the major bundled into the bus, handbags in hand, and were off.

"Portland seems to be a pretty nice town," drawled the author of *Tom Sawyer*, as the bus rolled down Sixth street, "and this is a pretty nice, smooth street. Now Portland ought to lay itself out a little and macadamize all its streets just like this. Then it ought to own all the bicycles and rent 'em out and so pay for the streets. Pretty good scheme, eh? I suppose people would complain about the monopoly, but then we have the monopolies always with us. Now, in European cities, you know, the government runs a whole lot of things, and, it strikes me, runs 'em pretty well. Here many folks seem to be alarmed about governmental monopolies. But I don't see why. Here cities give away for nothing franchises for car lines, electric plants and things like that. Their generosity is often astonishing. The American people take the yoke of

Mark Twain interviewed by Lute Pease in Portland, Oregon, 9 August 1895.
Courtesy of Kevin MacDonnell.

private monopoly with philosophical indifference, and I don't see why they should mind a little government monopoly."

"What about that book of travels you are going to write on this trip, Mr. Clemens? Will it be something like *The Innocents Abroad,* or the others?"

"Well, it won't describe the same places by any means. It will be a lazy man's book. If any one picks it up expecting to find full data, historical, topographical, and so forth, he will be disappointed. A lazy man, you know, don't rush around with his note book as soon as he lands on a foreign shore. He simply drifts about, and if anything gets in his way of sufficient interest to make an impression on him, it goes into his book. General Sherman told me that when he made his trip abroad, he found just about what he needed in my old books to guide him to what interested him most. He said it was too much bother to wade through the conventional guide book, which mentioned everything, so he dropped them by the wayside. That's just what makes traveling tiresome, I think—that ever-present anxiety to take in everything, whether you can enjoy it and digest it or not—that fear that you won't get your money's worth if you leave anything mentioned in the guidebook behind. What's the use of making a business of traveling when you are out for pleasure? While I am not going to write a guidebook, yet if it can help people to enjoy the same journey, why, I shall think it something of a success." . . .

"I don't believe an author, good, bad or indifferent, ever lived, who created a character. It was always drawn from his recollection of someone he had known. Sometimes, like a composite photograph, an author's presentation of a character may possibly be from the blending of more than two or more real characters in his recollection. But, even when he is making no attempt to draw his character from life, when he is striving to create something different, even then, however ideal his drawing, he is yet unconsciously drawing from memory. It is like a star so far away that the eye cannot discover it through the most powerful telescope, yet if a camera is placed in proper position under that telescope and left for a few hours, a photograph of the star will be the result. So, it's the same way with the mind; a character one has known some time in life may have become so deeply buried within the recollection that the lens of the first effort will not bring it to view. But by continued application the author will find when he is done, that he has etched a likeness of someone he has known before."

## "Mark Twain and Major Pond"

*Tacoma Union,* 11 August 1895, p. 6

. . . Then Mark Twain (Samuel L. Clemens) joined the party. He slid into a chair sidewise, and on coming so near his eyes did not look so wild as they did at a distance. Twenty feet away they look not unlike burned holes in a blanket and appear to be entirely out of joint with Mr. Clemens' calm and slightly ashy face. . . . He puffed leisurely at a cigar, while Major Pond tried to make it appear that Mark Twain was only the runnet of the Clemens family.

"You ought to see Mrs. Clemens and Miss Clemens. They constitute the family," Pond said. "You don't know it, but in five minutes I could produce the cleverest person with a piano on the coast. Miss Clemens is a wonder."

Mark Twain smiled coyly. "You're trying to boom the big end of the show by making up the minor parts," he said, after Major Pond had exhausted himself praising Miss Clemens' abilities.

"You can't deny it," Pond urged.

"Oh, no," replied Mr. Clemens, "but it's only transmitted genius."

Someone asked Mr. Clemens if he really enjoyed knocking about the country on one of Major Pond's lecturing tours.

"He's got," put in Pond before Twain could reply. "He got to like it. We won't have it otherwise."

Twain smiled, and seemed glad to have someone else talk for him by proxy. . . . He smiled just the same each time, even when he went into details about palmistry. He knew much about the subject, and told how Editor Stead of the London *Review of Reviews* had had his hands photographed once when Twain met him on an Atlantic liner. Twain was making one of the fifteen ocean voyages made by him during the past four years, and Stead was to submit the photos to a man who would read and report on the character of the subject.

Several men examined the photos, and Mr. Clemens said two of them were quite accurate in their reports, others were not so accurate.

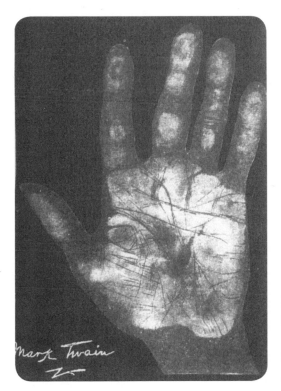

Mark Twain's palm print
from Welland, *The Life and
Times of Mark Twain,* p.
89; also in Milton Meltzer,
*Mark Twain Himself,* p. 151.

But here, as elsewhere, he mixed things up so a wooly west man could not decide with satisfaction to himself when it was proper to laugh. "The laugh" kept bobbing up at unexpected points, and it seemed impossible to decide about its genuineness.

For instance, Mr. Clemens went on to say that when a man looked at your hands and gave you certain information which you know all about yourself, and no one else knew it, not even members of your own family, you had to acknowledge the corn.

Well, one of the experts who examined those Stead photos of Mark Twain's hand reported "this subject has no sense of humor."

Mr. Clemens did not say whether this was so or not.

Then he talked about "doubles," and said all his doubles were around the country lecturing without giving him any of the proceeds. One had secured four bits, he said, at San Francisco by saying he was Mark Twain.

"He got the money in a saloon," added Mr. Clemens, "and I think he was a mighty sharp fellow to raise half a dollar in that way."

## "The Same Old Twain"
*Seattle Post-Intelligencer,* 11 August 1895, p. 7

As Mark Twain sat in the smoker of a northbound Northern Pacific train yesterday, . . . a *Post-Intelligencer* reporter approached him and soon drew him on to give such a random, jolly, enjoyable talk as only Mark Twain can.

Of course Mr. Clemens was pleased with the Northwest. . . . "One feature which has struck me as differentiating this section from those other parts of the West where I have passed before," said Mr. Clemens, "is its notable lack of desert lands. In other states the great stretches of sand and alkali lands are neither picturesque nor pleasant. The lands here are all cultivated or cultivable, and vast tracts of pasture land take the place of the California and Nevada deserts."

Mr. Clemens was equally enthusiastic about the scenery through which he is now passing. In speaking of the almost endless areas of level grain fields about Winnipeg, he instituted a comparison between the scenic effect of such a mass of waving green and that produced by the ocean. . . .

"The eye, in fact, cannot judge of distance unless it has some familiar object to set up as a sort of gauge," continued the great humorist; and then, with that peculiar drawl in his voice and twinkle in his eye which stamp him as the price of raconteurs and herald the flashes of fun for which he has become famous, he went on to tell how once during his early life on the plains he had stood with a group of comrades and gazed at a mass of approaching objects without a single rock or tree on which to base an estimate of distance. Indians, suggested one of the party, a

Mark Twain at his hotel in Olympia, Washington, 11 August 1895.
Courtesy of Kevin MacDonnell.

keen-sighted pioneer and experienced hunter. Wild horses, ventured another. Buffalo, hazarded a third. All thought the objects fully two miles away. "And what do you think they turned out to be?" asked Mark Twain, with as much zest and animation as if he were telling a ghost story to a wondering child. Then with his peculiar drawl: "They were nothing more than a lot of j-a-c-k-r-a-b-b-i-t-s."

Then, with all the soberness of a sworn witness, he went to tell how he once saw a man in New Orleans stand on the sidewalk and declare he saw a squirrel moving about in an upper room across the street, and the squirrel turned out to be a louse on a hair hanging from the man's hat. With equal facility he reeled off a yarn from the days when he was a pilot's cub on a Mississippi river steamboat. He and the pilot, side by side at the wheel, each and both distinctly saw one night what they supposed to be a man performing the foolhardy feat of climbing the whistle-pipe, a slender tube that reached far up the side of one of the tall smokestacks of the boat, some sixty feet from the pilot house. They commented on his strange conduct, and, concluding he must be a lunatic, were starting to capture him when he turned out to be nothing but a rat climbing a bell rope only a few feet distant from their eyes.

The mention of those old days of piloting naturally led the reporter to ask Mr. Clemens as to the truthfulness of the current story that tells how he came to take his well-known *nom de plume.*

"Like many others of its kind," he answered, "the story has become somewhat warped from being often told. The facts are about these: Old Isaiah Sellers, back in the '50s, was by odds the oldest pilot on the Mississippi. He used to write up the changing stages of that fickle stream for the columns of the *True Delta,* and now and then he would intersperse his short reports with startling statements of how things used to be fifty or sixty years before. I wrote my first skit as a burlesque on his reports. It covered a column and a half in the *Delta,* sometime in 1857. It was a crude effort, but it served its purpose. It played sad havoc with some of old Sellers' pet islands and channels, fairly knocking them galley-west, and telling how some century or so ago they used to occupy places in the far interior of the country. The old man never wrote another report. The name over which he used to write was Mark Twain. Time rolled on, and when the news of Sellers' death was borne to me in Carson City, I was doing up the Nevada legislature, embalming the members in a weekly letter. They did not relish some of my criticisms, and they were continually rising to a question of privilege to denounce the man whom they were pleased to call the 'unreliable correspondent of the *Territorial Enterprise.'* From the frequency with which they denounced me, I concluded it would save time if I gave them a shorter phrase than that, and when I heard that Isaiah Sellers was dead, I deliberately robbed his corpse and signed my next letter 'Mark Twain.'"

## "Mark Twain to Pay All"

San Francisco *Examiner*, 17 August 1895, p. 2

Sam L. Clemens (Mark Twain), who is about leaving for Australia, in an interview concerning the purposes of his long trip, said:

"I am idle until lecture-time. Write, and I will dictate and sign. My run across the continent, covering the first 4,000 miles of this lecturing tour around the world, has revealed to me so many friends of whose existence I was unconscious before, and so much kindly and generous sympathy with me in my financial mishaps, that I feel that it will not be obtrusive self-assertion, but an act of simple justice to that loyal friendship, as well as to my own reputation, to make a public statement of the purpose which I have held from the beginning, and which is now in the process of execution.

"It has been reported that I sacrificed, for the benefit of the creditors, the property of the publishing firm whose financial backer I was, and that I am now lecturing for my own benefit. This is an error. I intend the lectures, as well as the property, for the creditors.

"The law recognizes no mortgage on a man's brain, and a merchant who has given up all he has may take advantage of the rules of insolvency and start free again for himself; but I am not a business man; and honor is a harder master than the law. It cannot compromise for less than a hundred cents on the dollar, and its debts never outlaw.

"I had a two-thirds interest in the publishing firm, whose capital I furnished. If the firm had prospered, I should have expected to collect two-thirds of the profit. As it is I expect to pay all the debts. My partner has no resources, and I do not look for assistance from him. . . .

"The present situation is that the wreckage of the firm, together with what money I can scrape together, with my wife's aid, will enable me to pay the other creditors about 50 percent of their claims. It is my intention to ask them to accept that as a legal discharge and trust to my honor to pay the other 50 percent. as fast as I can earn it. From my reception thus far on my lecturing tour I am confident that if I live I can pay off the last debt within four years, after which, at the age of sixty-four, I can make a fresh and unencumbered start in life.

"I do not enjoy the hard travel and broken rest inseparable from lecturing, and if it had not been for the imperious moral necessity or paying these debts, which I never contracted but which were accumulated on the faith of my name by those who had a presumptive right to use it, I should never have taken to the road at my time of life. I could have supported myself comfortably by writing, but writing is too slow for the demands that I have to meet; therefore I have begun to lecture my way around the world. I am going to Australia, India and South Africa, and next year I hope to make a tour of the great cities of the United States.

"In my preliminary run through the smaller cities on the northern route, I have found a reception the cordiality of which has touched my heart and made me feel how small a thing money is in comparison with friendship.

"I meant, when I began, to give my creditors all the benefit of this, but I begin to feel that I am gaining something from it too, and that my dividends, if not available for banking purposes, may be even more satisfactory than theirs."

## "Mark Twain Talks"
### Vancouver *Daily News-Advertiser*, 20 August 1895, p. 5

The scribes found Mark Twain in bed when they called on him last Sunday morning at the Hotel Vancouver. . . . The scribes expressed a hope that R. M. S. *Warrimoo* would convey the humorist and his family in safety to their destination and apropos of the subject mentioned the *Miowera's* predilection for running on to hidden rocks. At the same time they did not forget to add, no lives were ever lost and beyond the damage to the steamer itself, these several experiences were unmarked by casualties. Mark Twain said he was looking for a ship of that kind—a ship with the rock habit, and one which never allowed such mishaps to disconcert her, but always got off again. The conversation gradually

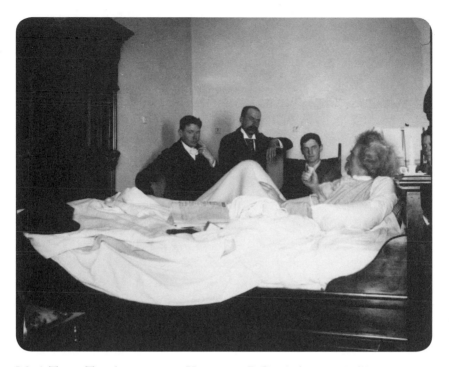

Mark Twain T and reporters in Vancouver, B.C., 17 August 1895.
Courtesy of Kevin MacDonnell.


turned on Thursday evening's lecture and the inability of some people to
perceive the point of a joke. Thus one well-known citizen would insist
on giving the lecturer's flights of fancy a literal interpretation. Mark
Twain ascribed the effect of a lecturer, humorous or otherwise, to the
audience as much as to the lecturer. "When you have a crowded house,"
he said in substance, "some subtle magnetic influence seems to permeate
the atmosphere, so that the recognition of the speaker's intention by the
audience is unanimous. It often happens that when one is telling a joke
to three or four listeners, only one out of that number will perceive its
meaning, but with a large auditory, it is invariably the large majority. The
depressing influence of a small audience is due to several causes. In the
first place, the individual members of that audience feel sorry for the
lecturer. Mentally they put themselves in his position and sympathize

with him—such is the charitable disposition of most people. But should the lecturer become scared and rattled their attitude changes from sympathy to contempt and contempt is fatal. The sympathetic attitude is hard to fight against and the ability to do so only comes with experience. Personally some of my most enthusiastic audiences have been small ones." . . .

Major Pond took advantage of a favorable moment to adjust what Mark Twain calls his "cartridge box," to wit a kodak, . . . before he touched it off at this interesting if unconventional group.

### "Twain Very Ill"
New York *World*, 4 September 1895, p. 8s

Samuel L. Clemens sailed yesterday for Sydney. . . . Before sailing, the invalid received a party of newspaper men.

"I am glad to see you," said Mark Twain. "I am somewhat of a newspaper man myself, and we are a hard-up, happy, carefree lot, take us altogether. I do not want to tell you of my business troubles. I have never wanted to do that to anyone since one day years and years ago. The foreman of the horse-bill department of a publishing house with which I was connected printed a card with the legend: 'I have trouble of my own; don't tell yours,' and hung it up where those who ran might read. That card was a corrosion to my soul and seemed to eat into me, and the impression that it made has never been effaced. The whole world knows that I have been in financial difficulties. I have given my newspaper friends for publication a personal statement of how I stand and what I intend to do, so that I need not weary you with any further reference to tales of foreclosures or creditors.

"Just what to talk to you about is a difficult thing to decide," he said. "If I were before an audience I could size them up and know what to say, but you will talk to audiences larger and more diversified than ever was gathered in a hall to listen to me." . . .

"But about audiences. I remember very well, indeed, giving an

Mark Twain, Clara Clemens, and Olivia Clemens aboard the *Warrimoo*, 23
August 1895. Courtesy of Kevin MacDonnell.

address in the Exchange Building in the city of St. Louis. The Exchange
Building was something like a barn that had gone to seed—one of those
great, big, hollow, broad, expansive buildings all on a level. The whole
would seat something like 1,500 people.

"The night that I spoke in that hall—it was in 1865, I think—there
were twenty people gathered to hear me. I am not sure about their being
gathered. I have a kind of an idea that they were people, the kind that
lived in the hall—were fixtures, as it were, like the benches. But, anyway,
I determined that, fixtures or not, I was going to give them that lecture;
so I asked them all to come and sit on the front bench, and then getting
over as near the front of the platform as I could I talked right into their
faces.

"Behind them stretched that fearful row of barren benches. It was like talking to people on the edge of the great Desert of Sahara, but we had a good time. The lecture was timed for an hour and a quarter, but we got along so well together and were having such a good time that I talked to those people over two hours, and they were the most enthusiastic audience I have ever had the pleasure of holding conversation with."

Mark Twain here put his hand behind his head and in doing so knocked down the candle set at the foot of the bed. . . . "There goes that confounded candle again," said he. "I look on that candle as a sort of link between gloom and darkness; it is not very closely connected in my mind with the idea of light. I remember very well when most of the hotels were lighted with coal-oil lamps. They were not bad; and if you could get the hall porter to let you have half a dozen of them you could generally decipher the difference between the outlines of the bed and bureau.

"When gas became more generally used I hailed it as a glorious innovation, but I soon discovered that the economical landlord has a way of dealing with that gaslight that left you a little bit worse off than you were with the lamps. Then came the electric light. I thought that when that came into general use we had at last got into an era of a good bedroom light, but I find that I have again been deceived. They put up a nice electrolier with about four burners on it, but you generally find that three of them have that smoky appearance that betokens a burnt out filament. You send word to the office to have it repaired. For this they keep a bellboy dressed up in overalls so as to look like an electrician. In response to your call up comes this suit of overalls with the bellboy inside of it and monkeys with the burners that won't light up. He pretends to fix them, but he never does. They continue non-illuminant up to the time of your departure.

"Besides that, I find that in most of the towns they run their electric light on a fixed-hour system. The light comes in at a certain time and goes out at a certain time. In this hotel, for example, we have to go to bed as a rule with the candle, because the light quits at 2 A.M. In these fixed-hour towns it does not make any difference how dark or gloomy the afternoon may be or how early the shades of evening gather round, you cannot get your light until a certain hour. If it gets dark at 6 P.M. you have to amuse yourself chasing shadows until 8."

# Australia and New Zealand

## Sept 17 1895–Jan 4 1896

Twain, his wife Olivia, and daughter Clara arrived in Sydney on September 16, 1895. Despite illness, his fifty performances between September 1895 and early January 1896 were well-received and earned thousands of dollars.

### "Mark Twain in Sydney"
Melbourne *Argus*, 17 September 1895, p. 5

Mark Twain landed in Sydney today. . . . Intellectually he is like many another humorist; he seems cast in a somewhat somber mould.

"Life," he said, looking from beneath his fair shaggy eyebrows, "is not at all a humorous thing. I have never found it a joke, and I am serious if nothing else. Man as a normal creature is serious now and then. One of us, say a scribbler like myself, pen in hand, may get a moment of enlightenment. A sudden thought may slip in, and then comes humor. That, however, is a contribution which the gods have sent his way, and which really is not of man. It comes from some place, the key of which he does not possess to open it at his will. Yes, life is serious, and man is the most serious part of it.

"Now you have heard," he continued, "that I am the laziest man in the United States, yet I tell you, and I believe, it is perfectly demonstrable that there is no such being as a perfectly lazy man. Just consider that every man has a gift either large of small. It may be to play billiards or to imitate Paderewski. Whatever that gift is man takes a native delight in exploiting it, and it is a most difficult thing to prevent him from exercising that gift. There are hundreds of interests that the human race possesses. In the case of any particular man ninety-nine out of a hundred of these interests may not appeal to him, so that so far as they are concerned he is the laziest of beings. He is too lazy to do this, too lazy to do that, but when you arrive at his gift he is not lazy. It is difficult then to keep him from working night and day. So I frankly admit that in regard to many human things, I am, if you like to use the term, phenomenally lazy, lazy in every way that you can possibly imagine, until it comes to writing a book. Then there is no more industrious man in the world than myself. Let me alone and I will work with my pen until I drop from fatigue. Then the only trouble my family have with me is digging me out of my chair when my day's work is done. To the extent I describe, then, I am lazy or industrious just as you please. Understand, I don't philosophize. I leave that for newspapers to do. I simply state a fact."

. . . "[I]f you ask what man has impressed me most, I hardly know what to say. Still I think above all men I would put General Grant. His was a grand figure and his was a noble nature. It was so simple and so beautiful. Standing face to face with him you looked at a man with a mighty record, and yet it was not the knowledge of that fact, but the man's latent power that was so impressive with him. . . . Of course, General Grant had great contemporaries. There were Sheridan and Stonewall Jackson, the latter with his deep religious fervor—just such another as Gordon, and the former with his profanity. Oh, my! he could swear. Still, I suppose, after all, that was merely a matter of environment. If he had the same training and the same surroundings as General Jackson I suppose he would have been much the same.

"Do I mind saying what I think about Bret Harte?" said Mark Twain in reply to an inquiry. "No. But mind if I speak strongly it is merely a personal opinion. I detest him, because I think his work is 'shoddy.' His forte is pathos which does not come out of a man's heart. He has no heart, except his name, and I consider he has produced nothing that is genuine. He is artificial. That opinion, however, must be taken with some allowance, for, as I say, I do not care for the man."

Mark Twain uttered this sentence with an emphasis that left no doubt as to his earnestness, and then went on to say, "I have no objection to my views being known. It is purely a personal criticism. I dare say, when I go to London, I shall meet him, but what of that? I am most moderate in my dislikes. There are only three or four persons in the world to whom I have had any antipathy, and the Almighty has removed most of them. It does seem wonderful that I should not have been allowed to get at them before they died."

## "Visit of Mark Twain / Wit and Humour"
### Sydney *Morning Herald*, 17 September 1895, pp. 5–6

When you sit down to "interview" Mark Twain he makes a remark that recalls the stock observation of the member of Parliament who is about to inflict himself disastrously on time and space. "I have very little to say," he begins. But this is where the simile—which no doubt is as unsatisfactory as similes generally are—begins and ends. . . .

"What is humor?" he says with a laugh, as some suggestive sidewind of conversation takes his mind that way. . . . "It is easy enough often to say what it is not; but an exact scientific definition—it seems like trying to transfix a sunbeam. I suppose no man ever knew why he had humor, and where he got it from, exactly what constituted a humorous idea, or in what way it first appealed to him. Life has been finely defined as 'a tragedy to those who feel—a comedy to those who think.' That is a very fine definition of the main qualities that go to make the humorist. I maintain that a man can never be a humorist, in thought or in deed, until he can feel the springs of pathos. Indeed, there you have a basis of something material to go upon in trying to comprehend what this impalpable thing of true humor is. Trust me, he was never yet properly funny who was not capable at times of being very serious. And more: the two are as often as not simultaneous. Whilst a man sees what we call the humorous side he must have ever present the obverse; those who laugh best and oftenest know that background."

You don't believe there is such a being who simply laughs, as the poet sings, because he must?

"The true and proper laughter, 'the sudden glory of laughter' as Addison has it, doesn't come in that causeless way. Look at all the humorists and their creations, their subtle contrasts and their exquisite breaks of laughter—can't you see behind it all the depth and the purpose of it? Look at the poor fool in *Lear*, look at Lamb, getting the quaintest, most spirit-moving effects with the tears just trembling on the verge of every jest; look at Thackeray and Dickens, and all the bright host who have gained niches in the gallery of the immortals. They have one thing always in their mind, no matter what parts they make their puppets play. Behind the broadest grins, the most exquisitely ludicrous situations, they know there is the grinning skull, and that all roads lead along the dusty road to death. Ah, don't think there is such a thing as a mere 'corner man' in literature any more than there is in any other department of life. I say that the clown rolling in the sawdust at a circus to the shrieks of the children knows and feels the truth that I have tried to explain. Don't you remember what Garrick said to a friend, 'You may fool the town in tragedy, but they won't stand any nonsense in comedy.' It is so true! Any pretender can cast up the whites of his eyes to the heavens and roll out his mock heroics, but the comedian must have the genuine ring in him. Otherwise he couldn't be a comedian."...

"Let me say that Gilbert seems to me a perfectly delightful and exquisite humorist. How perfectly charming is the lambent play of his fancy! and when I read his operas I am struck dumb with astonishment. It seems to me marvelous that a man should have this gift of saying not only the wittiest of things, but of saying them in verse! I don't think there are many better examples, in their way, of my philosophisings about humor up above than Gilbert's Jack Point. There you have the humor mingling and floating in a sea of pathos. Lewis Carroll always appealed to me as a true and subtle humorist; but I must fain confess that with the years I have lost much of my youthful admiration for Dickens. In saying so, it seems a little as if one were willfully heretic; but the truth must prevail. I don't know where it is exactly, but I cannot laugh and cry with him as I was wont. I seem to see all the machinery of the business too clearly, the effort is too patent. The true and lasting genius of humor does not drag you thus to boxes labeled 'pathos,' 'humor,' and show you all the mechanism of the inimitable puppets that are going to perform. How I used to laugh at Simon Tappertit, and the Wellers, and a host more! But I can't do it now somehow; and time, it seems to me, is the true test of humor. It must be antiseptic. . . .

"About American politics? Well, I have been out of the run of them for some years. Of course, we have found out that an omnipotent democracy is not an unmitigated blessing; but America is not governed by the people, as you seem to think. She only seems to be—it is her politicians who do the governing. Once upon a time, about 14 years ago, we had a strong third party, and that party attracted some of the best men in the country to it. The Mugwumps, as they were called, went down in a subsequent Presidential election before the folly of the people, and it hasn't reappeared. But it's wanted badly enough. It seems to me that you've got right at the basis of things if you have that strong third party with the best men in it. It doesn't matter what their views are, so long as they are the best men."

## "A Chat with Mark Twain"
### Sydney *Sunday Times*, 22 September 1895, p. 4

. . . I found him enjoying a peaceful pipe in his private room and opened conversation by expressing a hope that he was not altogether weary of being interviewed.

"Oh, no," was the reply. "The only difficulty is saying things that one should not say."

In reply to a question as to his impressions of the public men he had met here, Mark Twain said: "It is easy to see that they are able men, and remarkable men, or they would not be in those positions. The fact is it may be conceded that when men are politically prominent, no matter whether they are full of virtues or full of demerits, the chances are they are men of large abilities. I have found it so in all countries, and I never expect to see commonplace men in high positions."

"And what do you think of your audience?"

"There could not be a choicer audience or more satisfactory one to me, and I have found the same characteristics here as in England and Canada, that they adopt a friendly and uncritical attitude at the beginning, whereas it frequently happens in America that they only get into that attitude after one is fairly at work. The American audience is delightfully responsive and sympathetic, but not always in the very beginning. Foreign lecturers have noticed that and spoken of it."

"But is not the warmth of your reception chiefly due to your reputation as an author?"

"That may be the case, but I had not much reputation when I lectured in England 22 years ago. I found the attitude of the English audiences exactly the same as here. They give one confidence at once, instead of waiting for one to earn it, but it is impossible to talk much on that subject without thinking it out. It would amount to an essay."

"There has been some criticism regarding your published opinions of Bret Harte's work. They have been referred to as spiteful utterances."

"That's what it was. I said that a criticism of Bret Harte from me could have no value, as it would be tainted with prejudice. That is just one of the infelicities of interviewing—that you in the rush of talk intrude your private feelings upon the public, and no one has a right to do that. If I were writing about Bret Harte, and was betrayed into saying ungracious things of him or his work, that would not disturb me, because I should know that next day this flash of passion would have passed, and that piece of writing would find its appropriate place in the waste basket. No man who is ever interviewed, perhaps, fails to say things which are not proper things to be said to an unoffending public, and I am not less liable to these mistakes than would be the persons who find fault with me, if they were being interviewed without the opportunity to weigh their words. Since I have been out on this tour, now two or three months, I have expressed opinions in a great many interviews about authors foreign and domestic, and I have said no harsh word about any of them but three. It is a good enough average—constituted as I am—and I did not constitute myself. It is no merit that I said no hard things about the others, for there were no harsh feelings concerning them stored up in the place where I keep my bile.

"It would be inexcusable in me to expose my spleen publicly if I did it deliberately and with full opportunity to reconsider the matter and be courteously silent." . . .

At this point Mrs. Clemens entered the room, and the interviewer having been duly introduced Mr. Clemens mentioned that we had been talking about Bret Harte.

"Ah!" said Mrs. Clemens, with a smile. "I hope it was nothing critical. That was a great mistake you made. I think it would be better if your wife saw your interviews in print before they were published."

"The offence," said Mark Twain, "was committed against the reader; it is that which troubles me, not the offence against Harte himself."

## "Mark Twain on Prohibition"
### New South Wales *Licensing Guardian*,
### late September–early November 1895

"What do I think of Prohibition? Nothing, for the simple reason that there is no such thing. When men want drink, they'll have it in spite of all the laws ever passed, when they don't want it, no drink will be sold. Without wanting to know the experience of America, you people in Australia have an object lesson in temperance legislation. There is supposed to be no drink sold on Sundays in Sydney and Melbourne. Yet I, a stranger, can see that plenty of it is sold, that the most inveterate boozer can get all he wants while he is able to pay for it. Now, if Prohibition cannot be enforced on one day of the week, it cannot be enforced all the year round, and year after year. If men cannot do without a drink from

Saturday night till Monday morning it is certain that they cannot wait longer. The way in which your Sunday closing law is evaded will give you an idea of the so-called Prohibition districts in America. The front door is closed, but the back is opened; instead of open honest drinking, you have sly boozing; instead of having the traffic under the supervision of the law, and conducted in the interests of order and morality, there is no supervision at all, and the trade is conducted under the most demoralizing conditions. The manner in which these absurd liquor laws are broken breeds contempt for law in general. Then, while intensifying, instead of eradicating the evil, these laws give rise to smuggling, and informing, and perjury. So now you see why in the States and Canada, they are often repealed on the very first opportunity. . . .

"Ah," sighed our distinguished visitor, "Why don't the temperance agitators remember Edmund Burke's words? 'Lawful indulgence is the only check on illicit gratification.' Abolishing matrimony would not stamp out fornication. Well, what marriage is to morality, a properly conducted licensed liquor traffic is to sobriety. In either case, a certain human propensity is regulated so as to be a blessing; while left to itself, or subjected to repressive efforts, it would be a curse." . . .

Asked what he considered the best means of solving the vexed problem, Mark replied, "Ask me something easy. The solution of this problem may come with the Millennium, when there will be no crime, and we'll all be angels with wings instead of sinners in pants, and bloomers, and skirts, divided and otherwise. But no man can now point out a remedy. It is doubtful whether even the Temperance preachers believe in their own remedies. If they did, they would not be so ready to make them known. No man cares to find his own occupation gone. Perhaps, the professional Temperance man dreads that universal sobriety, which would force him to turn to another calling and keep the lamp of his nose burning by some other means. You must not think that because I'm in the lecture line myself, I'm prejudiced against these Temperance preachers, but if what one hears be true, then some of them are awful shams." . . .

"Of course many, perhaps the majority of them, are sincere and earnest, even to fanaticism. But there is a great objection against even that class. . . . In fact, the temperance people are selfish in one respect, they want a pleasure which they deny themselves, branded as illegal, though it may be agreeable and even beneficial to others. There is a lot of conceited self-sufficiency about these Temperance people. It is gratifying to directly rail at other people's vices, or pity their weakness, and so indirectly extol their own virtues and strength. The union of the churches with the Temperance party will never come off. The use of wine is sanctioned by the Bible. Teetotalism is supposed to have been invented as a blow at Christianity. Speaking of Mahomet, Schlegel, the German historian, tells us, 'Even the prohibition of wine was, perhaps, not so much intended as a moral precept, which considered in that point of view, would be far too severe as for answering a religious design of the founder, for he might hope from the express condemnation of a liquid, which forms an essential element of Christian sacrifice, that it would necessarily recoil on that sacrifice itself, and thus raise an insuperable barrier between his creed and the religion of Christ.'"

On the connection between the Temperance agitation and woman suffrage he was still more emphatic. "Woman suffrage is favored because likely to add to the voting power of the Temperance Party. But why should women have a vote to put down a practice that does not concern them, except in rare cases? It's the men who drink. Woman now complains of her political bondage, yet would celebrate her liberation by an act of tyranny."

Here Mr. Mark Twain—where is the middle initial of the Yankee name?—looked at his watch and said, "Time is pressing; come, let us solve the liquor problem in our own way. What are you going to have? Isn't it curious how drinks always follow the flag? For instance, I take a cocktail wherever I go. That doesn't suit the British constitution. In those German forests where the British constitution was reared, beer, according to Tacitus, was popular. Here's luck to *The Guardian* and confusion to tee-totalism."

## "Mark Twain"

### Melbourne *Evening News*, 26 September 1895, p. 2

... I found myself sitting opposite Mark Twain, and we shook hands. He introduced me to two ladies, his wife and daughter ... And I lapsed into silence in the presence of the man who had set the world's table in a roar whenever he exclaimed, "Pass the mustard." ...

"I have no literary work in contemplation at present beyond a book of my present Australian travels. I know that new countries are always a little touchy with respect to their critics. Dickens, in *Martin Chuzzlewit* and his *American Notes*, told us a great many unpleasant truths, but they were truths undoubtedly; and lately, when I have re-read them, I cannot see why so much fuss was made over them. The Americans didn't take kindly to them. Now, however, the case is altered. A lot of foreigners have cribbed Dickens' stale facts, and re-written his disapproval of things which no longer exist! I shall be a mild critic!"

Mark Twain was deeply moved by my next question. "What are your opinions of the British Empire?"

He gazed pitifully upon me and said, "Must I really answer that? It is such a large subject for an infant to try and talk about. I have long wished to receive a considerable gift of prophecy, but, oh, I know so little of politics. Yet it is to be hoped that in the event of trouble the common bond of the English language and literature would lead to practical sympathy in time of need."

"These matters of detail," said Mark, "remind me of a story. I had a friend who grappled with great subjects in a general, comprehensive kind of a manner, which was a sure indication of his grasp of the subject. When trying to explain the otherwise inexplicable, he would seek shelter behind forms and figures of speech. He was reckoning up a political antagonist, and making poor headway in the encounter, when he settled it to his own satisfaction by summing him up as a d——d fool, which he was careful to explain to the fool's friends was a mere matter of detail." ...

"It is hard to realize that this is spring at the end of September. I see the bursting buds and the flower blossoms on every hand, and I know that I am in a different country from my own, though the houses and fences and people are alike, and I might be in Kansas or South Carolina. But, then, I have been awake all night, and perhaps that increases the illusion. Fancy American May and Australian September being the same!"

Then with a troubled sigh, he moaned: "Two batches of Spring poets in a single year!"

## "The Tramp in Melbourne / A Morning with Mark Twain"
### Melbourne *Herald Standard*, 26 September 1895, p. 1; 27 September 1895, p. 4

It commenced with a yawn, did this interview.

"I'll tell you what it is," said the humorist; "I'm really fatigued. I didn't sleep well in the train on the way from Sydney, and when I did at length doze off, they woke me up at five o'clock this morning in order to change trains and bring me on to Melbourne. I must say I believe in early rising—for everyone but myself. Personally, I can always excuse myself for not getting up so very early."

It was Mark Twain who was speaking. . . .

"How do you like Australian railway traveling as compared with traveling in America?" . . . It is remarked to him that the carriage in which we are riding may suggest America to him, seeing that the seats were covered with buffalo.

"Ah," he says, "but not buffalo-buffalo. There are no buffaloes in America now, except Buffalo Bill. A wonderful man is Buffalo Bill, and a very fine show it is that he gives. I can remember the time when I was a boy, when buffaloes were plentiful in America. You had only to step off the road to meet a buffalo. But now they have all been killed off. Great pity it is so. I don't like to see the distinctive animals of a country killed off."

"It is the same in this country. The kangaroo is gradually becoming more and more scarce."

"Ah! I suppose so. And what a queer animal the kangaroo is. I haven't seen one, but I suppose it is. I did see one of your native creatures while I was in New South Wales. That was the laughing jackass. It sat on a tree, and I stood looking at it. But it wouldn't laugh for me. I tried to make it laugh; indeed I did; but it respectfully declined."

"Probably it didn't think you were funny," put in Mrs. Clemens who was sitting in the opposite corner of the carriage.

"Probably not; but I did my best. . . . Just think," he adds, "of the awful deceit I have been practicing for so many years!"

"The public, Mr. Clemens, is quite content that you should go on deceiving them in the same way."

"Thanks. But talking of Sydney, we had a splendid time there. The weather was perfect, and we had some excellent views of the famous Harbor. What did I think of Sydney Harbor? Well, I will say of it that its beauty justifies some of the most extravagant things that have been said of it. The way it is broken up, with its hundreds of little forks and tongues of water breaking into the land—fringed round with blue inlets—reminded me of a figure used by Marcus Clarke in that masterly work, *For the Term of His Natural Life*. The figure I refer to I regard as one of the most striking in the whole of literature. He is speaking of the Harbor at Hobart, you know, and he says—I have always remembered it—that the way the water spread round and indented the land was like 'melted lead spilt in water.' That is, I say, one of the most perfect figures I have ever read. You know how melted lead, when you drop it in water, shoots in all directions—radiates—and that figure came forcibly to my mind when I was looked at Sydney Harbor."

"Is Marcus Clarke's novel read much in the States?"

"By some, no doubt; but it is a work that is bound to be one of the most read as it becomes known, because it is a great work of art." . . .

"You haven't given the world any book since *Pudd'nhead Wilson* was born, have you?"

"Yes, one; it was not published under the name of Mark Twain, though. Oh, I am not going to tell you the title of it. That is my little secret at present. . . . I'll tell you the reason why I published this book anonymously. It is not in my usual vein. It is a story of quite another kind. Perhaps you have read my book *The Prince and the Pauper?* You have? Well, that is a story that is not in my usual vein. At first I intended to publish it anonymously, but I was persuaded not to do so by my family, because they liked it. But afterwards I was sorry I did not. Mind you I like the book myself, but what I felt about it was that the signature Mark Twain is a kind of trademark. The public buying a book by Mark Twain expects to get a book of a certain type. And I felt it was not quite fair to my readers to publish a book of quite another type under that signature. I may be wrong; but that is how I look at it. If a man puts a certain trademark upon a certain brand of cloth he has no right to sell the public another sort of cloth under that same trademark."

"But authors as a rule do not look upon a *nom de plume* as a trademark, do they?"

"Perhaps not, but I do. Mark Twain is my trademark."

"Your Twain Mark one might almost say."

But it seemed to hurt his feelings.

"Talking of authorship, how do American authors regard your copyright law now that it has been in working several years?"

"I think it works very well now. I was at first in favor of giving the British author absolute protection for his books sold in America, but you have to remember that in the course of years all sorts of vested interests are created and have to be considered. There was the vested interest of the printer, and of the publisher, and of all the others who had profited by the free publication, without copyright, of an English authors' books in the States. The Copyright Act passed by Congress was the best Act it was possible to get passed at the time, and, as it gives the protection of copyright to the author who has his books printed in the States it treats him very fairly, I think." . . .

On the subject of his present tour he says that it is the third lecturing season he has undertaken. "And," he quaintly adds, "as my first lecture was given twenty years ago I fancy you will own that is very mild dissipation." The conversation wanders on to a whole lot of subjects of various kinds. He speaks at one moment of his old days as the river pilot on the Mississippi—"the delightfulest life in the world and there never was anything like it," he declares. The British Empires commands his admiration, though, as for his views about it, he considers "a large subject for an infant to talk about." The American civil war he thinks did a good deal for forming the American character by raising up noble men and nerving them to great deeds. And so he talks on, until the train shoots from the environment of the green country laced with silver creeks to the brick and wood-shanty skirts of the city.

## "Mark Twain Put to the Question"
Adelaide *South Australian Register,* 14 October 1895, p. 6

. . . As we went into the private parlor of the South Australian Club Hotel . . . I asked him how he managed to smuggle his carbuncle past the Customs officers over the Border, [and] he guessed that they did not know that he had it concealed about his person. "It sits on me like the nation," he said; "it keeps quiet awhile, but at times it gathers itself together and gives an almighty hard twist. It's pretty vigorous." Remarking about the ordeal by interview he said drily, "I think interviewing as an institution is good enough where the man under torture has something to confess, and the torturer knows how to worry it out of him. Now I haven't got much to reveal."

"There is a lot of rubbish forced upon a long-suffering public through the competition in the interview business?" "Just so. It often happens that the interviewed has nothing to say, and the interviewer does not know how to make him say it. So times in despair they write up a lot the man never said, never intended to say, and couldn't say if he thought of it; but an accurate interview is a good thing. The interviewer has his interests to serve, and feels he must get something somehow. It may be that he is no better equipped with material than the man he wants to get the column out of." . . .

Mark Twain and Carlyle
Smythe in Australia,
September 1895.
Courtesy of the Mark Twain Project,
University of California, Berkeley.

"What about the racial feeling in America?"

"Well, that's a big question. Much of the talk is exaggerated by windy agitators and stump orators, and does not represent the real feeling. Away back there was talk of deporting the negroes to Africa, and of disfranchising a large number, but you do not hear much of it now. I expect agitators are much the same breed all over the world. Chinamen, the yellow agony; well, most of my acquaintance with them is amongst the washerman class on the Pacific slope; and as for the Japs, those I have met have been highly cultured gentlemen educated in our Colleges. The Jap is a superior person, and wears his English clothes of the latest cut with all the ease of an Englishman born to them. I was never disposed to make fun of the Chinaman; I always looked upon him as a pathetic object; a poor, hardworking, industrious, friendless heathen, far from home, amongst a strange people, who treated him none too well. He has a hard life, and is always busy and always sober, therefore I never could see anything to make fun of in the Chinaman. No, he is not wanted in America. The feeling is that he ought to go, but America is a place for all people, it seems."

## "Mark Twain in Hobart / Some Impressions and an Interview"
### Hobart *Mercury,* 4 November 1895, p. 4

. . . When I asked him if he would talk with me for a few moments he looked whimsical and said, "Well, I've nothing to say; but if it's of use to you I'm quite willing to say it." . . .

"You're really leaving Australia for a time today, Mr. Clemens," I said at length. "Are you sorry?"

"Yes," he said slowly. "I didn't come to stay, but I'm sorry—downright sorry. In this Australian trip the change to me has been delightful. I've met a good many people, and they've all been hearty and friendly. The same thing applies to my audiences, who have all along welcomed me in a fashion which is exceedingly pleasant to a stranger. All my impressions of the country and of the people are of a pleasant sort, for the reason that it is the human element that makes a country beautiful or otherwise. All this now (and he indicated Mount Wellington and its environment)—all this is very beautiful, but it seems to me that this could not be beautiful of itself. Scenery by itself is all very well; but the weather can damage scenery. You must have the pleasant human element to counteract the effects of climate and circumstance. Any country is pleasant, if the people are pleasant; any country is beautiful if the people receive you kindly. There'd be no perceptible beauty to a lone man in a tropical sunset if there were irreconcilable cannibals in the foreground; there is no scenery in the world that could be beautiful in the circumstances. The idea that scenery is beautiful of itself is mere nonsense; in one way or the other it is—it must be—modified by the human element."

With the memory of certain "artistic" discussions hot at heart it seemed to me that we were getting into devious ways. So I changed the subject. "Now you are an American, Mr. Clemens." (He bowed.) "I have heard it said that the people of Australia, and particularly of Victoria, are not unlike your own people. Can you express an opinion on the point? Considered as a British offshoot, would you regard the people of Australia as developing traits of character and manner differing from those of the insular English, and approximating more closely to those that obtain among the citizens of the States?"

"Unquestionably. One notices that at once. In speech and manner you Australians have a sort of frank and friendly way that lacks something of the English reserve. They differ, as you suggest, from the English people in England; and, just in proportion, they develop a certain similarity to the people of the United States. That is so." . . .

There was another silence here. Mark Twain is eminently companionable. Presently he began, inconsequently,—

"Ah, those maps! what erroneous ideas they give one! Before I came over on this tour I'd seen Australia and New Zealand on the maps. Glancing at the maps I had an idea that there was probably a small ferry boat running eighteen or twenty times a day between Melbourne and New Zealand. When I came to inquire about the name of the ferry boat, it was taken as the remark of an ignorant person. That's the trouble with maps: they get a lot of stuff into a small space, and give one an inadequate idea of distance. There was an old lady ran out of a gate to me once in Bermuda—came bounding out of the gate, and said, 'That's your ship that's lying in the offing there? An American ship? You belong in America?' 'Yes,' I said, 'I belong in America.' 'Ah,' she said, 'I've got a nephew there—a journeyman carpenter—and he works down in the lower part of New York City. His name's J. M. White: perhaps you've met him?' And she wanted me to hunt him up. Now that looks silly, but coming from a person who's only looked at a map it was perfectly natural."

"You're going to India, Mr. Clemens. Been there before?"

"Never. But I have received the pleasantest kind of letters from people connected with the civil and military administrations in India for years past. I shall find people in India whom I have not previously met, but who are still my friends."

"As you do everywhere?"

"Well, yes, as I do everywhere, since you are kind enough to put it so. A book? Why, on such a trip as this, one could write a library of books! If I do subsequently write a book it will be an incident consequent on the tour rather than any attempt at dealing fully with the tour itself. Of course on a lecturing tour one has to combine business with pleasure, and I can't say that they harmonize very well. Then I have had a succession of carbuncles—have one, just about spent, on my leg now—and they keep me rather lame. The only good times I have had—times, that is to say, when I have been entirely free from pain—have been on the platform, talking to my audiences. At such a time one's mind is fully occupied, and one has not attention to waste on pain. Yes, I naturally look forward to my visit to the East with anticipation more than ordinarily pleasurable, although I've only heard positively of one Asiatic who took what I may call a literary interest in me. He was a Chinaman, and a friend of mine who was American Consul at Singapore recommended him to read my *New Pilgrim's Progress*, venturing to praise the book as interesting and funny. The Chinaman got a book, written in his own language and illustrated with quaintly forcible woodcuts of fights with Apollyon, Christian's experiences in the Valley of the Shadow of Death, and that sort of thing: it was the original *Pilgrim's Progress*, published sometime ahead of mine, and differing a little in tone and treatment. The Chinaman read it, and seeking my friend the consul (one cannot account for the literary tastes of the Chinese) protested in a pained manner, as one who would deprecate a practical joke, that there was not a funny idea in the book from one end to the other."

## "Mark Twain / A Talk with the Famous Humorist"

Christchurch, New Zealand, *Lyttelton Times*,
13 November 1895, pp. 5–6

. . . Mr. Clemens's conversation ranged over a wide field; its subjects were many and diverse; and of all he knew much, and was anxious to know more. He spoke of labor matters in the United States, and remarked that the idea of the Knights of Labor, of consolidating all classes of workers into one body for mutual help in the effort to redress grievances, was a fine one, but that the organization had failed, because its leader could, from the nature of the organization, have no effective control over the members. It has done good, however, for as a result of its action the American State Governments are now turning their attention to Eight Hour Acts and similar legislation, matters to which, Mr. Clemens shrewdly remarked, governments are not inclined to pay much attention unless they are urged thereto by the continual watchfulness of the people—armed with votes.

The American militia system, by which the United States can now put several hundreds of thousands of fairly-trained fighting men into the field at a moment's notice; the negro problem, for which he frankly professed himself unable to see a solution, though he finds hope in the fact that the proportion of whites to blacks is increasing in the southern states; a ghastly story of the French astronomer who bound a book in the skin of a lady friend bequeathed to him by will; the superiority of Maoris to Australian black-fellows; the Mississippi River trade, prohibition, the differing characteristics of the English and Australian novel, the prevalence of crime among foreign residents in America, and the stones of Easter Island were some of the subjects upon which the versatile *raconteur* talked, and talked well and ably. . . .

The method of work of a celebrated writer is always of interest to his readers. Mr. Clemens' method is peculiar. He begins a book and works at it until he feels that the writing of it is becoming irksome, till he comes to a standstill. He at once lays it aside and begins on another, which in its turn may be put in the pigeonhole. He may thus have several "on the stocks" at once. After a while he takes one out, reads the last chapter or two, finds that his mind will again work freely on the subject, and goes on with the book "as a labor of love." An admirable plan he finds his for keeping his mind fresh and vigorous, and for preventing himself from becoming "played out." He is, as might be expected, a hard worker; and it is whispered that he is occupied on a book dealing with his present travels, a book colonials will look for with a good deal of interest. They need not, however, feel much apprehension that they will find themselves and their countries "slated" in this work, as they have been by some literary travelers. Mr. Clemens was most emphatic in his condemnation of the folly of hasty generalizations, of jumping to conclusions about a whole people because one has seen a few of the individual composing it. The Americans have had to suffer injustice from that kind of thing, and Mark Twain is particularly anxious to avoid doing like injustice to others.

Though a patriotic American, whose pride in his country is very evident, he has a soft spot, a large spot at that, in his heart for the Britishers. He especially likes an English audience. His best audiences, those whom he felt had "got with him" in the shortest time, were, he said, at Baltimore in Maryland, at London, and at Liverpool. His colonial audiences, however, pleased him well. *Apropos* of his audiences he told a story. His conversation, by the way, does not bristle with stories and jokes any more than that of any other educated and intellectual man. "When I was going over from America to England we had entertainments in the first and second cabins, and I was asked to give some of my pieces. The first cabin was full of Americans, but in the second cabin nearly all the passengers were English. I said to Mrs. Clemens, 'No, you'll find I shall have the most appreciative audience I the second cabin. She hardly seemed to think so, but I proved myself correct. The Americans in the first cabin were very good, but next night when in gave exactly the same pieces in the second cabin the English people there fairly carried it off with a whoop."

## "Mark Twain at Home / A Chat with Mr. Clemens"
Christchurch, New Zealand, *Press*, 13 November 1895, p. 5

"You ask me," said Mr. Clemens, "what I think of the colonies. Now, let me say right here that the man who attempts to describe a country which he sees for the first time after a brief visit to it, and before he has time to digest, as I may put it, is wrong. When you are in Rome you go into St. Peter's; there are many other churches about, and all that you know of St. Peter's different from them is that the dome is so many feet high, and so on. You come out, and the facts and statistics do not make much impression on you. By and by the time comes for you to leave. From the car windows you see the city disappear, but rising into the sky, a prominent figure, is the dome of St. Peter's. Now that is just the case with regard to the colonies. I am too close now to give any opinion. By and by, when I get further off—when I get a perspective so to speak of the colonies,—then I can form some idea of the country.

"You ask me what my impressions were of the colonies before I visited them, and whether they have been realized?—Well, I formed an idea of a physical Australia and a physical New Zealand before I left on this tour. You see, I had read a good deal about Australia. That was when it was before the world owing to the gold discoveries. I knew something of mining and mining camps, and though under different circumstances, I could construct pretty well a physical Australia; nor was I disappointed. It was all there as I had pictured it. But I was not prepared to see the populous cities which had grown up since Australia first came before the world owing to the gold discoveries. The writers failed to bring these before my mind, because they did not exist at the time they wrote. Strange to say, I had not conversed with an American who had visited Australia previous to my coming, so that my ideas of the country were purely physical, as I have said. But the growth of the cities I was not prepared for, and I was agreeably surprised. So also with New Zealand. I knew of the New Zealand of Tasman from reading but the New Zealand of today took me by surprise; therefore I may answer your question by saying that I had formed a correct idea of the physical appearance of the country, but there were points which did not suggest themselves to my mind. Men when describing countries give you as a rule statistics—heaps of them, till you are sick and tired of them. There are statistics on all kinds of subjects—extent of land, number of sheep and cattle, and population. But that does not convey any idea—any picture perhaps is the best way of putting it—as to the country as it strikes one when he reaches it. So it has been with me in Australia and New Zealand. I have read barrow loads of books on Australia and New Zealand, but they have not prepared me in any sort of shape or way for the actual appearance of the colonies as I find them today. . . .

"What is my experience of colonial audiences as compared with American and English ones? Well, there is a difference, and I will tell you what it is. The colonial audiences at once are friendly with you. They encourage you to give your best. You feel as soon as you step on the platform that they are your friends, that they wish you to succeed, and that puts fire and mettle into you, and puts you at once on terms with them. In Australia, aye, and in New Zealand, too, this was my experience. I went on the platform a stranger, but in a few minutes I found that I had a number of warm friends in front of me who were enthusiastic, and wanted me to do well, and I set to work at once without the least fear of success. This is the same with regard to English audiences. When I first went to London I naturally wished to make a success, and felt a little, well not nervous, but anxious as to the result. But I had only been speaking a few minutes when I felt that I had a houseful of friends, and immediately I was at home. Now, with us in America the audiences are different. They come prepared to demand that you give them the best you have got, and they will therefore feel to you somewhat critical. You must get them when you start in, or perhaps you will not get them again. You must attend strictly to business. They have made a contract with you to give them something and they hold you strictly to your part of the bargain, and all the time they are watching to see that you don't go back on it. But if you find that you don't get them fast at first there is no use in getting fussed. Give them something better a little further on and it is all right. Knowing you have got this then you are sure that in the end the audience will be with you. That is just the difference between an English or colonial—which is one and the same thing—audience and the American. The colonials are warm to you from the first, the Americans size you up and sample what you have got."

## "Mark Twain/Arrival in Auckland"
Auckland *New Zealand Herald,* 21 November 1895, p. 5

Who has not read Mark Twain? Who has not reveled in his humor? And who has not felt a longing to meet such a man face to face? Auckland people will have that pleasure for a couple of nights or so. A *Herald* representative had that pleasure yesterday evening. . . .

"Ah, yes," he said, "American humor is different entirely to French, German, Scotch, or English humor. And the difference lies in the mode of expression. Though it comes from the English, American humor is distinct. As a rule when an Englishman writes or tells a story, the 'knob' of it, as we would call it, has to be emphasized or italicized, and exclamation points put in. Now, an American story-teller does not do that. He is apparently unconscious of the effect of the joke. The similes used in America may be a little more extravagant than in England, but the method of treatment is modified. The method is quieter, more modified, and more subtle. Josh Billings said 'never take a bull by the horns; take him by the tail, and then you can let go when you want.' In any other country but America the part at which you should laugh would be put in italics and with exclamation marks."

Americanisms then cropped rip in the conversation, for many of these contain a big bulk of meaning, and expressed just what one wants to say.

"Yes," said Mark Twain, "there are many expressions said to be American and slang. Many are local, but here and there a phrase comes that just fits into what is wanted. And many so-called Americanisms come from the English. Take the expression, 'Fire him out,' which has come into use during the last few years. That expression was used by

Shakespeare in one of his sonnets. Then most people suppose that everyone who 'guesses' is a Yankee; the people who guess do so because their ancestors guessed in Yorkshire."

Then, naturally, the word "boom" came in, of which the man supposed to have first used it, in a newspaper, has said that he got the idea for the use of the term from the designation given the rise of water in the Mississippi.

"The sound of the word," said Mr. Clemens, elaborating this in his quick way, "has a good deal to do with the adoption of a term. If it has a good strong sound, and that sound seems to express the thing you want, then it has a chance to live."

"You a little while ago said," remarked our representative, "that American writers may be extravagant in the construction of their phrases, while an English writer would use exclamation marks or italics to bring out the 'knob' of his story. Would not the one counterbalance the other?"

"I was not saying that extravagant similes should not be used. Simple extravagance would be utterly reprehensible. But where a thing is happily phrased you do not care whether the figure is extravagant or not. For instance, what fault could you find in this: A captain of a ship is describing the perils his vessel went through; 'Why,' says a listener, 'You must have shipped a great deal of water.' 'Sir,' says the captain, 'we pumped the Atlantic Ocean through my ship sixteen times.' How are you to find fault with that? It is extravagant; but it is good fun, and does no harm." . . .

Mr. Clemens . . . went on to speak of the difference in writing now. If Harriet Beecher Stowe was writing *Uncle Tom's Cabin* now, it would have been written differently—that is, not so diffusively. And the same might be said of Dickens. They wrote for their time.

"And how did the change come?" said he. "That is a change to which everyone contributes. These things are contributions of Time. I was once idiot enough to ask the partner of Mr. Bell as to who was the inventor of the telephone. The reply I got was, Do you not know that 1500 men had been at work on the telephone for 5000 years—do you suppose that anyone could invent any such instrument in any one lifetime? It is the same with literature. English writing has been a good deal bound up with conventionalism; American writing has been less so. Though conventions exist in all countries." . . .

"A good many people think you do not show any very great reverence for subjects they regard reverentially. Take your *Innocents Abroad* for instance."

"Yes, I know. I once wrote an article for an American literary journal that has a vast circulation amongst young people. I was asked to change something in that article. I asked the editor what he wanted changed. He said I had put a clergyman in a ridiculous position. My reply was he had put himself there. If he liked to strike the clergyman out he could. But I could put no one in his place. It was a story I would have told in the pulpit, if they would have given me a pulpit to tell it from."

## "A Chat with Mark Twain"
### Wellington *New Zealand Mail,* 12 December 1895, p. 51

Mark Twain arrived from Wanganui last night at 10 o'clock, and was kind enough to receive me after supper. . . . I asked after the birth and life history of "The Jumping Frog," which had enlivened the young bloods of the world some time in the sixties.

He saluted the name with a certain comic air of parentage. "Oh!" said he, "I gave 'The Jumping Frog' to Artemus Ward who wanted something to fill up one of his volumes. But the volume was got out before 'The Jumping Frog' arrived. So Artemus Ward's publisher passed it on to Henry Clapp, the proprietor of the *Saturday Press,* a New York weekly journal. He said he could have it for nothing, which was lucky, as Henry Clapp never could pay for anything. On which terms 'The Jumping Frog' was published. . . . But 'The Jumping Frog' got even with Henry Clapp. After that Saturday that paper of his never appeared again. It was the very last issue. Henry Clapp announced that in that number. He couldn't help it; he had to." . . .

Then came *The Innocents Abroad.* . . . When I got with the book to New Zealand, I found several clever fellows who declared that there was never any ship called the *Quaker City,* who insisted that the book was just vamped out of books of travel and encyclopedias.

"I have heard that very thing said eighteen times in a week," said the author of the *New Pilgrim's Progress,* rousing.

"These fellows said it was very easy, sir."

"I wish I could do it," says he directly. "I wish I could do all my traveling that way."

And then he came out of his dream. "You see there's a Freemasonry about dealing with things you see yourself which can't be counterfeited. There is an ease and certainty of touch in describing what you see which you can't get artificially. . . . And how did Defoe write his plague of London? He knew London as well as you know this city of Wellington, every spot and corner of it. He had nothing in the way of local color to supply; it was all there before him. He got his details of the plague at first hand, from people who had seen. He made his studies in hospitals and by sick beds. What he saw he described, only changing here and there features of disease to suit the accounts of the plague. Defoe described what he saw, and added the equivalents which he had observed, and so he got his wonderful study. But to do a book of travel in that way, you would have to know every city in the world as well as Defoe knew his London. Only in that way could you get the firmness of touch, the Freemasonry I have spoken of, the thing which depends on your personal observation. How could a man describe that battered and faded Last Supper of Leonardo de Vinci's who had not seen it? His touch would be uncertain, his grasp weak, his description faulty. To describe the thing properly he would have not only to go to the works of other men, but to take their very language." . . .

He throws further light on this problem as he walks about in more hurried eagerness. I had mentioned the Mississippi pilot, referring to the changes on the face of that great stream, and the perpetual watchfulness of the steersman. "Yes, you can see the ripples," he says, "and the eddies and all the moods of the rapid river. But you can only see as an amateur.

There is a light line of ripples, which no amateur can understand: a harmless-looking line of ripples, quiet and easy, which to the pilot means the death of his ship if she gets there. You must see these things with the pilot's eye if you want to do justice to them.".…

One story he tells of editorial enterprise. "'Mr. Clemens,' said a New York editor in chief, 'will you write us your obituary?' 'Much obliged,' says I. 'But I would rather leave myself in the hands of your staff.' 'Well, if I give you 250 dollars will you give us your last words?' 'Right you are.' So I gave him my last words. But I haven't done with those last words yet. I am always improving on them, telling the fellow to strike that out and put in something better which I am sending them. And I intend to send him the last yet awhile."

## "With Mark Twain"
### Sydney *Bulletin*, 4 January 1896, p. 8

… I went to interview him at his hotel.…

"I would not like to say what I think is my best book, for I like them all; and I could not say what I think is my worst, for I don't think there is one of them like that. But the book of mine which gave me the greatest pleasure is *Huckleberry Finn* because years after I had written it, and long after it had been wholly erased from the pages of my memory, I took it up and read it to my daughter, who was ill. It was new to her; it was new to me. As the reading progressed, I didn't know what to expect—a surprise came as a genuine surprise—a genuine pleasure.

"The books which gave me the hardest time to write were *Tom Sawyer* and *The Prince and the Pauper*. In the middle of both I came to a dead stop—a blank wall. Couldn't get on at all; rooted round a long time—a damnation long time, for incidents, for ideas—couldn't strike any. Gave it up—gave it up for twelve months. Came back then with the tank full, broke down the wall, story flowed on. The other books were written fairly easy—working daily from 11 to 3 five days a week—tearing the work up, if necessary, afterwards—and always keeping Saturday and

Sunday sacred. *The Yankee at the Court of King Arthur* was as easy as any. *Life on the Mississippi* is my biography; it is a collocation of facts. As I have shown in that book, it is marvelous how the memory can be developed. When I ceased piloting and started reporting I could go all day, remembering everything. And when I brought my catch in towards evening I had it all there in my mind—every trifling detail, every figure. I had only to empty it out. But as the fashion was for reporters to use notebooks, I took up with one, and the first time I put a note down in that notebook, I wrote the death-sentence of my memory. . . .

"But my books are all founded on facts; every character was a living being; every incident or germ of that incident has occurred; every plot had actually grown, or nearly grown, within my experience. There was selection, grouping, blending. And in writing a book its characters lived always; day and night, day and night. I'd go to bed, but they'd stay up talking, talking, talking; acting, acting; always in character—spoiling my sleep, yet never doing or saying anything that was rational or valuable or even usable. . . .

"It is not true that owing to my lack of humor I was once discharged from a humorous publication. It's an event that could very likely happen were I on the staff of a humorous paper—but then I'd never get into a fix like that. I'd never undertake to be humorous by contract. If I wanted my worst enemy to be racked I'd make him the editor of a comic paper. For me there must be contrast; for humorous effect I must have solemn background; I'd let my contribution into an undertaker's paper of the London *Times*. Set a diamond upon a pall of black if you'd have it glisten.

"Dreams are more vivid than realities. The dreamer sits beside his glass of wine and accidentally causing it to begin falling lives seventy years, then stops his wine falling—drinks. Give Zola's *Downfall* to the day's imagination! how feeble are the reproduction of those blood-stained photographs of war's horrors! But at dead of night, when the reason is locked in the seclusion of oblivion, how the dreamer's imagination flashes upon the sensitive plate of the mind—armies, charges, battle scenes and incidents, perfect, horrible, magnificent. . . .

"And I have dreamt of something so exquisitely humorous that the seventh heaven of bliss could be only a side-issue to it—and the ecstasy of it has awakened me. And sitting up and taking pencil and paper, I have there and then written out that subtly humorous thing—lain back, deliciously happy, and gone to sleep. But in the morning what a reversion! That paper! that paper! gave me not a precious treasure, but words, words, words—creatures of irrationality—jotted down—strung together—meaningless—hopelessly meaningless. . . .

"I have a passion for the theater but seldom gratify it, for whenever I go there is sure to be someone before, or behind, or beside me who persists in talking loudly to his neighbor and ruining my pleasure. It is the same in America, in England, in Australia. There is always the human beast that talks; that is destitute of every artistic feeling, and of every sympathy with artistic feeling. Often have I thought of Sir Walter Raleigh's peaceful happiness in jail; often have I thought it a bitter thing that a man must first exterminate a talker in a theater, must become a criminal in order to gain seclusion."

# Bombay to London

## Jan 23 1896–Oct 14 1900

Twain continued his speaking tour across south Asia and Africa, from Bombay and Calcutta to Johannesburg and Cape Town. After completing these fifty-five dates, he settled in London with his wife and daughter while he wrote his memoir of the tour, *Following the Equator* (1897). Following the death of his daughter Susy in Hartford on August 18, 1896, Twain remained in Europe to mourn. He repaid the last of his creditors in 1898. He finally returned to the United States in October 1900 and promptly launched a verbal assault on American imperialism.

### "Mark Twain on His Methods of Work"
Bombay *Gazette*, 23 January 1896, p. 5

"It would have served me right to be left alone as I was for twelve hours, and then to be drowned as an idiot!" Mark Twain passed this severe judgment on himself because of his indiscretion in contracting a severe cold by lying asleep on board ship in an exposed place, and the words were uttered yesterday afternoon.... "I have seen nothing of Bombay," continued the great humorist, advancing to the window and pointing outside, "all the time I have been here, excepting these trees, which sadly need dusting, two or three cabs, and those towers. Yes, I am decidedly better than I was, and might even venture out now, but I shall not do so;

neither shall I leave my room tomorrow, as I don't want a recurrence of this cough, and want to make sure of being all right on Friday." . . .

After Mark Twain, with characteristic hyperbole, had assured our representative that for five hundred years it had been the dream of his life to visit the Golden Orient, a reference was made to the new book for which he is now collecting material. In answer to a question respecting his methods of work, the famous American said: "I have what would be called pretty lazy methods in the matter of preparation for my books. It is a troublesome thing for a lazy man to take notes, and so I used to try in my young days to pack my impressions in my head. But that can't be done satisfactorily, and so I went from that to another stage—that of making notes in a notebook. But I jotted them down in so skeleton a form that they did not bring back to me what it was I wanted them to furnish. Having discovered that defect, I have mended my ways a good deal in this respect, but still my notes are inadequate. However, there may be some advantage to the reader in this, since in the absence of notes imagination has often to supply the place of facts.

"I said just now I was lazy in preparation," said Mr. Clemens, "but I won't admit that I am lazy in writing. No, I don't write rapidly, for when I did that I found it did not pay. I used to spend so much time next day correcting the manuscript, that it went to the printer a veritable forest of erasures, interlineations, emendations, abolitions, annihilations, and revisions. I found I should save time by writing slowly and carefully, and now my manuscript gives the printer no cause to blaspheme. You ask me how it is I have not written more largely. Well, the fact of it is that for many years while at home, in America, I have written little or nothing on account of social calls upon my time. There is too much social life in my city for a literary man, and so for twenty years I gave up the attempt to do anything during nine months of the twelve I am at home. It has only been during the three months that I have annually been on vacation, and have been supposed to be holiday-making, that I have written anything. It has been the same during the five years that I have been away from America. I have done little or no work. I wish now," he added regretfully, "that I had done differently and had persisted in writing when at home. I could easily have done it, although I thought I could not. I seemed to think then that I was never going to grow old, but I know better than that now. In my vacation I have steadily done four or five hours' work every day at a stretch; and if they would only have let me alone, I would have done seven hours a time without getting up from my chair."

Asked the amount of copy he turned out during these vacation periods, Mark Twain pondered deeply, and having half-aloud worked out a problem in mental arithmetic, continued: "Well, my average would be from ten thousand to twelve thousand words a week. But I have numerous interruptions, and so, instead of turning out from forty-five to fifty magazine pages per month, I do not do more than thirty. Yes, I am very fond of literary work, and nothing would please me better than to be allowed to be kept at a book for six months." . . .

After assuring Mr. Clemens that anything that he might write would not be allowed to remain in manuscript after his death, unless he strictly interdicted its publication, our representative asked him whether he had as great a fondness for lecturing as for writing, and in answer received an emphatic shake of the head. "I like the platform when I am there, but the thought of it makes me shudder," said Mr. Clemens, momentarily collapsing into his chair; "the prospect of it is dreadful."

"Then I presume you prepare carefully for your lectures?"

"Yes, I am not for one moment going to pretend I do not. I don't believe that any public man has ever attained success as a lecturer to paid audiences (mark the qualification), who has not carefully prepared, and has not gone over every sentence again and again until the whole thing is fixed upon his memory. I write my lectures, and try to memorize them, but I don't always succeed. If I had a better memory it would be worse in some respects, for when one has to fill up an ellipsis on the spot, there is a spontaneity about the thing which is a considerable relief. I ought really to write the whole thing beforehand, but I don't do it, as I prefer to use material which has appeared in my books. The extracts, however, are seldom exactly the same as they are printed, but are adapted to circumstances. No, I don't localize, because to do that you want to be well posted up, and know exactly what you are about. You must be exactly prepared beforehand. I never pretend that I don't indent on my books for my lectures, for there is no object in doing that. It is all very well to talk about not being prepared, and trusting to the spirit of the hour. But a man cannot go from one end of the world to the other, no matter how great his reputation may be, and stand before paid houses in various large cities without finding that his tongue is far less glib than it used to be. He might hold audiences spell bound with unpremeditated oratory in past days when nothing was charged to hear him, but he cannot rely on being able to do so when they have paid for their seats and require something for the money unless he thinks all out beforehand.

"You ask me whether my memory has deserted me on the platform sometimes? Yes, it has sometimes entirely. And the worst of it is that, as I prefer to select things from my books, my remarks are often in the narrative form, and if you lose yourself in the narrative it is not very comfortable, because a tale should have an end somewhere. Still I have generally managed to get out of the difficulty in some way or other. It is really very curious to see what a man can do on the platform without the audience suspecting anything to be wrong. A case in point occurred in Paris a year ago. I began some opening remarks at one of my 'At Homes' there with an anecdote, as for some reason or another I wanted to fill up the time. I began telling the anecdote, but I found when half-way that my memory regarding it had gone. So I switched on to another line, and was soon leaving the half-told anecdote far behind. My wife and daughter were present, and I afterwards asked them whether they remembered the breakdown. They replied in the negative. I then asked whether they heard the finish of the anecdote with which I had begun my remarks, and they at once replied they had not. As you say, if anyone would be likely to discover a flaw, it would be my wife or my daughter, and when I found that they were unaware of the defect, I was quite satisfied that the audience in general knew nothing about it."

# "Interview with Mark Twain"

Bombay *Times of India*, 23 January 1896, p. 5

A representative of this journal called upon Mr. Clemens. . . .

"How did I make my first start in journalism, you ask? Well, I first stumbled into it as a man falls over a precipice that he is not looking for. I wasn't, as far as I could see, intended for a journalist, but out in Nevada in those early silver days it was a struggle—a scramble from pillar to post—and one had to get a living as best he could. I was invited to take a place on the staff of a daily newspaper there—the *Territorial Enterprise*—and I took it. I should have taken command of a ship if it had been offered, for I wasn't particular in those days. I had had no training, but yet they offered me the post of first officer, not the Chief Editor, but a subordinate post, and I remained in the journalistic profession for four years in Nevada and San Francisco together. On the *Territorial Enterprise* I was what they called the City Editor. It was a large title, but the pay was not correspondingly great; in fact, the name was merely for style. In reality the City Editor should have been called the local reporter. The post was, so to speak, flung at me. I didn't ask for it. There was a Chief Editor, a news-Editor, and a telegraphic-Editor, and in those days they gathered in from the San Francisco and Sacramento papers a good part of the reading matter of the journal. We were expected and supposed to furnish facts pure and simple for the columns of the *Enterprise,* but there were not facts enough to fill the required space, and so often the reading material was largely a matter of imagination—sometimes based on fact, but not always. After about four years in these parts I went off to the Sandwich Islands to write a series of letters concerning the sugar industry there for the *Sacramento Union.* I was gone about five or six months, and when I came back I concluded to deliver a lecture or two on the Sandwich Islands, and I did so. It seemed an easier way of making a living than by journalism; it paid better, and there was less work connected with it, so I dropped journalism and took to the lecturer's platform for two or three years.

Then I went on an extended tour in Europe, which lasted for five or six months, and when I returned I was asked to write a book. I did so, and from that time on I have written books mainly. Up to the present I have stepped out of silver-mining—that, by the way, was my first start in Nevada—into journalism, from journalism into lecturing, and from lecturing into book-making, each of these steps being not forced in any way, but the one leading to the next by a short of natural sequence."

The conversation having turned to his method of work, Mr. Clemens remarked: "I work very regularly when I work at all. I work every day and all night from after breakfast till late into the night until the work is finished. I never begin to work before eleven in the morning, and I sit at it till they pull me away from table to dress for dinner at seven at night. They make me stop then for a while, as they think I might overwork myself, but I don't think there is any fear of that, for I don't consider the kind of writing I do is work in any way: it is in no sense a labor with me. The mere physical work would not hurt me or anyone else, you can sleep that off. The mental part of it is nothing but amusement: it's not work. I always write my own copy. I have tried a typewriter and also a phonograph, but I couldn't get along with either."

"You do not find dictation any help, then?"

"I couldn't learn the art. I could conceive that for commercial correspondence it would be easy to do, but there's no inspiration about that. There's nothing to help inspiration or whatever you may call it, like the sight of your own work as it goes along. I am not a *very* rapid worker, but when I sit down to it I get through a fair amount in a day." . . .

"What do you find most helpful in your work?"

"Tobacco," replied Mr. Clemens, picking up a capacious briar-root pipe which was kept busily engaged as he paced up and down the room, enveloped in a rich cloud of smoke. "I always smoke when at work. I couldn't do without it. I smoke by necessity. I did stop smoking once for a year and a quarter, but in that year and a quarter I didn't write anything. I have no works in contemplation just now, but as soon as I get at leisure I shall go to work again. There are two or three things I want to write and I may—no doubt shall—write some sort of book on this excursion, but I always leave myself quite free in these matters. I never make any promises to myself or anybody else, because I don't like being hampered by the feeling that something has to be done when perhaps I am not in the mood to do it."

## "Mark Twain on the Relations Between England and America"
Bombay *Gazette*, 24 January 1896, p. 5

Although Mark Twain is of the opinion that remarks made to an interviewer on the spur of the moment are mere surface talk, unworthy of being printed, we venture to assert that the observations he made to our representative on Wednesday, respecting the relations between England and America, so far from being looked upon as of little or no value, will be generally regarded as important contributions to the discussion now raging around the Monroe doctrine and the Venezuelan question. . . . Mark Twain was speaking in high terms of the Australians whom he described as "a live bright people, energetic and modern, in every way up to date"; and said they reminded him of the Canadians. "I am intensely interested in them," he added, "as one ought to be in any community that speaks the English language, because they are becoming growingly important in the shaping of the world's destinies. When you think what the English race is today compared with one hundred years ago and how much ground it has since covered, and the immense influence it wields amongst the peoples of this earth, you cannot fail to be struck with how much it has accomplished in a very short time. Now, on the other hand, look at the case of France. There were, if I remember rightly, twenty-eight millions of people in that country at the time of the French Revolution. But this number has not since doubled; it has only gone up by fifty per cent. At that period Great Britain had a population of eighteen or twenty millions; it is now thirty-nine millions, and her sons have overflown into all parts of the globe. France had just as good opportunities as England, but has allowed them to slip from her grasp.

America has progressed in a still more marvelous manner. A hundred years ago we had a population of three millions in the United States, and now we have seventy millions. We have in that period flung in two Frances and the United States has now three times as many people as France had a century ago. "

This monologue on the greatness of the British naturally brought the conversation round to the existing relations between England and America, and Mark Twain, walking vehemently backwards and forwards, spoke in this wise: "I think it would be criminal now to interrupt the old friendly relations. I cannot conceive of any greater disaster to the world than a war between these two great countries. There can never be a sufficient excuse for so great a crime."...

"Then you think, Mr. Clemens, that most of the American people are of this opinion? You must have read that your friend, Mr. Stanley, after touring in America, has stated that there is an intense anti-English feeling in America—that is, the America outside New York and its money market?"

"I do not believe that the people of America as a whole are unfriendly," said Mark Twain decisively. "All that I can make out of Mr. Stanley's remarks given in the *Bombay Gazette* the other day is that the explorer got his information where you or I would get ours if we were traveling abroad, that is to say, from the newspapers, which are not always a safe guide to public opinion."

"At any rate in America?" suggested our representative.

"In any country governed on party lines," was the prompt reply.... "There is no anti-English feeling in the towns among really solid folk. People that Stanley would hear or you or I would hear if we were traveling in America would be the most noisy people. They are the ones that get themselves heard in any and every free country in the world. Now, in my own town of Hartford, which has a population of sixty thousand people, I know every sound and valuable citizen. But I cannot call to my mind one of these men, who would talk in such a way as to give Mr. Stanley the impression with which he returned to England. What is the case in Hartford is the case elsewhere; and travelers mistake the noisy clamor of a few men for the voice of the people generally."

Mark Twain is one of those rare American authors of note who have no grievance against the English pirates, notwithstanding his immense popularity in Great Britain. He explains the reason thus: "From 1861 to 1878 I did not get any remuneration for the copies of my works printed in England; but it was my own fault. I could have got copyright of my works, but was ignorant of the fact."

## "Sporting Notes &c."
Calcutta *Asian*, 7 February 1896. p. 398

Mr. Clemens, or as he is better known by his *nom de plume* of Mark Twain, arrived in Bombay last week.... I had the privilege of spending an afternoon in his company, and though one cannot attempt to set down on paper one-tenth part of the good things he said, yet, perhaps, a few gleanings from the sheaf of humor may be acceptable to your readers. ... Mr. Clemens is a finished speaker and one of the best raconteurs it has ever been my privilege to meet. My first question naturally was, "Well, Mr. Clemens, what do you think of India?" Pat came the answer: "Well, you can't show me much in climate and scenery"—this, to a man who has passed years of his life amongst the Rockies and been grilled upon the prairies of the West, is quite possible. "But, sir, the people—the people—the brilliant colors, the heterogeneous mass of humanity, the constantly recurring yet ever changing kaleidoscopic views, the never ceasing stream of types of so many different nationalities and race, that you have gathered up in this great city of yours. Why that is enough to make a man long to sit down and write about it all till he is quite tired."

Directly after this Mr. Clemens in his best manner started upon a recent experience of his. "I came down from Poona this morning, and got upon the cars before daybreak in the beautiful bright soft Indian moonlight. Shortly after we had started the sun got up, and the whole panorama was changed. Looking out of the window I said to my companion, 'Why, this can't be the same country we came through yesterday. Are we going the same road? Yesterday afternoon the whole country appeared to be a dry arid sterile waste—this morning it is a beautiful, glossy, green, and rolling prairie. The hills yesterday, which stood out bleak and bare, without a particle of vegetation, are now a mass of verdure. How do you account for it?' He immediately pointed out that the blue glass of the window, acting upon the old gold color of the sandy tracts we were passing through, caused the optical illusion. 'Well, then,' I said, 'When I want to trade off a back-lot of this country, I shall see that the man who prospects it wears blue glasses.'" . . .

Shortly after this conversation turned upon fame and notoriety. Mr. Clemens said: "I thought I was pretty well known at any rate in America, but I found it wasn't so. The other day in New York I went into a store that was simply plastered from cornice to floor with photographs of celebrities: I asked the young man running that store if he had a photo of Mark Twain. He ran his eyes up and down the walls and then drawled out 'I don't know. Where is she playing?'"

Mrs. Clemens capped this by another experience in which she used the *nom de plume* with equal ill success. Having bought some things in London and giving the man directions, she said "that as they were going by the Cunard line he had better send the goods for Mark Twain." "Very well, Mum," he said. "When does she sail?"

## "Mark Twain Interviewed / First Impressions of India"
### Calcutta *Englishman*, 8 February 1896, p. 5

A man of middle height, with erect, well-set up figure, and abundant head of gray hair, Mark Twain paces up and down the room in a leonine fashion as he converses. . . . "We went to see a recluse. . . . A man who is worshipped for his holiness from one end of India to the other. On the way we saw various images of this saint, and when I saw him coming out of his hut, I at once recognized him from the really excellent likenesses which these images afforded. Look here. This is a portrait of the man, and this is his book."

He showed the interviewer the book. It was the Vedic translation by Sri Swami Bhaskara Nand Saraswati, with a photograph of the translator as a frontispiece. The holy man is represented sitting cross-legged and scantily clothed. He is said to be over sixty and is certainly a well-preserved man, with a keenly intellectual face. The *Englishman* representative remarked on this.

"Yes," said the humorist. "That man started with a grand head on his shoulders, and after thinking and reading and improving upon his initial advantages he came to the conclusion that the greatest object in life is—that."

He pointed to the photograph, but neither in mockery nor contempt. It may surprise his many readers, but when Mark Twain is serious he is very serious. He described in graphic language how he stood at the hut of the hermit, and wondered what there was in him to worship.

"Suddenly a man came up who had traveled hundreds of miles for this very object. As soon as he approached near enough he prostrated himself in the dust and kissed the saint's foot. I had never realized till then what it was to stand in the presence of a divinity."

"Because," Mark Twain pursued, with great animation, "he is a divinity. Not even an angel. At the age of seventeen, I am told, he renounced his family ties and embraced the asceticism in which he has lived these forty years and over."

"And what effect have these practices had upon him? Is there anything peculiar in his voice, his talk, or his actions?"

"Nothing at all. It is just as though you had taken a very fine, learned, intellectual man, say a member of the Indian Government, and unclothed him. There he is. He is minus the trappings of civilization. He hasn't a rag on his back. But he has perfect manners, a ready wit, and a turn for conversation through an interpreter."

Turning to the fly-leaf of the book, Mark Twain pointed to certain Sanskrit signs and relapsed into the humorous vein.

"That is his name," he said. "He is so holy, that before his name can be written it must be repeated 108 times. I thought that too much even for a god. I made 104 times do. We traded autographs. I said I had heard of him, and he said he had heard of me. Gods lie sometimes, I expect."

"On the contrary, it is extremely probable that your books may have cheered him up in his loneliness."

Mark Twain laughed. "Hardly, because they would required to have been translated into Sanskrit first."

"In that case, Sanskrit is almost the only language, I should suppose, in which they have not appeared." . . .

"The subject of caste," the humorist proceeded in reply to further inquiries, "seems to me a great mystery. It's a fascinating mystery. Anything more uncongenial to the Western mind and training could not be conceived. When I am told that this man will not drink out of that man's *lota*, because if he does so he will be defiled—these are simply so many words to me. I can't grasp the idea. When, again, you say that the man with a special cord round his neck is a Brahmin, and twice born, and that because of the cord and what it implies he is to be groveled before, I ask how is it? And I can't for the life of me imagine."

"When, too, I see a Hindu—the very man, perhaps, who fears defilement so much through the other man's *lota*—when I see him going down to the muddy, filthy Ganges, and washing himself in and drinking out of water only fifteen yards away from where a dead body is lying—I can't help thinking he is at least sincere. . . . It is my belief that in the development of the world the strongest race will be and by become paramount—the strongest physically and intellectually. Now if we look round upon the nations we find that the English seems to possess both these qualifications. It has spread all over the earth. It is vigorous, prolific, and enterprising. Above all it is composed of merciful people, the best kind of people for colonizing the globe. Look, for instance, at Canada.

"Look at the difference between the position of the Canadian Indians and the Indians with whom the United States Government has to deal. In Canada the Indians are peaceful and contented enough. In the United

States there are continual rows with the Government, which invariably end in the red man being shot down."

"And to what cause, Mr. Clemens, do you attribute this difference?"

"I attribute it to the greater humanity with which the Indians are treated in Canada. In the States we shut them off into a reservation, which we frequently encroached upon. Then ensued trouble. The red men killed settlers, and of course the Government had to order out troops and put them down. If an Indian kills a white man he is sure to lose his life, but if a white man kills a redskin he never suffers according to law."

"Is not the negro difficulty somewhat allied to the Red Indian question?"

"No doubt. But I am of opinion that in course of time that difficulty will settle itself. The negroes at present are merely freed slaves, and you can't get rid of the effects of slavery in one or even two generations. But things will right themselves. We have given the negro the vote, and he must keep it."

"Is there, then, any likelihood of intermixture?"

"Not the slightest. The white and the black population, however, will in time learn to tolerate each other and work harmoniously for the common good. They will co-exist very much as the different races in India have done for centuries."

## "Mark Twain in Madras"
### Madras *Standard*, 1 April 1896; rpt. in
### Calcutta *Reis and Rayyet*, 11 April 1896, pp. 176–77

. . . A Calcutta daily giving him the tip as to the celebrated humorist's departure from the City of Palaces on Thursday night last, a representative of the Madras *Standard* proceeded on board yesterday afternoon to interview him. . . . "Mr. Clemens, I presume," said our representative laying his card upon a handy tea-stand within focus of Mark's glasses.

"The same, sir; glad to meet you, I am sure; sit down."

"Not wearied yet with interviewing, I hope."

"Well, no, I have had the last three or four days myself occupied nursing a cold, and I don't mind meeting press people anywhere. We are brought up to regard interviewing across the water as part of our lives, you know." . . .

"Did I find India precisely the place it was represented to be? Well, hardly. You seem to know of course that this is my first visit to India. I came here like many others with only a very vague idea of the country, and I am bound to confess that I did not find it the immensely wealthy place it has been described as. But I am not surprised at that at all, because it is the showy side of the globe that reaches the remotest region, whether that showy side exists or not. In California, for instance, people have an idea that the gold dust is merely to be scooped up. Go there and you realize the nakedness of things. A feature that has struck me very forcibly in India is the poverty of the country. This was something I knew of only vaguely before. It is poverty compared with the poverty I have been acquainted with, and it is also a poverty based upon a certain value which does not exist in the country I come from. Somebody on this very ship told me that it doesn't make any difference how low wages in India are, the working-man will save something out of it. He said don't deceive yourself when people talk to you about low wages. Take the case of a man who earns Rands 7 a month—he pointed out one to me—and lower than that sometimes, I should think it would cost that man all that to live and yet leave him something to lay by. Wherever that is the case, then I would not say it was abject poverty, but then this is looking at it all through a false medium—the values are not the same here as they are in other countries. We think the Italians are very poor until we have lived in Italy; then we readily find that there are really no poor Italians. When you come to examine their circumstances they have enough in life to live upon and to save. . . .

"Yes, I have been interested in the recent 'situation' between England and America, but I never doubted for a moment that the warlike talk was based upon nothing. The latest news is, I see, that they are getting into a rational and satisfactory state. Arbitration is to be resorted to after all. I knew that common-sense would get the advantage of all concerned presently. It was absolutely silly to think that America and England would ever fire a shot at each other."

## "Mark Twain on Tour / Arrival in Cape Town"
### Cape Town *Cape Times*, 7 July 1896, p. 7

. . . With the object of ascertaining some of his impressions of the country he is soon to leave and his views on the remarkable political situation recently developed, a representative of this journal called on the famous author yesterday. . . .

"The trouble with the outsider in the Transvaal," he remarked in reply to a question, "suggests the simile of a person walking around a monument which changes its aspect with every step he takes. It changes its form and its expression, and by the time he gets around to the point he started from he is likely to say that he had a wrong focus, and at the same time he must admit that, his time being short and his eyes not as good as the eyes of men on the spot and familiar with the matter, he has probably still got a wrong focus."

"When I first arrived in the country it was in absolute ignorance of what had been going on, and the whole affair of the Jameson raid was a big surprise. Since then I have moved through a tossing sea of varying opinions and information, and for a while I supposed that, if the Jameson raid had for its purpose the overthrow of the Transvaal Republic, it was inexcusable. By this time I have considered the peculiar grievance of the 'uitlanders,' which make that position uncertain and pretty nearly untenable. . . . It is very like our old quarrel of the American Revolution 100 years ago, which is a sort of parallel case I should say. The three millions of Americans who existed in that day, and who were really Englishmen and regarded themselves as such, were really 'uitlanders.' To put it in a single phrase, it was the old story, taxation without representation. That is just the exact trouble at Johannesburg. In America they were hampered in all sorts of ways. The country—

such as it was—was run solely in the interests of the Mother Country, and finally there was a Jameson raid at Concord and Lexington, in Massachusetts, on April 19, 1775. We had a little fight and the 'uitlanders' won. They were more fortunate than Jameson. The object of that raid, however, was not the overthrow of the English Government, but it was the beginning of that sort of a revolution where the persons beginning it cannot foresee the lengths to which it is going to reach. It was a year or more after that before anybody dreamed of throwing over the British rule. They wanted their rights under the British Government, that was all that Lexington and Concord were fought for, and if the English Government had acted wisely it would have gone no further. If they had allowed those American prisoners certain perfectly fair privileges which they asked for, the United States of America would be a province of the British Crown today. It is one of those vast political mistakes which Governments can make, and which the Transvaal Government can easily make. That Government can drive the 'uitlanders' into revolution if they go on and just follow the English example in the matter of the revolution in America."

"That has been the case with every revolution in this world. The thing could have been stopped if it had been taken in hand at once. There was no necessity for the French revolution, which would never have happened if the Crown had made concessions."

"Kimberley and Johannesburg," continued Mark Twain in reply to the usual question, "are the striking features of South Africa. I have seen plenty of gold-mining towns, but Johannesburg does not look like any I have seen, because it is so substantially built. Kimberley is of course different. In the old California days when the gold-washer washed out two or three ounces of gold it had a distinct value. It is not so with diamonds, and they would have ruined the diamond business if everybody had been in it. I went over the Kimberley mines and very interesting it was. I found a diamond about as big as the end of my finger, but there were so many people watching me that I did not bring it away."

## "Mark Twain Amused"
Frank Marshall White, *New York Journal*, 2 June 1897, p. 1

Mark Twain was undecided whether to be more amused or annoyed when a *Journal* representative informed him today of the report in New York that he was dying in poverty in London. . . .

The great humorist, while not perhaps very robust, is in the best of health. He said:

"I can understand perfectly how the report of my illness got about. I have even heard on good authority that I was dead. James Ross Clemens, of St. Louis, a cousin of mine, was seriously ill two or three weeks ago in London, but is well now. The report of my illness grew out of his illness.

"The report of my death was an exaggeration. The report of my poverty is harder to deal with. My friends might know that unless I were actually dying in poverty I should not live in poverty when I am receiving offers to lecture by every mail. The fact is that I was under contract to write the book that I have just finished or I should have accepted these offers."

## "Mark Twain Smiling Through His Tears"
*New York Herald*, 13 June 1897, IV, 1

"Of course I am dying," Mark Twain smiled grimly. "But I do not know that I am doing it any faster than anybody else. As for dying in poverty, I had just as soon die in poverty here in London as anywhere. But it would be a little more difficult, because I have got quite a number of friends, anyone of whom would be good for a month's provisions, and that would drag out the agony a fairly long time.

"No, I assure you I am as well as ever I was. You see you must not attach too much importance to my wife's remark that I was not in a condition to receive visitors. That simply means that I was in bed. Now most women think that if a man does not get up before twelve o'clock there must be something wrong with him, and as I never get up before then, my wife thinks that I am not in good health. As a matter of fact when you were announced I told her to have you shown up to my room, but you can never persuade a tidy woman to show a stranger into an untidy bedroom, and so that did not work.

"I said to her, 'Show him up, send some cigars up. I am comfortable enough!'

"'Yes,' she said, 'But what about him?'

"'Oh,' I said, 'if you want him to be as comfortable as I am make him up a bed in the other corner of the room.' That did not work, either, so I thought the best thing to do was to get up and come to see you.

"Poverty is relative. I have been in poverty so often that it does not worry me much. A more serious matter is the money owing to other people, not by any fault of mine, and yet owing to them by me. But I do not trouble about the rumors that go about in regard to me. Why should I? The rumor will die itself if you will only give it three days. Start any rumor, and if the public can go with its curiosity unsatisfied for three days something else will spring up which will make the public forget all about the first one. Therefore when people talk about my dying, or as really happened a few days ago, about my being dead, I do not take the slightest notice. I know perfectly well that the public will forget all about it if I let it alone. I keep on ploughing away and working and working and hoping and hoping, but the idea of being in poverty does not either trouble me, or frighten me."

What are you working about, just now?

"Oh, my journey about the world. Everybody has done his little circumnavigation act, and I thought it about time I did mine, so I have been getting it ready for the press since I have been here, and therefore, for the matter of that, the book is just my impressions of the world at large. I go into no details. I never do for that matter. Details are not my strong point, unless I choose for my own pleasure to go into them seriously. Besides, I am under no contract to supply details to the reader.

All that I undertake to do is to interest him. If I instruct him that is his fate. He is that much ahead." . . .

When do you expect [it] to appear?

"Oh, about Christmas. Christmas is a good time to bring out a book. Everybody is thinking about Christmas presents, and the pious are praying that Divine Providence may give them some clue as to what to give for a present, and the book if it comes just at the right time, is about as good a thing as one could desire. It must come just at the right time though. . . . If the impulse to kill and the opportunity to kill always came at the same instant, how many of us would escape hanging. We have all of us at one time or another felt like killing something, and we have all of us at one time or another had the opportunity to kill something, but luckily for us, impulse and opportunity did not coincide. If a man is rich and he does want to kill something he can take his gun and go out and shoot. He lets off steam in that way, and the sore place gives over hurting. I used to have a rage and let it expand in the letter box.

"If anyone had done something to me that annoyed me or put me out, I would sit down and write a letter to him, and I would pour out all my thoughts and all the bitterness and anger and contempt and indignation and invective in my heart, and when I had cleaned myself out thoroughly I would put that letter in the box and my wife would see that it did not go.

"She used to say when she saw me sitting down: 'What are you going to do?'"

"'I am going to answer this letter. I would—'

"'But you know you won't send it.'

"'I know that, but, by George, I am going to write it.'

"I have been very sorry many a time that those letters were not kept, because when a man is in a thoroughgoing temper, he finds things to say worth preserving."

## "Mark Twain's Bequest"

London *Times*, 23 May 1899, p. 4

Mr. Samuel Langhorne Clemens (Mark Twain) has been obliged to postpone his departure from Vienna until the 26th. . . . The Emperor Francis Joseph will receive the distinguished American author in audience on Thursday next. . . .

Mr. Clemens has kindly given me permission to telegraph to *The Times* some particulars of a pet scheme of his to which he has already devoted a great deal of his time and which will occupy a great part of the remainder of his life. In some respects it will be unparalleled in the history of literature. It is a bequest to posterity, in which none of those now living and comparatively few of their grandchildren even will have any part or share. This is a work which is only to be published 100 years after his death as a portrait gallery of contemporaries with whom he has come into personal contact. These are drawn solely for his own pleasure in the work, and with the single object of telling the truth, the whole truth and nothing but the truth, without malice, and to serve no grudge, but, at the same time, without respect of persons or social conventions, institutions, or pruderies of any kind. . . .

In Mr. Clemens's opinion, a work of the kind he proposes is only possible under the conditions he has laid down for himself. To use his own words: "A book that is not to be published for a century gives the writer a freedom which he could secure in no other way. In these conditions you can draw a man without prejudice exactly as you knew him and yet have no fear of hurting his feelings or those of his sons or grandsons. A book published 100 years hence, containing intimate portraits, honestly and truthfully drawn, of Monarchs and politicians, bootblacks and shoemakers, in short, of all those varieties of humanity with which one comes in contact in the course of an active life of 50 years, cannot help being then valuable as a picture of the past. I have written a great deal of this book since I came to Vienna. During the rest of my life I mean to write in fresh portraits whenever they come vividly before my mind, whether they be of the present day or old acquaintances. To make such a book interesting for immediate publication it would be necessary for me to confine myself to the men of note. As it is, I choose them from my whole circle of acquaintances and the undistinguished have about as good a chance of getting in as the distinguished. The sole passport to a place in my gallery is that the man or woman shall have keenly excited my interest. In 100 years they will all be interesting if well and faithfully described. We have lost a great deal in the past through a lack of books written in this way for a remote posterity. A man cannot tell the whole truth about himself, even if convinced that what he wrote would never be seen by others. I have personally satisfied myself of that and have got others to test it also. You cannot lay bare your private soul and look at it. You are too much ashamed of yourself. It is too disgusting. For that reason I confine myself to drawing the portraits of others."

## "Mark Twain in London"
### London *Chronicle*, 3 June 1899, p. 3

Mark Twain has just arrived in London, and he gave me an audience yesterday. . . . "Well, now," I had asked him, "what brings you to London—why have we such luck?"

He seemed to like it put that way; anyhow, I thought I caught a twinkle in his eye. It was banished almost before it had arrived, and I argued with myself, "Why, he is serious enough for a Scotch humorist."

He was, for he went on, "You see, my American publishers are about to issue an *edition deluxe* of my books in twenty-two volumes. I have come to London to arrange for the issue of a similar edition through my publishers here, Messrs. Chatto. The volumes will include all my writings, which I have revised for the purpose. The publishers are trying to make the books nice—as fine books as they can. The two editions will be limited to a thousand copies each—limited, mark ye!

"Yes," he soliloquized, "I fancy it's the limitation to a thousand copies that is the chief charm and value of an *edition deluxe*. I don't expect to read this *edition deluxe* myself, although you needn't tell that to anybody else. Frankly, you know, I don't suppose that anybody ever reads an *edition deluxe*. No one puts bric-à-brac to any very practical purpose. There's some human instinct which makes a man treasure what he is not to make any use of, because everybody does not possess it." . . .

"What is the real story of that German speech of yours which was to be delivered to the Emperor Francis Joseph, but which you forgot?" . . .

"Necessarily," he almost rebuked me, "anybody prepares for an audience with an emperor, because it is essentially formal. You prepare yourself to say the right thing in the best words. I made that preparation, and there were only eighteen words in the sentence. That was very short for a German sentence, which generally covers a good deal of ground. Mine was a compressed sentence."

"You had rehearsed it all beforehand—gone over the field, so to speak?"

"Wouldn't you? But, you see, the Emperor at once began to talk in an entirely informal way, and I didn't remember, until some little period after, that I had a speech in stock. We were indulging in a pleasant talk; no ceremony about it. Then I recollected, and I blurted out to the Emperor that I had memorized a very good speech, but that it had gone clean out of my head. 'Oh,' he said, agreeably, 'it isn't necessary.' Strangely enough, I can't recall the seventeen words yet, though a minute ago I fancied I had them." . . .

After the Emperor, Vienna and the Viennese, and Mark Twain testified handsomely of both. He had chatted of the Emperor in words as ready as they were hearty. He tackled the Emperor's capital with an equal flow of expression.

"You cannot live a couple of years in Vienna," he said, "without becoming pretty thoroughly saturated with the fascination of both the people and the city. The disposition of the citizen of Vienna is commonly described by the German word 'gemüthlich.' This is not quite translatable into English, but perhaps our nearest word to it is 'genial.' One soon becomes contented in Vienna, and is never quite willing to go away again."

Finally, I asked Mark Twain, as one who had viewed it from the distance, what he thought of the great coming together of England and America? He straightened himself up, feeling the whole Anglo-Saxon man, lit a fresh cigar, and delivered verdict.

"It has always," his words were, "been a dream of mine, this closer relationship between England and America. I hardly expected to live to see that dream realized, but it has gone far enough towards realization to furnish me with contentment. As far as the English people are concerned, I knew that this friendly feeling was already blossoming four years ago—when I was in Australia."

"During your tour round the world, of course?"

"Yes. Mr. Cleveland had just issued that proclamation which threatened for a moment to embroil the two countries. But the people in Australasia and in India were as friendly and as hospitable to me as if there were not a suggestion of gunpowder in the air. Neither in social gatherings nor in the lecture hall did anyone say anything which could remind me that friction existed between England and America."

"You might have been at home?"

"Practically. The Australian and Indian papers never spoke of this episode with anything like bitterness, but were always moderate in tone, rational, kindly. Therefore, as I say, this English feeling is not a new birth, but is already four years old as evidenced in my personal experiences."

## "Mark Twain Talks"
### Curtis Brown, *Buffalo Express*, 30 July 1899, p. 1

Mark Twain has just set out for a sojourn in Sweden with his wife and two daughters, and will not get back to London till fall. At least, those are his intentions; but, as he observed, in a rather extraordinary talk I had with him the other day before he left, "I am full of intentions. I don't believe I've had an intention in months that I've fulfilled. Why, it isn't safe to have an intention. You mustn't have anything more than just the vaguest germ of an idea that maybe you'll do something or other if when the time comes you don't happen to do something else. You mustn't be a bit more definite than that, and if you get as far as having a real intention you are lost."

Mark Twain isn't often interviewed. He is always a hard man to find, in the first place. System and regularity are not numbered among his sins; and in the second place, after he has talked awhile to a favored newspaperman, he is likely to say, as he did on this occasion: "Now, see here, it won't do to publish any of that. I ought not to be telling about my affairs. It isn't quite right. It doesn't look well."

Whereupon I argued, and with fervor enough to win consent to the publication of some of the talk, although Mark Twain reiterated that he didn't believe the public would care much about his "fool intentions." He added: "You see, it's the vanity of the thing that worries me—that everlasting vanity that every mother's son of us has. If you can manage to cover it up somehow—if you can be deceiving enough to make it appear that the vanity wasn't there—why, go ahead and print some of the things I've been saying; but don't you print all of 'em." He pulled one hand from under the bedclothes and shook his finger impressively, thrusting the warning home with a sharp glance from two of the keenest blue eyes that were ever put into the head of man.

Mr. Clemens was in bed taking a bite now and then from his morning roll, and getting a sip of coffee between times, although it was 11 o'clock in the morning. . . . Naturally, one of the first questions was about the remarkable book which Mr. Clemens is writing, but which is not to be published for 100 years. It evidently worries him to think that he can't be taken seriously. "It's no use talking about it," he said, slapping his hand down on the bedclothes and giving the pillow an extra hitch. "There isn't a living soul, so far as I can discover, who can understand my purpose. My best friends don't grasp the idea. I begin to think even my family don't quite understand me. You couldn't get the idea either. Nobody could. And yet I suppose that the one thing I could do was to talk plainly. I don't use any big words. I don't sprout any flowers of speech, and yet I suppose I have read comments about it in 50 English and American papers, and not one of 'em seemed to know what I was driving at. And yet I have made it a rule to say exactly what I meant to say. I try to be clear, and let all the other graces go.

"When I say I have earned a vacation and am going to spend it in my own way, they get up and say to me, 'But what a waste of time it is to write a book that you won't sell!' Oh, the sordidness of the idea! And yet I am not pretending to work for nothing. I am no better than anybody else. I shall get my pay in pleasure. I have a right to get my pleasure in my own way, haven't I? Now, it is my idea of a good time to write a book that nobody now living shall ever see. If it is expensive to write a book that I shall not let anybody buy in my day, all right. It's my little copper penny, and if I want to spend it in a new way it doesn't need to worry a man who might spend his little copper penny some other way.

"Some say I want to advertise myself. What should I want to advertise myself for? I'm through writing for publication. Anyway, that's my intention, although it isn't safe to have an intention.

"Some say: 'That's not a new idea; Talleyrand did it.' Why, there isn't any such thing as a new idea. There isn't a man alive who ever had a new idea. Nobody ever did have a new idea. Adam himself never had one. When a critic goes to a play and then goes and writes about it that it wasn't based on a new idea, all he should mean is that the old idea didn't have a new coat of paint, that it wasn't rearranged. The mind of man isn't capable of producing a new idea. All it can do is to take the material already at hand and work it over into a little different form. We can't even boss the job. We can't tell our minds what to do and what not to do. All we can do is just to stand around and admire the workings of our mammoth intellects and think how moderately smart we are. . . .

"We all think we are swimming out vigorously on the ocean, while, as a matter of fact, we are each of us paddling around in our own little mud puddle. If you try to get a man out of his private, individual mud puddle he is lost. No man can swim in another man's mud puddle, so when I have a plan that is different from other people's plans they can't understand it, and I have to swim around alone in my own puddle.

"However, I'll tell you what it is I want to do. The difference between what I am writing and the ordinary biography is as marked as between an ordinary flat photograph and one of those—what-d'ye-call-'em—cinematograph pictures. Biography is a patchwork of flat photographs, each of them giving the prejudiced view of some particular observer. Perhaps one of the photographs would be the prejudiced recollections of the hero's mother, another the prejudiced observations of a man who hated him, another the stories told of him by Tom, Dick, and Harry—all of them distorted by some sort of prejudice. Along comes the biographer to patch all of these prejudiced views together, and, lo, he, too, is prejudiced. The cinematograph picture, on the other hand, shows the man complete, all around and in action.

"But you can't show all sides of a man without prejudice while he is living or while his friends or children are living. If he is a friend, you are inclined to paint him up a little, whitewash him a little; if he is an enemy, you are inclined to put a little black paint on him. If you know a story about him that reveals one whole side of his character, but that would hurt the feelings of his family, you will not be able to compel yourself to use it; but if it isn't going to be published for 100 years, it can be told without offense to yourself.

"Now, I'm writing on this book at odd times—and I have been at it for several months—just as if I were writing about people I had known 100 years ago, and as if they and their children were buried. I'm writing as much as possible, as if time had smoothed down all my prejudices; as if I'd got far enough away from my subject to see it in the proper perspective. Yes, I'm writing as if I were a Rip Van Winkle, and as if the things I remembered as having happened yesterday had really happened 100 years ago.

"If a publisher should come along and offer me an incredible sum I should say, 'Get thee behind me, Satan!' Why, that would spoil the whole thing. I am unhampered now, but as soon as the idea of publishing that book in time for anyone now living to read got into my thoughts, anyone can see that I couldn't go ahead as I had started out.

"I'm not going to write autobiography. The man has yet to be born who could write the truth about himself. Autobiography is always interesting, but howsoever true its facts may be, its interpretation of them must be taken with a great deal of allowance. In the innumerable biographies I am writing many persons are represented who are not famous today, but who may be some day.". . .

The Clemens conscience was much troubled at the time of the interview by the hat of Canon Wilberforce. The American humorist and the famous English divine had been fellow guests at a dinner two nights before, and Canon Wilberforce was called away early by his Parliamentary duties, and when Mark Twain came to go later on he found that his hat was gone. "I tried every hat in sight," he said, "and at last found one that fitted every idiosyncrasy of my cranium. It is a strange and mysterious circumstance that it turned out to be the property of Canon Wilberforce. After I had had it a day I was obliged to write hastily to the canon and explain that my family had become seriously alarmed by my condition. Ever since wearing the canon's hat I had been unable to take property that did not belong to me; had found it impossible to stretch a statement beyond the bounds of truth and had shown such a complete change in morals that the advisability of sending for a doctor for me was being seriously considered.

"When I reflected that this was, no doubt, the influence of the clergyman's hat, I became badly frightened at the thought of what must be the effect of my hat upon him. He must have been telling lies right and left, ever since he picked out my hat—'Mark Twain' was written in it, too, in big letters; I wrote it myself. Judging by the number of moral beauties brought out in me by the canon's hat, the number of vices awakened in his bosom by my hat must have been appalling, and I must get up this minute, have that hat nicely ironed, take it down to Westminster and get mine away from the canon before it plunges him into some awful disgrace, if it has not done so already."

## "Mark Twain Returns After Nine Years"
*New York Herald*, 4 October 1900, p. 3

Mark Twain will leave London on Saturday, to make his home in the United States, after a nine years' residence in Europe. . . .

"I am not here for my general health," he said, "but for lumbago. It isn't the ordinary kind of lumbago, either, but what is called 'private hotel lumbago.' One gets it from the beds. They are unnecessarily firm and their main characteristic is of a geological nature. They are composed of Silurian, superimposed upon red sandstone, and still contain the imprint of the prehistoric man. The English private hotel was once the best in the world. It is still the quietest, but its other merits are in decay. It is lingering upon its bygone honorable reputation. Many elderly English people still cling to it from inherited habit and arrested development. Rich Americans frequent it through ignorance and superstition. They find in its austere solemnity and Sabbath repose a charm which makes up for the high charges and mediaeval inconveniences. Pretenders who can't afford to live in Dover street at all affect the lumbago because it conveys the impression that they live in private hotels there."

## "Mark Twain, the Greatest American Humorist, Returning Home, Talks at Length to *The World*"
New York *World*, 14 October 1900, p. 3

If it were the good fortune of the journalist to have only Mark Twain to interview his lot would indeed be cast in pleasant places.

When *The World* correspondent called upon him today at his London hotel he was received with that charming courtesy and dignified geniality which are the outward stamp of the noble personal character of the greatest living humorist. . . . "Why, of course I am very glad to speak for *The World*. Whenever I arrive in a new place or whenever I leave it I always make it a point to answer as well as I can any questions that may be put to me by the boys. But between seasons I never talk. The same rule guides me in connection with public appearances. I have to work, and I like to do it as systematically as I can."

"Have you been busy with your pen amid the distractions of London?"

"Well, London, you see, doesn't distract me. I find it about the best possible place to work in. I like it too as a place of residence better than any I know outside Hartford, where I am always happiest and feel best. Here I meet men of my own tongue and I have many friends. For although seemingly I live a retired life here, I am constantly going out to dinners. You can understand that at the close of a day's work it is a big luxury, a great relaxation, to dine in pleasant company, in absolute privacy, where you can say what you like with the knowledge that it will not get into print. These dinners I enjoy; it's the luncheons that break in upon your time and upset your working arrangements. But dinners! Why I can do with millions of dinners!"

"Is it true that you have resolved never to leave the United States again?"

"Not a word of truth in it. Perhaps we may spend the rest of our days at home. I don't know and no consideration on earth could induce me to give a pledge about that or anything else. That is another of my rules of life. I never give pledges or promises about things of that sort. If I felt myself under the constraint of a pledge the situation would become so irksome to me that only on that account alone, I should be irresistibly compelled to come away again. No—as far as I am able to speak about a subject on which other people have the controlling voice more or less—I propose to stay the winter in New York, and then go back to Hartford in the spring."

"But do you really think it possible that such an indefatigable traveler as you have been can settle down at home? Won't you feel restless?"

"An indefatigable traveler! That's where I am misunderstood. Now I have made thirty-four long journeys in my life, and thirty-two of them were made under the spur of absolute compulsion. I mean it—under nothing but sheer compulsion. There always was an imperative reason. I had to gather material for books or sketches, I had to stump around lecturing to make money, or I had to go abroad for the health or the education of my family. For love of travel—never any of these thirty-two journeys. There is no man living who cares less about seeing new places and peoples than I. You are surprised—but it's the gospel truth. I had a surfeit of it.

"When I started out in 1867 for a six months' tour in the *Quaker City* I was a voracious sightseer. With nearly all the rest of that gang I said to myself: 'This is the opportunity of my life—never again shall I have the chance, the time or the money to see the Old World.' We lived up to that idea. We went in for seeing everything that was to be seen. In a city of inexhaustible treasures like Rome we got up at 6 in the morning and throughout the whole day, in rain or shine, we made a perpetual procession through picture galleries, churches, museums, palaces—looking at things which for the most part did not interest us one cent but which we thought we had to see. And we saw them. If our meals interfered with our seeing any old thing our meals were put aside. At 9 or 10 at night we returned to our hotel, our brains and our bodies reeling with fatigue and utter exhaustion. My head used to ache, my eyes to swim, but I would not succumb to the terrible temptation to throw myself on the bed, as if I did so I could not rise from it again before morning. I had to resist because we had to see something else by moonlight or because there was no moon or some other foolish reason. The only rest we had was when we went a short voyage from one port to another in the Mediterranean, and then I slept all the time. What was the result of this insensate sightseeing? Why, that I was so fagged that I lost the capacity to appreciate most of what I saw or to carry away any coherent idea of it. Since then only hard necessity has ever driven me traveling. When I went around the world, five years ago, it was because I wanted money to pay off debts that were a nuisance to me—they burdened my conscience. People say that it was to relieve my creditors. Not at all. It was far more to relieve Clemens than creditors. I could not be happy until I got rid of that debt. I have never recovered from the *Quaker City* surfeit of sightseeing, and don't think there is any reasonable prospect of my doing so now."

"Don't you find theatres as much of a relaxation as dinners?"

"No: that is another mistake. I had a surfeit of theatres, too. My family are fond of the play and go very often, but they don't enjoy themselves as much as they otherwise would when they persuade me to go with them. You see, when I was a reporter on the San Francisco *Call* I always had a full day's work. I had to do all the police reports, together with any other odd assignments that might turn up, always finishing up by going to seven theatres every evening. I had to write something about each of them, and as a reporter yourself you can understand that with the fag end of my day's work to finish and seven critical notices of high-class performances of the most varied kind to write up, I could not devote that leisure to each play that as a conscientious dramatic critic I should like. Ten minutes here, a quarter of an hour there—that was all I could afford, because there might be a couple more night assignments waiting me at the office. I was very hurried all the time. The result is that when I go to a playhouse now and I have been there about fifteen minutes or half an hour, I begin to fidget around, thinking, 'I shall get all behind if I stay here any longer; I must be off to the other three or four houses, and I have still that murder story to write.' So that the family don't care much about my company at the theatre. That is another example of how bad a surfeit is."

"How long did you continue to keep the San Francisco *Call* going?"

"Let me see—just about twelve months. At the end of that time I was reduced to such a pitiable condition of mental destitution, was so completely worn out and impoverished in mind and body by the responsibilities of my position, that the editor invited me to resign. I didn't want to be ungrateful to a man who had allowed me to learn so much of different kinds of newspaper work in so short a time, so I resigned. And, mind you, there was very little chance of another job, either—in fact it was three or four months before I got one." . . .

"And what do you think about the American campaign?"

"Well, you see, I have only read scraps and snatches of news in the papers here, not sufficient to stir my prejudices or partialities. I am going back to vote—I mean, I shall vote, as I shall happen to be there when the election comes on. I have been paying taxes all the time I have been away, so I suppose I am entitled to exercise the franchise."

# Man of Letters

## Oct 16 1900–Oct 14 1901

In the full bloom of his celebrity, Mark Twain was a public intellectual, his opinion sought on a variety of issues, from civic corruption to football and copyright. Still, his views were often considered "quaint" rather than serious expressions of belief.

### "Mark Twain Home, An Anti-Imperialist"
*New York Herald,* 16 October 1900, p. 4

Mark Twain, sometime known as Samuel Clemens, returned home last night. . . .

"I have had lots of fun," remarked Mr. Clemens, as he came down the gangplank. "I have enjoyed myself, except for a twinge of dyspepsia now and then, in every country and under every sky. Fun has no nationality. It has the freedom of the world. But I think I had most fun in Vienna, with the poor old Reichsrath. I was there for a year and a half, and had plenty of time to take it in. It was one of the biggest jokes I have ever seen, and I enjoyed it immensely.

"Fate has its revenge on the humorist," said Mr. Clemens, after he had got well ashore and felt his legs more secure under him, and could risk a more serious tone. "Now, I have lied so much, in a genial, good-natured way, of course, that people won't believe me when I speak the truth. I may add that I have stopped speaking the truth. It is no longer appreciated—in me.

"I have found that when I speak the truth, I am not believed, and that I have never told a lie so big but that some one had sublime confidence in my veracity. I have, therefore, been forced by fate to adopt fiction as a medium of truth. Most liars lie for the love of the lie; I lie for the love of truth. I disseminate my true views by means of a series of apparently humorous and mendacious stories.

"If any man can do that, and finds that he can disseminate facts through the medium of falsehood, he should never speak the truth— and I don't.

"The English, you know, take everything that is very serious as an immense joke, and everything that is really side splitting as terribly dull. They even pretended to think me jesting when I spoke about writing a history to be read one hundred years after it was written.

"If ever I spoke truth—and at that time I had not given up the habit of resorting to it occasionally—I spoke it then. I was in dead earnest, but of course the English set it down as a great joke." . . .

"Mr. Clemens, have you had time to give any thought to the grave question of imperialism?" I asked. . . .

"I left these shores, at Vancouver, a red-hot imperialist. I wanted the American eagle to go screaming into the Pacific. It seemed tiresome and tame for it to content itself with the Rockies. Why not spread its wings over the Philippines, I asked myself? And I thought it would be a real good thing to do.

"I said to myself. Here are a people who have suffered for three centuries. We can make them as free as ourselves, give them a government and country of their own, put a miniature of the American constitution afloat in the Pacific, start a brand new republic to take its place among the free nations of the world. It seemed to me a great task to which we had addressed ourselves.

"But I have thought some more, since then, and I have read carefully the treaty of Paris, and I have seen that we do not intend to free but to subjugate the people of the Philippines. We have gone there to conquer, not to redeem. We have also pledged the power of this country to maintain and protect the abominable system established in the Philippines by the Friars.

"It should, it seems to me, be our pleasure and duty to make those people free and let them deal with their own domestic questions in their own way. And so I am an anti-imperialist. I am opposed to having the eagle put its talons on any other land.

"But I want to say that I cannot conscientiously support Mr. Bryan. I am not so much of an anti-imperialist as that. I have been told that I cannot vote in this election, but if I could I should not vote for Mr. Bryan. As to what I would do I cannot say, as I am a mugwump, and a mugwump won't vote until he has had plenty of time to look the thing over.

"And then, I don't want to commit myself too far, as, if I find that I cannot vote, I shall run for President. A patriotic American must do something around election time, and that's about the only thing political that is left for me."

"Have you any books about ready for publication?"

"No; but I have several on the way. I wrote myself out in the line of anecdotes and humorous sketches in my last book. I ran short even in that and could barely find enough material to fill it. I am now falling back upon fiction; but, as I have said, my fiction is different from the fiction of others. No matter what I write in that line people will think that I am hiding some truth behind the stalking horse of a story."

"Will you have an American story?"

"You see, I write the story and then fill in the place, like blanks in a railway form. The places don't count so much. The story is the thing."

"But you will give your people some of their own types, with characteristic dialect, will you not? And won't that require you to select your scenes first?"

"No, not entirely. Even that can be filled in. It is astonishing how much can be filled in. I rewrote one of my books three times, and each time it was a different book. I had filled in, and filled in, until the original book wasn't there. It had evaporated through the blanks, and I had an entirely new book. I shall write my story, and then lay the scene where I want it, and, if necessary, change other things to suit the places.

"I shall very probably write a story with the scene laid in this country, or I shall place the scene of one of my present uncompleted stories here. This can be done rather handily, after the whole story is written.

"But I am not going to publish another book for at least a year. I have just published a small one, and a book every two or three years is enough."

"Will you have any more like *Huckleberry Finn* and *Tom Sawyer?*"

"Perhaps," and Mr. Clemens smiled as he thought of these creations. "Yes, I shall have to do something of that kind, I suppose. But one can't talk about an unwritten book. It may grow into quite a different thing from what one thinks it may be."

When I asked Mr. Clemens to tell some of his experiences of travel, he replied: "That is another old story, and almost everything I saw or thought or imagined during my trip around the world has been told in my books. . . .

"In Pretoria, also, I had some little fun. It was with the Jameson raiders, who were in jail when I reached there. They were very disconsolate, expecting to be shot, or something of the sort, every morning. I went down to cheer them up a bit.

"I talked to them. I told them that they didn't seem to appreciate the privilege of being confined in a jail. Bunyan, I told them, would not have written the *Pilgrim's Progress* if some one had not shut him up in a cell, and that we should not have had the pleasure of reading *Don Quixote* if Cervantes had not spent several years in prison. Some of the fellows smiled sadly. They didn't appreciate the point of view. I told them that some men went through life without having the privilege they were enjoying."

## "My Impressions of America"

New York *World*, 21 October 1900, p. E5

*The World's* clever caricaturist, Kate Carew, was sent the other day to get Mark Twain's impressions of America. . . . Here is the interview which Miss Carew obtained. . . .

"The trouble with us in America," said Mark Twain, "is that we haven't learned to speak the truth."

He was sitting at breakfast opposite an exceedingly embarrassed young woman who was taking pains to keep her pencil and sketchbook below the level of the table, because she did not wish to excite the curiosity of the waiter—though he would be a bold waiter that betrayed curiosity in the presence of Samuel L. Clemens.

What led up to the remark about truth was that others were clamoring to see Mark Twain, and the embarrassed young woman had ventured to say: "Don't you find that one's time is more respected on the other side?"

"Well, yes," he replied, after a pause occupied in carefully breaking the end off a roll—and I wish I could convey the solemnity of utterance and the long, oft-broken drawl. "Well, yes. I guess—perhaps—it is. Now—in London I always had—a—regular time set for myself. But there—I'd—go—'way down into the—city—and people—would know where to find me, and wouldn't—know—my other address. . . . Except friends, of course—but then—no one would think of calling—at—ten in the morning—there; and if—they did—one wouldn't hesitate—to—say—'I'm at—breakfast'—or—'I'm—about—to breakfast.'

"But here—well, of course—our—friends are anxious to see—us, and they—come—whenever—they think they can—find us. And—the—trouble with us in America is we haven't learned how to—speak the truth—yet.

"If we had it would be—a—pleasure for me to—tell—my friend—that he was intruding, and he would be—benefited—and not injured.

"Now, it is an—art—high art—to speak the—truth so that the object—does not object—does not become offended. The trouble—is—

Kate Carew sketches from the *New York World* for 21 August 1900.

with our social laws. The only—way to get reform is to educate—both sides—one to—give, the other to—receive; one to tell the truth, the— other to—listen to it without—getting—mad."

A pause. A longer pause than usual. An abominably protracted pause. A pause hovering on the abyss of irretrievable silence. Heavens! Would he say no more? He whom it had been so much trouble to coax into speaking at all? It was a desperate chance. I broke in, hardly knowing what I was saying: "But I always thought that the art was in telling lies, and—and telling the truth seems so easy!" . . .

"Don't believe it," he said, dropping his napkin to his knee. "Lying—is not an art—not that I have ever been able to—discover—and I have— tried—hard all my life. It is a—device—of primitive intelligences. The best—liars—are savages and—children. The most cultured—people speak the truth as often as they—think about it, and enjoy—hearing it spoken by—others. In heaven I shouldn't wonder but they—use—the truth—most of the time."

I had been listening too hard to do much work, though there was never a more tempting head for pencil or brush than this silver-crowned one. . . .

Of his experiences in Vienna and his friendships there—not a word. Paris, London—the same.

New York? If I could only get this most taciturn of humorists and philosophers to tell his impressions of America—not a whole budget of impressions, just one or two tiny ones that might escape his determination not to be interviewed!

Ah, what a master of the art of silence is Mark Twain! The skyscrapers? Not a word. The torn-up streets? Not a word. Rapid transit? Not a word. Politics? Not a word. Noise? Let me see.

"Don't you find New York very noisy after the quiet of European cities?" I ventured.

"No; it doesn't annoy me," he said. "I don't—hear it. You don't have to hear—noise—unless you want to. The only time I hear the elevated— is—when it—stops."

The waiter flitted back with a note. Another caller.

"They don't do this—sort of—thing in London," he remarked. "There one can—breakfast—between 10 and 12 in beautiful—safety. I don't know why I breakfast at—the same hour—here. It's just habit, I guess. The early breakfast habit is one of—the American institutions—I admire most—when I am abroad.

"But these early morning—calls—are meant in a kindly spirit. They touch my heart, even when—the coffee gets—cold."

It would be impossible to exaggerate the composure and gravity with which Mark Twain utters his quaintnesses—and I'm sure he wasn't in much of a mood for quaintnesses that morning. . . . He had occasion to send for the head waiter and ask him why something hadn't been done, or why it hadn't been done sooner. He didn't scold, he just said: "You understand, it's better—for me to—know about these things, so I'll know what to do about it next time."

The tremulous head waiter explained that there had been something the matter with the speaking-tube by which the original order had been transmitted.

"Oh, that was it, was it?" said Mr. Clemens. "I just wanted to know." And then, turning to me, he added: "I don't suppose we—have a right—to know as much as cooks and—waiters, anyway."

## "A Day with Mark Twain / Funniest Man in the World"
*New York Journal and Advertiser,* 11 November 1900, magazine supplement, p. 18

Mark Twain disapproves of interviews, but in his talk with a correspondent the other day he said some things that were as interesting and full as a nut is of meat. . . .

"When it comes to a serious interview—I feel—er—as though I might be able to write my impressions as well as the reporter.

"And—er—make more money."

A little later Mr. Mark Twain gave painful evidence of his lack of enthusiasm for American newspapers.

"Now, Sunday morning," he said, in his slow drawl, "I wanted a paper to read while I was eating my breakfast. I am such a tremendously hearty eater that it takes me more than a week to eat enough to last me from breakfast to lunch time. I said so to the man at the newsstand when he showed me an enormous stack of paper.

"'One copy!'" he cried, and then, seeing I was green, added, 'costs 5 cents.'

"'Oh, I don't want the whole thing,' said I. 'It's too expensive, and besides, I haven't my carpetbag here to carry it in. Just give me a little installment of it that I can carry into the diningroom by myself. Let me pay for it in proportion. I guess about a cent's worth will do me today.'

"But actually he wouldn't do it!

"'Why not?' said I. Then, to persuade him, I added: 'If you're saving any particular part for someone else I don't care; I'm not particular. Give me anything; a little bit 'off the top,' the outside, the inside, or anything you've got handy.'

"Still he said he couldn't do it.

"The result was we couldn't strike a bargain and I couldn't read a Sunday paper."

Mark Twain's opinion of newspapers recalls the time when a reporter was sent to interview him as the leading author. . . . He received the reporter with his customary politeness and elusiveness. The reporter, however, summoned all his wits and asked the question which was to point his article.

"Mr. Twain," he asked, "to what one thing, most of all, do you owe your marvelous success in literature?"

He waited for the humorist to answer "My newspaper training."

Instead Mr. Twain burst forth decisively:

"To the fact that when I was young and very ambitious, I lost my job."

"May I ask what was your job, Mr. Twain?" exclaimed the puzzled reporter.

"Certainly, sir, certainly," replied the humorist, with great suavity. "I was a reporter."

## "'This Beats Croquet,' Said Mark Twain at Football Game"

New York *World*, 18 November 1900, p. 3

Mark Twain, as the guest of Laurence Hutton, the writer, was an interested spectator of the Yale-Princeton football game. . . . Just before 2 o'clock yesterday afternoon Mr. Clemens, Mr. Hutton, and several Princeton professors were driven to the football field. Some Princetonians in the crowd recognized Mark Twain and he was the recipient of several long-drawn out "Sis-boom-ahs" as he climbed up the seats of the east stand. This was the stand where the Princeton singing societies were congregated. They were gathered near the northern end of the stand, and the mighty volume of sound they put forth seemed to delight Mr. Clemens, who smiled at their enthusiasm.

Mr. Clemens wore a huge yellow chrysanthemum in the left lapel of his long black overcoat. This tribute to the college was appreciated by the students nearby, who throughout the game gave an occasional "tiger" for "Mark Twain."

Mr. Clemens appeared deeply interested in the contest. It was the first college football game he had ever witnessed. He asked many questions of his friend Mr. Hutton and of others nearby concerning the plays and the players. He quickly mastered the main principles of the game and easily detected the superiority of the team from New Haven.

In the early part of the contest, when Princeton surprised her admirers by the strong resistance she put up, Mr. Clemens cheered lustily in unison with the other rooters for Old Nassau. He looked gloomy and sympathetic when Gould made an easy touchdown for Yale soon after the game began. But when Mattis shortly thereafter dropped a pretty goal from the field Mr. Clemens laughed loudly, clapped his hands, and exclaimed: "That's good! That's good! Perhaps Princeton will win after all."

When the first half closed with the figures standing 11 for Yale and 5 for Princeton, Mr. Clemens was one of the most eager of the mathematicians figuring how Princeton might yet pull the game out of

Katy Leary in Jean Clemens's room at Twenty-one Fifth Avenue in January 1905. Courtesy of the Mark Twain Project, University of California, Berkeley.

the fire. After the ten minutes' intermission were up, Yale's giants came lumbering on the field for the second half, and Mr. Clemens, who had been standing up and stamping his feet to keep warm, sat down again with a broad grin of anticipatory joy.

"Here's where Princeton gets even!" he remarked jovially to his friends. But Princeton didn't get even.

As the second half progressed and Yale's big fellows ripped the light Princeton line to piece for long gains Mr. Clemens' face was a study. He apparently was a sincere adherent of Princeton, yet he could not refrain from making remarks complimentary to the physique of the Yale eleven.

When the gigantic Perry Hale and the huge and gritty Gordon Brown, the captain of the blues, or the almost equally stalwart Stillman slammed into the Tigers, bowling them over on all sides, Mr. Clemens made such remarks as:

"I should think they'd break every bone they ever had!"

"Those Yale men must be made of granite, like the rocks of Connecticut!"

"Those young Elis are too beefy and brawny for the Tigers!"

"Well, say, this beats croquet. There more go about it!"

"That Yale team could lick a Spanish army!"

"The country is safe when its young men show such pluck and determination as are here in evidence today."

The eighteen thousand cheering people were a revelation to Mr. Clemens. As the Tigers were trawled deeper and deeper in the mire, when the score was standing 29 to 5 against them, toward the very close, the cheering clubs gave a grand exhibition of the "never say die" spirit for which Princeton has always been famous....

Yale might beat their football team, but the pluck of the Princeton men was undaunted. It was this feature which particularly impressed itself upon Mr. Clemens. He said, after the game, that the contest was one of the events of his life, and that he was proud to have been present at a game where Princeton men made such a splendid exhibition of spirit. He said he was proud of Yale, too, for Yale is in his State. He spoke of the splendid courage displayed by all of the Yale men, particularly Brown, who repeatedly hurled himself at formations and broke them up in a manner that overwhelmed the lighter Jerseymen.

Mr. Clemens said he was sorry football, as it was played today, was not in vogue during his schooldays, as he believed he would have liked to play it. He gave it as his opinion that it was the grandest game ever invented for boys—one which showed all their best qualities to advantage, and a game that must necessarily build up the mind as well as the body.

## "Mark Twain Bests a Grasping Cabman"
### New York *World*, 23 November 1900, p. 12

Seriously, semi-tragically, the plaint of Mark Twain against the cabmen of New York was told to the Mayor's Chief Marshall at noon yesterday, and as a result Cabman William Beck now has no license....

With Mark Twain came Kate Leary, who for eighteen years has

been a maid in his family, and Sherman Everett, butler for the Clemens household, who did the detective work in locating the cabman after he had given a false number. . . .

Mark Twain . . . leaned forward in his chair and began deliberately: "The salient features of the case are these: That this maid servant came to my study the evening of the 20th at 6 o'clock—along there some place—and said she had been brought from the Forty-second street station to my house, No. 14 West Tenth street, in this coupe, and that the driver required a dollar and a half for the service, and I went down to see about it, and he required the dollar and a half from me. I judged it to be an overcharge."

Marshal David Roche called the attention of Mark Twain to the fact that the distance was thirty-four blocks, and that the legal charge for the hackman was only fifty cents a mile.

"I haven't finished yet," interrupted the author. "There is another charge. I inquired of him his number. Instead of exhibiting his number, he gave me a false one with his mouth. Those are my two charges."

The Marshal wished to know how Mark Twain ascertained the false number.

"I ascertained it," replied Mark Twain, "through my colored man who serves us. I sent him down to the carriage to ascertain. I suspected when he did not show me his number that he was not telling the truth."

Marshal Roche asked the cabman to produce his license. When this was read Beck, the cabman, started in to make his defense. He said: "He engaged me from Grand Central Station down to No. 14 West Tenth street. I took the maid down there and thought I was entitled to $1.50."

. . .

The Marshal scrowled at the cabby. "It was an overcharge," he announced. . . .

Marshal Roche then delivered his sentence midway in the hearing.

"This man was required to exhibit his license and he failed to make his number known," said the Marshal. "It is against the ordinances and therefore we will have to suspend your license, my dear man, for this action. I will go further. I will hear out all the evidence and pay particular attention to this case."

Mark Twain smiled. It was the only time during the hearing that his deep seriousness left him. . . .

"I don't think the case warranted this publicity," spoke up the cab owner.

"May I speak?" suddenly asked Mark Twain, turning to the Marshal. When an affirmative reply came the author settled back in his chair, closed his eyes as if he was soliloquizing, and said: "Now, my dear sir, this is not a matter of sentiment. It is mere practical business. You cannot imagine that I am making money wasting an hour or two of my time to prosecute a case in which I can have no personal interest whatever.

"I am doing this just as any citizen who is worthy of the name of citizen should do. He has no choice. He has a distinct duty. He is a non-classified policeman, and every citizen is a policeman and it is his duty to assist the police and the magistracy in every way he can and give his time if necessary to help uphold the law. Now if nobody comes forward you have this result:

"Here is a man who is a perfectly natural product of an infamous system in this city. It is a charge upon the lax patriotism in this New York that this thing can exist. You have encouraged him in every way and allowed him to overcharge. No fault has been found with him. He is not the criminal here at all. The criminal is the citizens of New York and the absence of patriotism. They ought to be ashamed of themselves to allow such a state as this to grow up; and if they allow, it will continue forever.

"I am not here to avenge myself on him. I have no quarrel with him. My quarrel is with the citizens of New York that have encouraged overcharging in this way.

"Now you say it is not necessary that there should be publicity. In church and state and everywhere always the defense of a man with a weak case is to conceal.

"The only way to bring such things out and make them practical and give them force is to remove all concealment; make it a public offense when a citizen neglects his duty—when he should bring forward a charge.

"I believe that if the public knew how simple it is here to spend a few minutes and prove a case or lose it, they would do so. They don't appreciate that you take care of these things. If they knew that you were here always ready to carry out the law, more complaints, I am sure, would come to this office." . . .

The cab owner took a step forward. Mark Twain straightened in his chair.

"There are two sides to a question," said the cab owner.

"There is only one side to a moral question," answered Mark Twain. "A legal question is a moral one. There are not two sides to a moral question."

The voice of the humorist was loud. . . . "I will prosecute every case that comes to my notices, at any time or any place.

"This charging of extortionate rates caused the formation of the Pennsylvania hack service and the New York Central hack service, and after a time there will be no room at all for other hackmen."

"There is more back of this case," said the cab owner.

"What?" asked Marshal Roche.

"Well, if they get all the special privileges we must do something," said Byrne. "Why don't they give us some of the business those other people get?"

Mark Twain bristled up. His eyes flashed. "The pirate can make that argument," he interjected.

This caused laughter. The cab owner did not take it as a joke. His face became livid.

"You have been repeating parrot talk yourself," he exclaimed.

Mark Twain did not notice that "pirate" had been twisted into "parrot."

Marshal Roche was hammering on his desk for order. Several policemen who were outside edged in toward the room.

"Well, it's all over," said Mark Twain to the maid. "Let's go home."

## "Mark Twain Bearded in His New York Den by a Camera Fiend"

*New York Herald*, 20 January 1901, V, 3

... It so happened when I boarded the train that the author was looking over his mail. ...

"I can't do it. There isn't money enough in New York or Boston to go round."

He hadn't spoken to me, but had answered a condition of depravity in human nature that his letters had revealed.

"I suppose they can't help it; it's a dreadful habit, though."

"More requests for money?" I asked.

"Yes. I don't mind helping people I know; friends should depend on each other when the world doesn't treat them well, but no wonder the figures of Charity are made to look so haughty and stuck up in statues."

...

"We're all beggars, more or less, the whole lot of us. It is a depraved condition in all of us. One man, in good clothes, asks a favor, another asks for a quarter because he's hungry. I asked a man to give me the address of another man. He mailed it to me. I might just as well have found it out myself, but by begging I saved myself exertion and trouble.

"I remember a certain day in San Francisco, when, if I hadn't picked up a dime that I found lying in the street, I should have asked someone for a quarter. Only a matter of a few hours and I'd have been a beggar. That dime saved me, and I have never begged—never!"

He was distinctly proud of this fact, not for his own strength of achievement, but for a fortunate escape from violation of his principle. A good deal of fun has been made of Mark Twain's endeavors to arouse New Yorkers to a sense of their rights of citizenship. His recent resentment of a cabman's attempted extortion was only a shade of the principle and uprightness that make the ideal American citizen. ... The Postmaster of New York city loomed up in the unpleasant guise of an autocrat to the author's vision.

"Why do we have to go down to the Post Office and present an official with a carefully revised edition of our family tree before we can get a registered letter?" asked Mark Twain, glancing at me, as if I were the Postmaster.

"Abominable!" I said, soothingly. . . .

"No such trouble in Europe. A registered letter means important letter to the authorities over there, and they can't get it into your hands too quickly. Not only that, but you're not obliged to receive it if you don't want it. Nearly all begging letters abroad are sent by registered mail, so that you can't say you didn't receive them. I never accepted a registered letter unless the handwriting was familiar to me after awhile."

"Do they write begging letters in Europe?"

"Oceans of them. They have a habit of enclosing soiled and time-worn letters and documents of recommendation, signed by famous people who are not on earth to deny them. I used to leave them with the hall porter of the hotel, with a note thanking them for the opportunity afforded me of reading their testimonials, and stating that they could receive them intact from the hands of the porter. . . . All the professional beggars, or rather the men and women afflicted with the complaint, need are a name and address. They scan the newspapers for arrivals at the hotels, and labor diligently in this way to make a living."

He handed me a letter on which was printed the statement that the sender, having a "nice collection of autographs," would be quite willing to add Mark Twain's to the collection. A stamped envelope, addressed to Bloomington, Ill., completed the bargain so far as he was concerned.

"What gorgeous type," mused the author, grimly.

"There's another phase of human depravity, the organized autograph hunter. Now, I don't object to answering a letter if the writer will show me the common courtesy of using pen, ink and notepaper to address me, but when he goes to a printing machine, and seems to begrudge the time he must spend to write me personally, I don't feel compelled to answer him. I can't afford a printing press in my establishment to turn out my correspondence in colored inks, bound and folded automatically. I still have to use the primitive methods of correspondence. He's too rich for my blood," and he laid the letter aside.

"How often have you been photographed?" I asked, as I showed him the pictures taken in his den in New York.

"Twenty-three times in twenty-three minutes the day before yesterday," was the answer.

"Harpers wanted to be sure to get something lifelike," explained Mark Twain. "I felt as a moving picture must feel going at full speed. It's wonderful how ugly we are sometimes, too, when we get a real, good, faithful likeness. No one would have believed a horse was such a homely acting animal till we got a picture of him in action. It won't do for us to be too self-conscious in these snapshot days of inquiry. Now, I said a thing last night in a speech that I didn't mean to say. It just slipped out because I had been writing an article on the subject. I didn't intend to say it there."

It was in reference to the Presidential policy in the Philippines. I showed him the paragraph as reported in the daily papers. . . . "You do not approve of the policy of the administration in the Philippines?" I asked indifferently.

"If we desire to become members of the international family let us enter it respectably, and not on the basis at present proposed in Manila. We find a whole heap of fault with the war in South Africa, and feel moved to hysterics for the sufferings of the Boers, yet we don't seem to feel so very sorry for the natives in the Philippines."

"Another phase of depravity," I suggested.

"That's it. Human nature is selfish, and it's only real noble for profit."

"Have you been to the opera?" I asked.

"Once; the other night." He spoke with the slow utterance of reserved thought and a little sadly, I thought.

"You don't like it?"

"Yes and no. I think opera is spoiled by attempting to combine instrumental and vocal effects. I love instrumental music and I love a good voice, but I don't like them together. It's too generous. I can't fully take it in. Either the instruments spoil the voice or the voice spoils the instruments." . . .

I showed him one of the photographs taken at his desk.

"Now, if Mrs. Clemens had come in and seen that desk being photographed in this shape she would have been aghast at its apparent disorder. But that is not disorder. I know exactly where everything is, top and bottom, from a telegraph blank in its hiding place to a manuscript or a letter. What looks like disorder to some people is the best of order to others.

"My mother had the same disordered sense of order that I have. I might buy her reams and reams of the most magnificent note paper, blue, green, red, pale peacock, anything you like; it was no use. She never would write on anything but odd scraps. Many's the letter I've received from her written on uneven scraps of paper, different colors and qualities all bunched together in an envelope and unpaged. My mother's letters were as hard to understand as any problem book I ever read." For the first time since we had been talking Mark Twain laughed.

## "Mark Twain, Expert on Trade Marks, Has Fun"
### *New York Journal and Advertiser*, 14 March 1901, p. 1

"I hope you gentlemen will let me go soon," sighed Mark Twain, as he seated himself in United State Commissioner Shields' private office yesterday. "I have a most important engagement." And the lovable humorist resignedly settled himself in a chair and looked unhappy.

Presumably Mr. Clemens was called as an expert on the copyright law and literary trademarks, with which he has had some sad experiences. Rudyard Kipling's suit against R. F. Fenno & Co., alleging infringement of copyright, was to be heard, and A. T. Gurlitz, Kipling's counsel, had called Mark Twain.

Mr. Gurlitz began to question him about the trademarks used by Kipling's publishers.

"I object!" exclaimed Mr. Rives, counsel for Fenno & Co., and "'Bject!' 'Bject!' 'Bject!'" sounded after each of Mr. Gurlitz's questions.

"They don't seem to want me to talk at all," plaintively observed the man who wrote *The Innocents Abroad,* and he added, looking at the Commissioner, "I think I might smoke if I can't talk."

Mr. Shields, smiling, offered him a cigar. Mr. Clemens looked long and solemnly at the cigar, then at Mr. Gurlitz, then at Mr. Rives. Waving the cigar away from him, he said: "No, no. I guess I'd better not take it. They would 'bject,' I know. But"—regretfully—"it looks like a good cigar."

"Oh, there will be no objection, Mr. Clemens," the lawyers declared.

Looking much relieved, Mark Twain slowly put on his steel rimmed spectacles, lit the cigar, learned back contentedly, puffed away, then exclaimed: "Now, go on, gentleman. I'm ready to meet all your objections."

"Have you written in your career?" asked Mr. Gurlitz.

Mr. Clemens seemed as surprised as if the thought of writing had never suggested itself to him. Recovering himself, he replied, with mock modesty:

"A few stories."

Q. Do you consider that a book of stories of an author, published under a title selected by the author, can reasonably and generally be regarded as a book written by that author?

Mark Twain drew a deep sigh, as if to say, "That's a hard one."

"I should say yes. But it's no business of mine. I don't know whether that's a legal answer," he hastily added.

Q. Do you consider that a publisher, other than the one who originally published such a book, has any right to issue a similar volume of the same works?

"No, that wouldn't be square," answered the most entertaining of experts. "Nothing square about such a proceeding."

"A manufacturer who put up soap, beer, whiskey"—Mr. Gurlitz began.

Mr. Clemens, most temperate of men, pretended to be delighted by the mention of whiskey and looked around as if he were athirst.

"Put up soap, beer, whiskey, under the label previously used by another manufacturer would be guilty of counterfeiting, too?" the lawyer finished his question.

"Yes, no difference between counterfeiting, be it whiskey or a book," Mr. Clemens replied. "There's no substantial difference. I might be permitted, by the by"—this with much significance—"to explain why I think so. But you understand why." . . .

To Mr. Gurlitz, Mr. Clemens said he understood that, since his own suit, trademarks have become more valuable to authors. When his testimony was over Mr. Rives most politely said, to enable Mark Twain to keep his engagement, he would waive verification of his testimony nor need Mr. Clemens sign it.

"I will get Mr. Clemens to read it and make any needed corrections," suggested Mr. Gurlitz.

"You will have a hard time to get me to read it," retorted Mark Twain, gathering up his hat and coat.

"Don't you ever read your own productions?" laughed Mr. Rives.

The answer came like a flash, as Mark Twain hurried away: "Not when I can get a proofreader to do it."

## "Mark Twain Will Warmly Greet Robbers"
### *New York Journal and Advertiser*, 11 October 1901, p. 1

Mark Twain offers a warm welcome to the burglars who, for two months and more have been defying the police and preying on the rich and fashionable residents of Riverdale and Kingsbridge. . . . "If I were a burglar I would feel very much hurt that my confidence in the persons who occupy the residence around here should be so abused. Any decent burglar is entitled to something for his pains."

Mr. Twain here opened a drawer in his desk and fondled a highly polished revolver, repeating, "Something for his pains." Then he continued:

"It is unkind to deceive these industrious burglars by putting plated ware where they can get, when everyone knows they put themselves to the trouble of breaking into houses to obtain solid silver. The burglar, like anyone else, must make a living. I believe it unkind to discourage him in his peculiar efforts; perhaps he has a family to support."

At the thoughts of the burglar's family Mr. Twain seemed about to weep. But just then three great dogs, with large, white, sharp teeth came bounding into the study.

Mr. Twain restrained his tears, patted the dogs' head, felt the sharp points of their teeth, and murmured, "What a pity it would be if the burglar's family should be deprived of his invisible means of support." Then he continued:

"Sic 'em!" shouted Mr. Twain of a sudden. With distended, dropping jaws, the huge dogs hurled themselves into the grounds around the house.

"Or I may tie the burglars up, so that my dogs may not be interrupted in the repast," drawled Mr. Twain.

## "Mark Twain Would Convert Tammany Police"
*New York Herald,* 14 October 1901, p. 5

Mark Twain has declined regretfully to take the stump for Seth Low, because, he says, he cannot persuade folks to take him seriously, even in his most lofty flights of spellbinding eloquence.... "Sh-h-h! Not so loud," said the author of *Tom Sawyer,* with a warning finger at his lips. . . .

"You see, I have undertaken this proselytizing effort wholly on my own responsibility, and with only the tacit support of the fusion Campaign Committee.... I will tell you in confidence that I am much encouraged. I began my campaign on a Tammany policeman whom I met the other day at my gate. Personal suasion is my long suit. I am more successful at that than I am on the stump, though I used much good cart-tail eloquence on this particular policeman, and I could see that he was impressed. I convinced him that there was no authentic record of any Tammany man ever having gone to heaven. But, while he seemed measurably pleased by my attentions, I noticed that he appeared to restrain his enthusiasm. I soon saw that this was a very judicious policeman, the kind who does not blurt right out all the things that may be in his mind and so does not get transferred oftener than twice a week. . . .

"I don't know just when I will be able to approach the other men on the force, but I regard this particular policeman as a rather promising convert. At least, I have impressed him with a sense of my interest in his personal salvation, and I am pleased to think that he may keep a special eye on these premises, for you know there has been a band of burglars operating around here rather actively of late, and I have no means of knowing with which party they are affiliated.

"I am really fearful that Tammany may have heard something of my political activity up here. Certain of my new neighbors who are democrats are throwing out dark hints that they will challenge my vote if I attempt to poll it on election day. They even insinuate that I am no better than any other vulgar thirty day colonizer, and have just come up here to electioneer and then get in my vote. Of course it is a fact that I have not been thirty days in this district, and this may subject me to suspicion in the eyes of a partisan. I have tried to assure my neighbors that I am above such sordid motives, and that I will have lived here a full month before election day, but still they look at me askance and talk about watching the house to see if cheap cots are being carried into it.

"In one of the daily papers I saw a notice—not in agate, nonpareil or minion type, which is soft and soothing—but in the heavy, blackface characters which jar one, to the effect that I dare not register nor vote, because the last registration day is October 19, and unless I perjure myself I could not swear on that date that I had lived thirty days in Riverdale. Now, I do not wish to perjure myself unless there be strong provocation, and, being a good republican, I feel great respect for Mr. McCullagh's deputies. So I think of asking Mr. Croker to grant me a special dispensation and permit me to register all by myself on October 31."

When Mr. Clemens' attention was called to the rumor that Mr. Croker thought of taking a house in Riverdale for the winter, and so might become one of his neighbors, the author smiled delightfully, and said, with a twinkle of the eye:—"Wouldn't that be charming? I should then certainly ask the Tammany chief to take my family as lodgers and boarders. I should feel so much more secure from burglars, sneak thieves and second story men if I could only feel that Mr. Croker's protecting aegis were spread over us and our household gods. Think what such an arrangement would save me in the cost of burglar alarms, special watchmen, firearms, and patent electric doormats!"

# Sentimental Journey

## May 29 1902–June 9 1902

Awarded an honorary doctor of laws degree by the University of Missouri on 4 June 1902, Twain was feted in St. Louis, Columbia, and Hannibal during his last visit to his home state.

### "Mark Twain Here as St. Louis' Guest for the First Time Since 1861"
Robertus Love, St. Louis *Post-Dispatch*, 29 May 1902, pp. 1–2

... When I was admitted, Mark Twain was enjoying coffee, bread, and butter, his breakfast.... Then Mr. Clemens took occasion to explain how he happened to be cold on a reasonably warm night and hot on a cold night.

"The first night I was aboard," said he, "the porter thought it was going to be a hot night, naturally, because it is summer time. I had only one blanket on my bed. I got chilly. It was so chilly that I was uncomfortable, so I lay awake and read a good part of the night. That porter was mistaken—I did sleep some."

"Last night I determined to be prepared. So I ordered an extra blanket, which the porter brought me. But some offspring of an idiot turned on the heat, and I almost suffocated."

That is why Mark Twain went to sleep shortly after reaching St. Louis—not because the town reminded him of Philadelphia.

"The fact is," said Mr. Clemens, "I don't know anything about St. Louis except from memory. I haven't been here since 1861. That is to say, I haven't been here really to stay any time. I have flitted past once or twice. In 1885 I lectured here, in the old Mercantile Library Hall, but that wasn't a visit.

"In fact, I merely flitted past. I flit into many cities and flit out. I don't see the places, I just flit. I'm a flitter and have been one for a good many years."

"But this time, Mr. Clemens, you are not going to flit. You will stay with us for awhile, won't you?"

"I'm going up to Hannibal this time, but I want to come back by way of St. Louis and stay a day or two, if I don't get a telegram calling me back to New York. I have some relatives here whom I have promised to visit.

"But Hannibal is my main point. I am determined to see Hannibal this time. Practically, I may say that I have not been back to Hannibal, where I grew up, for 50 years. I have not been back there long enough to see the town and the people.

"Twelve years ago I went to Hannibal to bury my mother, but I was there only a day or a part of a day.

"Now I am going to see the place—perhaps for the last time. When a man gets to be 67 he is about ready to wind up. I don't feel old, but the years are upon me." . . .

Mr. Clemens showed heightened interest when his train reached the Mississippi river. He craned his neck to look up and down the stream, once so familiar to him as a steamboat pilot. . . .

"By the way, Mr. Clemens," I remarked, "an old raft pilot on the upper river told me the other day that you never made a good pilot. He thought you might have been a pretty fair one if you hadn't quit the business just about the time you had it learned and begun writing. It takes a man, he said, about 10 years or so to learn the business."

Here was where Mark Twain woke up. He saw a challenge and accepted it.

"I'll venture that man," he said, "was a mud clerk. I'll venture he never knew me, and had no opportunity to know whether I was a good pilot or a bad one. I'll venture he's a no account pilot himself, or he would not have shown his ignorance by making that remark.

"Rank on the river those days was very strict. The captain and the pilot had a rank of their own, at the top. Those under them never met them on terms of equality. There was one grade—and I guess your raft friend belonged to that—which was made up of mud clerks, cub pilots, and strikers. The mud clerk was the apprentice clerk. The cub pilot was the apprentice to the pilot, and knew nothing about the business till he spent several years at it. The striker was the engineer's apprentice. Those three were equals. They never got near the captain or pilot in rank.

"Your man was on the upper river, you say. Where did he see me? I was on the lower river altogether. What did he know about the lower river?

"Some men never did make good pilots, it is true, but that was because they didn't have the faculty. They were in the wrong business. They were not born to be pilots. Others made good pilots naturally." . . .

Mark Twain is proud of the proffer of an LL.D. degree from the Missouri State University.

"What do I think of such a degree?" he said. "Well, you can see that I think enough of it to travel more than 1000 miles each way, in my old age, to get it."

"But isn't it a fact, Mr. Clemens, that its value is enhanced because it comes from Missouri?"

Mr. Clemens tried to hedge on this question, but when I asked him if he would go 1000 miles up in Canada to receive an LL.D. he replied, with his honest smile: "You can rest assured I wouldn't."

## "Mark Twain Laughs in Grain Pits"
### *St. Louis Star,* 29 May 1902, pp. 1, 7

Mark Twain was given a big reception on 'Change. . . . "I wish now," said Mark, "that I were the clergyman I once started out to be, but I am not like the clergy.

"They are always talking for others, and not for themselves. Always seeking the salvation of others, and incidentally putting in a stroke for themselves. Had I followed the course of a clergyman, as mapped out when I was young, things might have resulted without the slightest disaster to you—and to myself. . . . I am on my way to Columbia to receive a degree of Doctor of Laws. The colossal part of this is my degree will cost me nothing, whereas other folks have to earn theirs. But Missouri is granting this degree to her most deserving son.

"After June 4 I shall be a doctor, and maybe I shall call on you good folks for your practice.

"I am glad to be back in Missouri, the State that gave me birth, and trusted me for it, never knowing how I would pay her back." . . .

At this point a slim, wiry man with a short, cropped gray beard appeared at Mr. Clemens' side.

"Why, hello, Bixby," the author exclaimed.

"Sam, Sam, old man," said Captain Bixby. "I didn't think you'd know me. Why, it's been more than twenty years since I met you last."

Captain Horace G. Bixby is known as one of the best river pilots alive today. He is the one who taught Mark Twain to guide a boat. Mark insisted that the old fresh water sailor should sit down beside him.

"This man talks about my not knowing him," said Mark, throwing his arm back in a reminiscent mood. "Why, he taught me the river. Do you know that he is one of the greatest pilots this old Mississippi has ever known? That he is, this same old Captain Bixby.

"How old are you, Bixby?" he said, turning to the old pilot, who was embarrassed by the glare of distinction which had fallen on him.

"Why, I am 62," said Captain Bixby.

"Lord, man, you were 62 it seems to me when I first met you in 1857," replied Mark. "Do you know that when I first met Bret Harte, years ago in California, with that crown of white hair, he seemed 62 years old and when he slips away from us in London the other day, I read in the paper that he is only 62 years old. It's a wonderful old world," sighed Mark, who is almost 70 himself.

"That reminds me," he continued, "a fellow's responsibility does not cease until he supports a monument.

"I expect I will be supporting one very soon. I've come to New York not to live, but to die. I know perfectly well that my allotted time is coming to a close, and all the things you boys can say doesn't make a bit of difference. But I always feel happy except when someone reminds me that I am still writing books.

"Now, do you know I am always writing new books. Not one book, but many books. The trouble is my interest ceases, and I find a new theme, and I start a new book, and I can't get the other book finished. I'm always starting new books, but I don't know when I shall publish one."

Someone wanted to know which was his favorite book.

Mark thought it over a minute and replied, without moving a muscle:

"Indications in the usual way make me think that *Huck Finn* and *Innocents Abroad* are the books most favored by the public. I mean, of course, by the financial returns. I have no favorite of my own.

"In fact, I don't know what's in my books. I haven't read one of them for years. Do you know that when I write the book and get it out of my hands and finish with the printer and proofreader I am sick of it? So sick that I don't want to see it for a year." . . .

"Did the river look familiar?" asked Captain Bixby.

"Old man," said Clemens, "it looked new in places. You know I came over the other bridge—not the Eads bridge.

"Well, I saw one old boat, a Wiggins Ferry boat, that I knew. I knew it because I had been on it often years ago. I think I even piloted it. I can't think about its name. But it was the boat, all right. Some men were painting it. If it had been painted before I reached here I wouldn't have known it at all.

"Now, do you know I didn't see the river front. Just about the time I was ready to take a look at it a pretty young lady whom I knew was bidding me good-bye, and she was so pretty that I forgot to look at anything but that young lady.

"The city is entirely new. I don't recognize any of it. Do you know that

I did not even take a look at your Union Station?"...

"I've been all over this small world—in India, Australia, Africa, way up in Iceland, down in South America, but do you know there never was such an old river as the Mississippi? It's been since '84 or '85 since I've been as far west as the Mississippi. It's good to be back again. But I'm not going to talk about the river until I get a better look at it."

## "'Mark Twain' Comes Back to Missouri"
### St. Louis Republic, 30 May 1902, pp. 1–2

Samuel L. Clemens ... was in St. Louis yesterday.

Old associates and one-time river comrades gathered round him by the score to shake hands and talk a moment of the days that are gone....

Being a humorist, it was apparent that many persons expected Mark Twain to be funny. He did say amusing things occasionally, but nothing which was obviously intended to be funny—he was too natural to act "funny now."...

At noon, George J. Tansey, president of the Merchants' Exchange, escorted Mark Twain to the exchange, where he was introduced to many, and where he made a short address. He said that the sudden call upon him had found him without a text upon which to base his remarks. Of Mr. Tansey's introductory words, the humorist quaintly said:

"It is very embarrassing to listen to personal compliments, but doubly embarrassing when the recipient of them feels that they are deserved. Mr. Tansey said very many nice things about me, but there are many other things which he might have said, but which, no doubt, slipped his mind."

After hastily lunching at the Planters, Mark Twain took a cab for Union Station, where he departed for Hannibal, his boyhood home, at 2:15 p.m. He looks forward with much interest to his two or three days' stay in Hannibal, and hopes there to meet many other old friends....

He seemed impressed with the dignity of becoming a Doctor of

Laws, which degree is to be conferred upon him June 4 by Missouri State University, and he was especially flattered since he did not have to work for it. "That is the colossal thing about it," said he.

"Have you ever doctored laws?" he was asked. "Yes, cab laws," he said. Further explanation requested, he continued.

"I doctored the cab laws in London and New York. The cabbies overcharged and I simply made them come down by calling official attention to the fact.

"The truth is, however, that the laws do not need to be doctored so much as the enforcement of them needs to be doctored." . . .

The story of Mark Twain's years upon the river, when he sought to rise high in the ranks of pilotism, is the story of a man with a sense of humor who tackled a "tough proposition." . . . When he found that his friend, the *Paul Jones,* was about to start for St. Louis, he "besieged a pilot," with whom he had scraped up an acquaintance on the down trip, and "after three hard days" the pilot surrendered. This pilot was Captain Bixby.

The Captain had his own way of telling of this siege. "A pretty good looking young fellow," said he yesterday, "was always hanging round the pilot house. Said he was going down in Central American or somewhere. But when we got down to New Orleans he came round to me and said that he thought he'd like to learn piloting; didn't think he'd go to Central America after all; asked if I wanted to teach him the river. I said that young fellows like him round were more trouble than use; couldn't think of it.

"He kept after me anyhow, and finally I agreed. He was to pay me $500 for teaching him the river between St. Louis and New Orleans. We drew up a contract, which was put away in the safe of the boat and neither he nor I have seen it to this day. Well, I was with him pretty much all the time for the next three years, or until he got his certificate as pilot. I know some say he didn't make much of a pilot, but I think he was about as good as any young fellow of his age—he was about 20 when I first met him.

"He was a quiet sort of boy at the time. Of course, he had some of

Posing before his boyhood home on Hill Street in Hannibal, 30 May 1902.

that famous drollery and humorous way of looking at things which is celebrated in his writings. I remember when I undertook to teach him I questioned him about his antecedents and other matters.

"'How are your habits?' I asked.

"'Fair,' he mumbled.

"'Do you chew?'

"'No, don't chew,' very deliberate.

"'Do you drink?'

"'No, don't drink.' At this he seemed a little uneasy, and with a slight twinkle of the eye, he continued, 'But I must smoke.'

"He must smoke to this day."

"After he left me in the latter part of '59 I saw little of him. He was on board the *Alonzo Childs;* was caught by the Confederates and had quite a time of it. Then he went out to Nevada and California, then to

Honolulu, then to New York, and all over the world."

"How about the five hundred?" *The Republic* reporter asked Captain Bixby; "did he pay that?"

"Paid three hundred," responded the captain. "You see, the war came on and there wasn't much money to be had. He didn't have any and I didn't. So we just called the other two hundred off."

## "Mark Twain Sees the Home of His Boyhood"
### Robertus Love, St. Louis *Post-Dispatch*, 30 May 1902, p. 1

Mark Twain at 10:30 o'clock visited and identified the old house on Hill street where most of his boyhood was passed.

"Yes, this is the house," he said, while a large crowd of adults and children gathered about him.

"I couldn't recognize the picture, but I recognize the house." He tarried only long enough for a photographer to preserve the incident to posterity's eyes, then entered a carriage . . . and was driven to Mr. Olivet Cemetery, where he saw the graves of his parents and brother. . . .

Many old-timers crowded about the great man to shake his hand in the hotel office. Among them were W. H. C. Nash, Charles W. Curts, and Edwin Pierce, all of whom he identified as old playmates.

"How are you doing, Eddie?" he inquired of Mr. Pierce.

"Like yourself, Sam," replied the schoolmate, "like a cow's tail going down." . . .

Mr. Clemens walked the one block to the Windsor Hotel. . . . Will Sutton, the hotel clerk, remarked: "Mr. Clemens, I was born close to your birthplace at Florida, and have been in the house where you were born, often."

"I was not born often—only once," responded the humorist, "but I'm glad to see you, all the same."

Thus early in his visit Mark Twain learned that he was back among the home folks. . . .

Ten minutes after his arrival Mark Twain went to bed. Room 27 was assigned to him and the porter took his leather traveling trunk thereto, having learned that it did not contain samples.

"I feel as if I ought to go out and walk around and see the people," said Mr. Clemens, "but I'm a little tired and will rest. Perhaps later in the night, when everybody is abed, I may go out and take a walk."

By invitation, I knocked on the door of No. 27 two hours later and found the great son of Hannibal lying on top of his bed covers, feet to the headboard, dressed for the night, with a long black cigar between his teeth and Mont Pelle puffs of smoke arising.

He was not asleep, but he was dreaming. It was a dream at sunset— and 67.

The mild blue eyes of this man who has viewed the rivers and mountains, the creeks and crags of many lands, were turned toward a high hill half a mile to the south, plainly visible through his one window.

At the eastern crest of the hill, far above the river, around a rounded yellow bluff out of the foliage of green trees on the slope.

"That," said Mark Twain, beckoning me to the window, "is Lovers' Leap. Many times when a boy I have climbed that hill and dangled my legs over the precipice. It has not changed—not that. It is handsomer than I thought."

## "Mark Twain Dines With His Sweetheart of Old Time Days"
### Robertus Love, *St. Louis Post-Dispatch*, 31 May 1902, pp. 1–2

. . . There is no doubt Mark Twain came here because he felt it to be a sort of sacred duty to come back to the starting point and review the journey.

How he feels about it, now that he is here, may be judged from what he said to me Friday noon while waiting for the hotel people to move his baggage into two connecting rooms nearer the bathtub than is No. 27. He was just back from the cemetery.

"It is very beautifully situated, that cemetery," said Mark Twain. "If I had the time I should look for the boys out there. That is where they are. I came here to see the people.

"I have met a good many more than I expected to meet. I find about 20 surviving, and am moved with gratification and gratitude for that.

"But most of them are out there in that cemetery. I could pick them out if I had the time to walk about and read their names.

"I came this time for the reason I was invited by the university of my native state to go to Columbia and be made a doctor of laws. I think I am well fitted for that avocation, and I am glad of the invitation to come and get an honorary degree which I have not earned. The chiefest of all the preparation I have had for the LL.D. I acquired in the old schoolhouse here that Mr. Cross used to take care of. He qualified me to be an LL.D. There were difficulties connected with it two generations ago. Here tonight I see a great advance in matters of intellectual taste over the schools of my boyhood. Two generations ago the quality of school oratory was bombastic, a pretentious, inflated oratory, words, abounding words, and words delivered with an immense energy, when the ideas were weak.

"The modern oratory, which deals with grace of expression and felicity of ideas, I heard in the Presbyterian pulpit for once in my life in Hannibal. Many is the time when, as a boy, I went to the Presbyterian Church by request.

"The desire I had to stand in the Presbyterian pulpit just once and help instruct those people the whirlgig of time has gratified and the ambition of nearly two generations ago has been satisfied. The character of those school exercises you have listened to tonight shows a great improvement. In those boyhood times we had children in school of all ages up to 25 years and of a dozen sexes, year after year. . . . In the old commencement exercises there was not a single line of original thought or expression. The programs were made up of recitations and nearly always poems, exciting poems. But these young ladies tonight had delivery, graceful and expressive, and they had written their own ideas. Here are the young gentlemen, too, and I don't see why the so-called superior sex is in such a limited quantity. This commencement is a mighty advance on what we did on the public square 60 years ago. If a boy then showed any original thought the people suspected that something was the matter with him.

"As I said, everything was recitation and those recitations were not selected from the wide field of English literature. There were three or four poems used and only one prose piece and that we had always heard every week. It was 'Give Me Liberty or Give Me Death.' I never ventured that."...

"But the standby of all, the boy that saved Hannibal to intellectual life, recited always 'The Boy Stood on the Burning Deck.' Today it has been so pathetic for me to meet, shake hands and look into the eyes of old white-headed men whom I know as boys in the old school and I could not help but imagine them repeating again 'The Boy Stood on the Burning Deck.'

"I shook hands today with half a dozen who used to recite 'The Boy Stood on the Burning Deck,' always in the same old way. They never tried to invent ingenuities and new departures. It is hard for me to conceive of taking that as a method to identify a Hannibal boy, but seven years ago coming in a ship from Ceylon to Bombay in the Bay of Bengal—no, let me see, my geography was learned here—in the Arabian Sea, on the deck stood a man who yelled, 'Hello, Mark.' 'Hello, yourself,' I said. 'Who are you?'

"'Don't you remember,' he said, 'the old Cross school in Hannibal?'

"'Yes,' I replied.

"'But who are you?'

"'Why,' he said, 'I'm the boy that used to recite 'The Boy Stood on the Burning Deck.'"

"There wasn't a boy in Hannibal that didn't do it. It was a cold day when he didn't have half a dozen boys standing on the same deck. In this presence tonight is that old mariner, Billy Nash. I have stood on the burning deck with him a hundred times, without fire insurance or anything."

## "Attention of Old Friends Move Mark Twain to Tears"
Hastings MacAdam, *St. Louis Republic*, 31 May 1902, p. 1

Touched by the deep attention which this community has evinced for
him, before an audience assembled in the Hannibal Presbyterian Church
to celebrate Decoration Day by religious observance, Mark Twain
wept. Sobs choking him, the man of laughs, in deep, heart-touching
seriousness expressed his appreciation of the tender regard in which he
is held. He wept manly tears. The audience, many of whom were old like
himself, yet had been young with him in Hannibal, likewise was carried
away by deep feeling, the truest expression of which was tears.

"I am profoundly touched," said the speaker, "by my reception here. I
have not only been moved, moved a number of times, by the cordiality of
my reception by the old, old men and women who knew me here when
I was a boy. I am overcome by the something more than friendship
which has entered into my reception—an evidence of true affection.
Affection! That is the proudest thing anybody can acquire in this world,
and in granting me that this city of my early life has paid me the highest
possible compliment."

Then Mark Twain spoke of patriotism, a theme appropriate to the
day, and his words were earnest and true.

"The patriot is the conscience-instructed man," said he, "the man
who is true to his convictions."

His theme led him to the Civil War and one of Mark Twain's the
author's inimitable narrators followed.

"My conscience directed me to take up the Confederate cause," said
he. "I labored for that cause just two weeks. In that period I tried to
help Confederate affairs. I think it was in the second week of June 1861
when Ed Stevens, Sam Lyons, and a lot of young fellows marched out
of Hannibal and camped at New London. We walked the ten miles
in four hours. We might have done it in three and a half, but were not
practiced up yet. We camped, as I said, and had a council of war—to
see what we could do toward inducing the Northern States to behave
themselves. We didn't do any fighting, but we didn't see that we could

aid the Confederates' cause any by being harassed by General Grant's soldiers—he was Colonel Grant then, Colonel of the Palmyra Regiment. We did no fighting because we couldn't get into a fight. General Grant's soldiers never showed their faces. They never got that near to us, though I think if they had there would have been trouble. After two weeks, we thought there wasn't any use bothering with the problem anymore—it was too big for us. We went down in Louisiana and dissolved ourselves. I still think that, if we'd have met Grant and that Twenty-first Illinois Infantry of his, there would have been trouble."

## "Mark Twain Tales a Drive with His Schoolmate's Pretty Daughter"

Robertus Love, *St. Louis Post-Dispatch*, 2 June 1902, p. 5

. . . Mark Twain also took a drive about Hannibal—the Hannibal of 60 years ago, the St. Petersburg of Tom Sawyer—with John Briggs, Sunday afternoon. . . . John Briggs was one of the young men who joined the Confederate army with Sam Clemens in 1860, undergoing the strenuous two weeks' campaign of keeping away from Colonel Ulysses S. Grant which the humorist loves to tell about.

"Briggs and I," he said, "were the best retreaters in the company." . . .

Mark Twain's sermon at the Baptist Church Sunday morning was a little different from what the people had expected. Hannibal folk have come to expect lachrymose scenes when the distinguished fellow townsman arises to talk.

For that matter, the Baptist Church service was lachrymose, but not Mark Twain's part of it. Rev. Everett Gill, the pastor, preceded Mr. Clemens by preaching a short sermon on "A Garland for Ashes," in which he said some things that brought out the trickling tear from hundreds of eyes. . . .

The pastor then referred to the guest of the city, the great man who has come back to say good-bye.

"Mr. Clemens," he said, "has not scattered the ashes of his own griefs upon the heads of others. He has kept them to himself, and all through his life has been bestowing garlands of joy. In doing this, he has been doing the work of Christ."

Mr. Gill then invited Mr. Clemens into the pulpit, "not to preach a sermon," he said, "but to say a few words, whatever might come to him to say."

"No," said Mark Twain, arising in the pew where he sat beside his old sweetheart, Mrs. Frazier, the Laura Hawkins of his boyhood. "No, I shall not come into the pulpit. I might do that on a weekday, but I cannot do it on a Sunday without bruising my own sense of the proprieties.

"But I must take issue with Rev. Dr. Gill, who says that I need not preach a sermon. What I say will be preaching. I am a preacher. We are all preachers. If we do not preach by words, we preach by deeds. What we do and say has its influence upon others, and in our daily life, though we be not clergymen, we preach to each other.

"The art of preaching is to influence. From the pulpit and from the mouths of all of us, the preaching goes on all the time. Our words and deeds are like the tidal waves of the seas that encircle the earth.

"They are not for ourselves alone, but for others. We forget that we carry influence, but we should remember it and we should see that our influence is of the good kind.

"Words perish, print burns up, men die, but our preaching lives on. Washington died in 1799, more than a hundred years ago, but his preaching survives, and to every people that is striving for liberty his life is a sermon.

"My mother lies buried out there in our beautiful cemetery overlooking the Mississippi, but at this age of mine, she still cheers me. Her preaching lives and goes on with me.

"Let us see that our preaching is of the right sort, so that it will influence for good the lives of those who remain when we shall be silent in our graves." . . .

And five minutes later, when the benediction had been pronounced, he stood in the aisle and shook hands with the hundreds who passed by,

Departing Hannibal,
3 June 1902.
Courtesy of Kevin
MacDonnell.

holding a few old schoolmates for a little space to discuss the teachers in the little old schoolhouse. . . .

Out on the sidewalk he asked Rev. Dr. Gill to walk down to the hotel with him. "It will give me a better standing in Hannibal," said Mark Twain, "to be seen on the street with a preacher."

### *Ralls County Record,* 6 June 1902;
### rpt. Hannibal *Courier-Post,* 6 March 1935, p. 5C

. . . On Sunday afternoon about 2:30 o'clock Mark Twain, John B. Briggs, and the *Record* man rambled over Holliday Hill together. Driving past his old home on Hill street, they went through the alley in the middle of the block, pointing out places where they played in their boyhood days. They commanded the driver to stop and Mark said: "John, the ell of the old house has another story on it. That's about the only change." As we drove by the gas works John said, "Sam, the gas works stand on the site of my old home." Going into Palmyra Avenue, they called to mind house after house where incidents of their early days had occurred. Going up Holliday Hill as far as the carriage could go, we walked the remainder of the way and stood on the summit. Looking up and down the Mississippi river, which spread out in its magnificent grandeur the hills on either side covered with tall trees, Lover's Leap standing like a huge sentinel in the distance, islands dotting the river here and there, waving fields of wheat glinting in the sunshine in the lowlands along the Illinois shore, Mark turned to Mr. Briggs and said: "John, that is the prettiest sight I ever saw. There is the place by the island where we used to swim. There is where a man was drowned, and there is where the steamboat sank. These things all come to my mind now. 'Twas fifty years ago, John, and yet it seems as yesterday." Pointing to various houses in the city and places among the hills, for the town lay spread out before us, he continued: "There is where the Millerites put on their robes one night to go up to heaven. None of them went that night, John, but no doubt many of them have gone since. John, fifty years have whitened our hair and warned us that we are growing old. We stand today amid the scenes of our boyhood days for the last time. Let us be boys again today, and live over the past for this is one of the happiest days of my life."

And there standing face to face, hands clasped, these two strong men, equally great in strength of character, and each imbued with a love for the other that had sprung up in their childhood and grown with the years, looked into each other's eyes while tears stole down their cheeks. Turning to John he said: "Do you remember the days we stole the peaches from old man Price?" "Yes," said John, "as if it were last week." "Well," resumed Mark, "you know he moved out here from Virginia and he had a raft of bow-legged negroes. He set out a big peach orchard over there" (pointing to the place) "and we invaded it one morning, filled ourselves with peaches, stuffed a lot of them in our shirts and started for home, when one of those bow-legged negroes set the dogs on us. We ran until the dogs came up, then we fought them back. Then we ran again, the dogs still following, when all of a sudden we turned, drove the dogs back and tried to catch the negro, but he was too swift for us and got away. Do you remember, John, that we intended to catch that negro and drown him? Why, of course we did."

Going over the hill, they came to the place where they pried a huge rock from the top of the precipice and sent it crashing down the hill, across the road, over a negro driving a wagon, and into a cooper shop. Arriving at the spot John said: "Sam, here is where we pried the rock loose, after digging the dirt out from under it for three Sundays." Mark said: "John, if it had killed that negro we would have had a dead negro on our hands with not a cent to pay for him. John, I believe there were only four of us in that devilment, yet from all reports there was a gang of forty. It seems we have more playmates today than we had then. After the crash, we escaped and played innocents at home, although the patroles gave us a close chase." Going down the hill, Mark and John keeping up a rambling chat about old times, of the people who were living fifty years ago, of those who had died and of the few left among the living, we came to a well on Palmyra Avenue with two old oaken buckets in it. Here as boy drew up a bucket of water from the cold depths below, when the lady of the house called to her son: "Tommie, get a glass for the gentlemen," when Mr. Clemens said: "No glass for me, John, we are boys today and we'll drink out of the bucket." So we all took a long draught out of the old bucket, and the water was good, cool, and refreshing. Driving along Palmyra Avenue, John Briggs pointed out the house where Barney Farthing, now of Paris, once lived. Barney is one of the original "Hucks." Then we drove down the river road to old Scipio. As we passed the bridge Mark said: "Here is where I swam the river when I was a boy. When I got near the other shore one leg cramped. I crawled up on the bank and rubbed my leg to get the cramps out of it. The sun was going down and the chill of evening was setting in and I had to swim back. After a while I started and when I got halfway across my leg commenced drawing up, then the other began to cramp, but I swam on. Once, when near the shore, I thought I would let down, but was afraid to, knowing that if the water was deep I was a goner, but finally my knees struck the sand and I crawled out. That was the closest call I ever had." Driving along the road, these boys for the evening pointed out the place where the haunted house once stood, but the house and ghost have long since gone. They told how Scipio was to be a great city and defeat Hannibal, repeating the history of the old Roman and Carthagenian days, but the order was reversed and today Hannibal is the victor and Scipio is only a memory. And thus these boyhood chums, one the greatest writer and humorist of the world, the other a prosperous farmer and good citizen, chatted and laughed, here calling up some incident, there looking for a spring at which they had slaked their boyish thirst, now dried up; casting longing looks at the hills, the river, and scenes here and there, drove back to the hotel and went to Mr. Clemens' room, where the conversation drifted into parting words. They stood up and shook hands, when Mr. Briggs said; "Sam, this perhaps will be the last time we will meet on earth and I reluctantly say good-bye. God bless you. May we meet in heaven and renew our long friendship." "John," said Mark Twain, "I am glad we have been together today. I have enjoyed it. It's been worth a thousand dollars to me. We were like brothers once. I feel that we are just the same today. Good-bye, John. If we never meet again here, I'll try to meet you on the other side." And with tears in their eyes and their voices trembling with emotion, they parted.

## "Dr. Mark Twain at a Smoke Talk"

Robertus Love, *St. Louis Post-Dispatch*, 6 June 1902, p. 2

And Mark Twain came back.

Friday he is back at his old trade, piloting a steamboat on the lower

Mississippi. With the Rochambeau party and other parties he is making an excursion on the city wharfboat, *Mark Twain,* so christened during this voyage.

"Mayor Wells," remarked Mark Twain, "sent me a threatening telegram today. He said there was a boat here without a name, and if I would come in time to make a trip on it with the other foreigners he would name it after me; otherwise he would name it after somebody else, himself I reckon. The threat scared me. I was doing very well at Columbia, but when I got that threatening message I replied at once, before I recovered from my fright, and accepted the conditions."

"What kind of a boat is it?" somebody inquired.

"I don't know," replied the humorist. "It ought to be a snag boat if it is going to be named after me."

"By the way," said a man from Pike County, "there's a town named for you up in our county. It's—"

"No, it isn't in your county," interrupted Mr. Clemens. "It's in my county—Marion, right in the lower edge of Marion. And it is not a town, either; it's a town site. When I was going up to Hannibal last week on the Burlington the brakeman invited me to stand on the rear platform of the tail-end car and see something. I stood there several miles and saw nothing in particular, until at length we whizzed past a shed with the name 'Clemens' lettered on the end.

"'That's it,' said the brakeman. 'See it?' I saw it. 'It's named after you,' said the brakeman. . . .

"There are no houses in my town," said Mark Twain, "but the place will grow." . . .

"How many cigars a week do you smoke?" I asked him last week in Hannibal.

"Just as many as I can," was the reply.

Mark Twain smokes two grades of cigars, both Porto Ricans, three-centers and seven-centers. He prefers the three-centers, because they are "just as good" and cost less.

"I am looking for a man who holds the commercial value of a cigar above its smoking value," he remarked. "At home I have a few cigars that cost $1.66 apiece, and I am keeping them in the hope that I can sell them to somebody who thinks the cost of a cigar has anything to do with its quality."

## "Mark Twain at Pilot Wheel; Bids Farewell to Mississippi"

### St. Louis *Republic*, 7 June 1902, p. 1

Mark Twain at the pilot-wheel for the last time, on the Mississippi he helped to immortalize. . . .

Doctor Clemens's farewell to the historic stream was impressive. Standing in the pilothouse far above the crowd on the decks, the river breezes caressed his frosty hair, the great wheel moved obediently to his master hand, while the kind, blue eyes of the celebrated humorist were lifted dreamily up the lazy current.

Then his hearty voice called: "Lower away lead."

"Mark Twain, quarter, f-i-v-e a-n-d o-n-e-h-a-l-f, s-i-x f-e-e-t," came the response from the lower deck.

"Mark Twain, Mark Twain," shouted the spectators who had surged to the bow and were frantically waving their hats and 'kerchiefs in the breeze.

"You are all dead safe as long as I have the wheel," answered Mark, taking three turns on the wheel. "There I have rested you," he said to the pilot, but the party on the deck raised their hands appealing and begged Mark to stand by them, and he did. He steered the harbor boat for a full half hour and enjoyed every minute of his task.

"That is the last time I will ever play pilot," were the serious words which fell from his lips as he slowly descended the steps from the wheelhouse. Something of solemnity cast its shadow over the gay party. Tears stood in the eyes of old rivermen. It was only a snatch of sadness. Doctor Clemens ordered refreshments for the crew.

"Something stronger than river water," he added. "A crew cannot perform its duty without something bracing." (See also "French Visitors Afloat," St. Louis *Globe-Democrat,* 7 June 1902, p. 1: "That's good enough water for anyone," said Dr. Clemens. "You couldn't improve it without putting in a little whiskey.")

## "'Mark Twain' Bids Missouri Farewell"
*St. Louis Republic,* 9 June 1902, p. 3

After two busy weeks in Missouri, Samuel L. Clemens, Mark Twain, departed yesterday for his home at Riverdale, N. Y., probably bidding a final farewell to the State of his birth and the Mississippi Valley, wherein were spent so many years of his eventful life. . . .

Mark Twain's slim appetite has been remarked by all who have met him, and he was induced to talk upon the subject after his brief sojourn at the helm of the harbor boat last Saturday, when he once more assumed the role of pilot.

"I have starved for twenty-five years," he said.

The newspapermen who had just watched him say farewell to the wheel looked into the placid face of the humorist and focused their eyes on the pink cheeks of 67 years.

"It has been that many years since I ate more than one meal a day," continued Doctor Clemens. "I do not count breakfast as a meal because it consists of one cup of coffee and a meager allowance of bread. My meal is at 6 or 7 o'clock.

"There is no principle involved in this abstinence, what many persons would call starvation. I discovered long ago that one meal is plenty for the man who does no more work than the brain-worker. Now if I were chopping wood, I probably would eat three times every twenty-four hours. The waste of muscular force in that sort of an occupation requires rebuilding.

"There are many advertisements nowadays that entice the man who does not use his muscles to build them up. There is not any occasion for it. Beyond light gymnastics to preserve healthy circulation, the man who labors with his mind to the exclusion of his muscles need not be alarmed because he cannot put a hundred-pound shot more than three feet.

"Oh, when I was a pilot, that was long before I stopped eating three meals," said Mark, in reply to a question. "The last time I was on the river—hum, let me recollect, it was in eighty, 1880 that Jimmie Osgood, the publisher, and myself made a trip down the river under fictitious names. We were gathering material for *Life on the Mississippi.* Knowing the riverman well, I concluded that the only way to get him to do and say things that would make the sort of material I sought was to catch him off his guard. If they had known it was Clemens, you can depend upon it that he would have gone into his shell and spoiled the whole scheme.

"Well, we were discovered right here in St. Louis. We registered at the Southern. The clerk there wheeled the old book around on its swivel and and gave me a pen. I think that I wrote down the name, J. Smith, from some place in New Jersey. That fellow turned the book around, just glanced at the name, and called:

"'Front! Show Mr. Clemens up to 236.' The rascal had known me when he was a clerk at a hotel down East. It was a little embarrassing to be caught disowning yourself."

# Dean of Humorists

## Sept 7 1902–May 12 1907

In the twilight of his career, Twain hired Isabel Lyon as his personal secretary. This period in his life is punctuated most forcibly by the declining health of his wife Olivia and her death in Florence on 5 June 1904. In January 1906, he anointed Albert Bigelow Paine his official biographer. He also began to dictate parts of his autobiography, and he lobbied Congress on behalf of a more progressive international copyright.

### "My First Vacation and My Last"
New York *World Magazine*, 7 September 1902, p. 3

Mark Twain, the great humorist, is spending his vacation at York Harbor, Maine. . . . The writer for *The World's Sunday Magazine* discovered the author of *Tom Sawyer* the other day walking slowly to and fro on the lawn. . . .

"So you want me to tell you about my first vacation?" he said. . . .

Very deliberately he took from his vest pocket a long black deadly looking cigar. Then, after groping for an interminable time in his coat pocket, he pulled out three matches and placed them side by side on the table. He was very particular about those matches, for he rearranged them six times.

"That was long ago."

A pause.

"That"—the matches again engage his attention—"was sixty years ago."

He lit the cigar—not placing it in his mouth, but assuring himself that he had a good light before the match was wholly consumed.

A pause certainly of three minutes.

He puffed at his cigar three or four times, but only mechanically. It became very clear indeed that he was away back in his boyhood days again with Tom Sawyer and Huckleberry Finn, wading in the Mississippi or playing leap-frog in the dusty streets of Florida, Missouri.

"Ah, I shall never forget that first vacation," he said. "It wasn't as long as this one, nor in some respects as pleasant, but"—very slowly—"what it lacked in length it made up in excitement.

"Do you know what it means to be a boy on the banks of the Mississippi, to see the steamboats go up and down the river, and never to have had a ride on one? Can you form any conception of what that really means? I think not.

"Well, I was seven years old and my dream by night and my longing by day had never been realized. But I guess it came to pass. That was my first vacation."

A pause.

"One day when the big packet that used to stop at Hannibal swung up to the mooring at my native town, a small chunk of a lad might have been seen kiting on to the deck and in a jiffy disappearing from view beneath a yawl that was placed bottom up.

"I was the small chunk of a lad.

"They called it a life-boat," said Mr. Clemens, "but it was one of that kind of life-boats that wouldn't save anybody.

"Well, the packet started along all right, and it gave me great thrills of joy to be on a real sure-enough steamboat. But just then it commenced to rain. Now, when it rains in the Mississippi country it rains. After the packet had started I had crawled from beneath it and was enjoying the motion of the swift-moving craft. But the rain drove me to cover and that was beneath the yawl. No. It was not a life-boat, for the manner in which that rain came pouring down upon me from the bottom of that yawl made me wonder if I was ever to return home again.

"To add to the fun the red-hot cinders from the big stacks came drifting down and stung my legs and feet with a remorseless vigor, and if it hadn't been a steamboat that I was on I would have wanted to be safe at home in time for supper.

"Well, it kept on raining and storming generally until toward evening, when, seventeen miles below Hannibal, I was discovered by one of the crew."

A very deliberate pause.

"They put me ashore at Louisiana."

Another pause.

"I was sent home by some friends of my father's.

"My father met me on my return."

A twinkle in the steel-blue eyes. "I remember that quite distinctly."

Then as an afterthought: "My mother had generally attended to that part of the duties of the household, but on that occasion my father assumed the entire responsibility."

Reminiscently: "That was my first vacation and its ending"—he bit his cigar—"and I remember both.

"So now, sixty years after that event," emphasis on "event," "I'm enjoying another vacation at the age, I believe, of sixty-seven.

"Fact of it is," he drawled, "the best part of a man's life is after he is sixty. I feel stronger, mentally, now, than ever before."

He lit another of those ominous looking cigars. Their mere appearance compels comment. You express surprise that the first one was not guilty of murder.

"No. Smoking doesn't seem to affect my health at all. Perhaps though, that's because I only take one smoke a day." A brief pause and with a flash of humor from his eyes—"That commences in the morning and ends just before I go to bed. But, Lord bless me! I like to smoke and have since I was seven years old. That first smoke was a fine one, but it made me very sick. I rolled a cigar from green tobacco and when my father found out about it he did the rest.

"I find," he added seriously, "that smoking aids me while I am engaged in writing."

He looked far out to sea.

"This bracing salt air makes me do good work," he said. "I work harder in the summer than in any other season of the year. Just at present, because of Mrs. Clemens' illness, I am not doing much writing, but up to the 11th of August I was busily engaged upon the novel that isn't finished yet, though I've been at it for four years. It's to be a fantastic book," he added, "not so serious as *Joan d'Arc*—it took me twelve years to write that—but up to the present I can't tell how the book is going to end. Confidentially, I won't know until it's finished.

"In fact," said the humorist, "that's the purpose of the book." . . .

He spoke of his recent trip to the scenes of his boyhood days, and told how he met his chum and playmate, John Briggs. . . . "What I consider a crime was the act of John Briggs and myself when we got hold of a boat along the Mississippi at Hannibal and painted it red over its coat of white. Just as we had finished our job the owner of the boat appeared and 'lowed that if that boat had been white he would have sworn that it was his own."

As to whether or not the boat ever got back into the hands of the original owner Mr. Clemens refused to say. He did talk freely, however, about his now famous letter written from his vacation retreat on August 14 to a Denver friend anent the attempt to exclude *Huckleberry Finn* from the Denver Public Library. "Now, that was a very funny thing about that letter getting into print," he said. "You see I sent it to my man marked 'Private,' and that was a sure sign that it was going to be published."

## "Mark Twain: His Wit and Humor"

James Montague, New York *Evening Journal*, 20 December 1902, p. 5

. . . We sat for a while and said nothing. The humorist puffed steadily on his reeking pipe, now and then stroking the papers on the arm of his chair lovingly, as if he longed to begin work upon them again.

"This hour," he said finally, "between a quarter past 10 and 11—it isn't an hour; only three-quarters of an hour, you know—is the only time I have for visitors. Then people can come and see me. After my breakfast is settled and I am ready to get to work.". . . The silence again became heavy.

At length I found it oppressive, and by way of lightening it asked him if he remembered that story about the Gold Arm, with which he used to terrorize people who came to hear him lecture.

"Now, I'm glad you mentioned that," he said deliberately. "You know, I delight to tell that story. I've retired from all public speaking entirely. I never go anyplace or appear in public unless I have to, but now and then I do love to tell that story."

And his eyes lighted reminiscently.

"Sometimes I go to the house of friends of mine in New York to get a chance to tell a story or two—I can't help doing it just once in a while. I go on condition that nothing shall be said about it before or afterward in the newspapers, for if mention was made of it people would say, 'That dad-blamed old liar said he was never going on the platform again, and here he is just the same as ever.' But I do love to tell that story. I'm going to talk to some friends before long—I have half an hour to fill—and that will fill up three of six minutes I was short. Now, if I can just get another story for the other three minutes I'll be fixed. . . . But I'm out of public life now," continued the author, lighting his pipe and puffing until his white head showed as in a fog, darkly. "I have a very happy time here, all to myself. I shall never go far away again.

"I should not have gone to Missouri last June if I had not gone to get a decoration. I think when an institution, especially in a man's native State, offers to confer a decoration on him it is equivalent to a royal invitation; it's a command. He ought to go if he has to go in a hearse.

"But when I see some of these old, these very old fellows, going from one side of the earth to the other to get degrees it does seem hard. Some allowance should be made for their years. The universities ought to mail them the decorations."

## "Mark Twain's Door Open to Burglars"
*New York Herald*, 15 June 1903, p. 6

Undisturbed by the recent activity of thieves in the Bronx, Mark Twain, at his home at Riverdale, in the extreme northern end of the borough, expressed himself yesterday as not averse to the powers that prey on his neighbors.

"I just wish I knew the fellows on my route," said the humorist, his eyes twinkling with merriment. "I have been expecting them about here, and from feelings of brotherhood, if for no more noble reason, I have been intending to give them a warm reception. My larder is open to them, and if they smoke they can have the best in the box. You know all we literary people and second story men have a good deal akin. We all travel in groups. We work one neighborhood until we feel that we have sapped the lemon dry and then we move on to more fruitful soil. . . .

"Burglary, like many other things, has got to be a science, and the man who is a success at it ought to be respected. He has a family to support, maybe—little babies and a wife, who need nice clothes and things—and it is only fair that he should be given a chance to ply his chosen trade. It is cruel to put him in jail with forgers and common swindlers."

## "Twain Off Shooting Shafts of Humor"
New York *Evening Journal*, 24 October 1903, p. 3

Mark Twain sailed for Europe on the *Princess Irene* today for a stay of one year in Florence, Italy. . . .

Bubbling over with good spirits and with his blue eyes twinkling as he gave forth one story after another Mr. Clemens talked to the *Evening Journal* today just as if he liked to be interviewed.

Before leaving the Hotel Grosvenor to take carriage for the Hoboken Ferry, he walked up to the desk and, pulling out a checkbook, observed: "I love to write my name to checks. It gives a man the impression that he can manufacture money."

Then turning to the *Evening Journal* reporter he drawled: "Getting ready to sail for a trip abroad requires a vast deal of trouble. I've always felt sorry for Noah; he had such an awful lot of worry getting all his animals on the Ark."...

When Mr. Clemens reached the steamship pier in Hoboken he busied himself with various matters connected with his departure.... Then turning to an *Evening Journal* reporter he answered a question concerning Aristophanes and Rabalais that had been propounded after he had read an article in which the humorist was heralded as the modern reincarnation of those two distinguished gentlemen.

"Remarkable statement, that," he drawled with a twinkle in his eyes, "and very handsome, very handsome; but if I tell you the truth I can't agree with the statement because I was only an empty vessel at the various times my friend William D. Howells says that Aristophanes lived. So you see, I don't know Aristophanes even if Howells has told me at various times that he was everything from a sailor with Sir John Hawkins in the British Channel to a Greek physician and an Italian virtuoso. But Rabelais! Ah, my dear young sir, I know Rabelais from the head down to the end of his toes and from his toes to the top of his head. Yes, I know Rabelais, and if I had lived in the fifteenth century I would have been Rabelais."...

Just at this moment an interruption occurred in Mr. Clemens' story, when a man with a Van Dyke beard and an effusive manner rushed up to Mark and introduced himself as a member of the centennial committee of the big celebration at Tarrytown one year from now, asked him if he was going to get back to America in time for the celebration.

"You know, you've been a taxpayer up there," he said, "and we want to have you back."

"Well," said Mark, with ever the same drawl, "I certainly intend returning to America after a year abroad, but I'm not sure whether I am going up to the celebration. I might get taxed for being there. They love to assess you in Tarrytown.

"Now," he declared with great emphasis, "I've hired this fancy villa over in Italy at a fancy price, but it is our house, and I am going to live in it for one year. I've got mighty tired of paying rent and taxes for four places and living in one."

The man with the Van Dyke beard nearly exploded at this sally of the humorist.

"Four houses and properties, that's it exactly, and only a chance to live in one. Let's see. There was the house at York Harbor, Maine; one at Riverdale, another at Hartford, and then the Captain Casey Place at Tarrytown where they love to assess people."

Another interruption occurred here when a number of newspaper men rushed up to Mr. Clemens and asked him if he had heard of the arrival of Henry W. Lucy, the noted English humorist, and famous as "Toby, M. P., of *Punch*." Lucy said he had come to this country to ask a settlement with Twain in the matter of *The Obituary*, a magazine to be devoted to publishing obituaries of men while they were alive and then selling the subject all the copies he desires, suppressing the rest of the edition. . . .

"Well, I'm glad that at least one Englishman can see the point," said Twain. "I was afraid that he wouldn't. You see, this idea of *The Obituary* was mine. I suggested it to Lucy at a dinner . . . in London several months ago. He jumped at the opportunity and we formed a partnership. Now he understands the joke, for he is living on hopes and I am living on accomplished certainties."

"You see," and Mark grew enthusiastic, "this was the greatest money-making contrivance ever devised and, as I was the originator, I naturally in my heart expected to reap the fruits of my originality.

"The scheme was simply this: We were to go to various men and offer to write obituaries of their lives before they were dead, for fifty guineas. There would be no money in a corpse, you know, and he would pay for the obituary while he was alive.

"We would say to the man: We can write a fine obituary of you; you pay us fifty guineas, we give you the right to have as many copies printed for you as you desire and then *we suppress the remainder of the edition*."

"It was great fun to see the way men would come to us. We were able to cover up—we are yet, that is, Lucy and I—all the dark spots in a man's life, and then even artistically shade them so they resembled the deeds of glory. "Things went beautifully until a little while ago, when Lucy wanted more profits, and, as I've said, I knew that for the money in it, the proposition resolved itself into the axiom of 'It is better for Twain than for two.'"

## "Mark Twain on the Law of Copyright"
London *Sketch*, 30 March 1904, p. 376

. . . On my entrance, I made some stumbling apology for my intrusion, and he said, rather severely, that he had made it a rule never to be interviewed between whiles, but that during the twenty-four hours preceding his departure from one country and the twenty-four hours after his arrival in another country he was open to all comers. I ventured to hope that my visit would not result in his undoing, and inquired if he knew Italy well.

"No," he replied, laboring with a recalcitrant pipe; "I should like to very much, but this is the only part of Italy that I know. A very pleasant race the Tuscans are, and I get on well with them in a deaf-and-dumb fashion; not that I did not carry on long conversations with every Italian I met when I was in Settignano eleven years ago, only I spoke English and the Italian spoke Italian, and neither of us understood what the other was saying. But we never bore malice and always parted friends." After applying a fresh match to his pipe he went on: "The world, of course, is the same all over, and I have my singular correspondents here, too. Today I have received a letter from a Florentine gentleman in which, as far as I can make out with the aid of my daughter, he asks me to pay him twenty francs for some copies of his paper which he sent to me and as recompense for five visits which he has made to my house 'at grave risk from your dogs.' I did not ask for his papers, I did not ask him to pay me those visits, and the dogs who threatened his life belong to my neighbor!"

Speaking of the followers of Mrs. Eddy, who do not reason but blindly believe, he said: "For the matter of that, the ordinary followers of any religion may be accused of the incapacity to reason clearly about it. The opinion of 'The Man in the Street' is worthless on a subject of which he has not made a special study. Lawyers, perhaps, and college professors may be listened to with attention on their own subjects, for their training has been long and in one direction, but this is true of scarcely any other men." The pipe was going easier now. . . .

I rose to go, and, looking out of the window at the incessant rain, expressed a regret that Florence was treating him so unkindly with her weather. "Well," quoth the humorist, "it is rather an incentive to imaginary rheumatism. Mother Eddy has not taught me yet to suppress my imaginings." Whereat I laughed, and so ended a long visit in which all my preconceived notions of the great writer had been upset, and a New Mark Twain showed himself to me, not solely humorous, but intensely earnest.

## "Mark Twain to Reform the Language of Italy"
### *New York Times,* 10 April 1904, p. 11

Reporter: And how do you like Italy again after your long absence from here?

Oh, Italy is right enough. The best country in the world to live in. Perhaps England runs it rather close, but here all is quiet, town and country alike. In England there is always London with its great unquiet pulse.

Reporter: And the Italians?

Right enough, too. I love to watch them, and to study their gestures and their ways. That is why I do not object to the slow pace of our horses, like my daughter there, even if they do take a time to land us in town.

Reporter: And the language?

I never get hold of an entire sentence. Just a word here and there that comes in handy, but they never stay with me more than a day.

There is one person who always understands me, and that is our old kitchen scrub. She was with us last time, too. We have quite long talks together and exchange no end of compliments. I talk English; she rattles along in her own lingo; neither of us knows what the other says; we get along perfectly and greatly respect each other's conversation.

*When the talk turned to books, the reporter said that he had never been able to read a novel by Sir Walter Scott.*

Just so. I was once ill and shut up and there was nothing but Scott's novels to read, so I had another try. Well, when I got through *Guy Mannering*, I wrote to Brander Matthews and asked him if he would be good enough to point out to me the literary and stylistic merits of the work, for I could not find them.

Fact is, nothing is eternal in this world, and literature is as much subject to the character of the times as any other intellectual manifestation. Books reflect the mental atmosphere in which they were born, and on that account cannot expect to live forever. Every generation has its own authors. Look at Dickens. At one time nothing went down that was not a little tinted with the Dickens style; now who would allow that? And the same for all the others. Is there a more tiresome and unnatural book than *Pendennis?* All the people are exaggerated, caricatures, with no intention of being so. It's like when they show us some weird old picture and say it's wonderful. I dare say it is wonderful, for its time; but its time is past.

## "In Genial Mood"
### *Boston Globe,* 6 November 1905, p. 9

"A man who is a pessimist before he's 48 is a fool—he knows too much. A man who isn't a pessimist after he's 49 is a fool—he doesn't know enough."

This was one of Mark Twain's reflections yesterday afternoon while chatting with a group of newspaper men. . . .

The famous humorist was discussing old age and his approaching 70st birthday, which comes on the 30th of this month, when he made the above remark.

Colonel Thomas Wentworth Higginson was present during the combination interview, which lasted more than two hours and during which time a wide range of subjects were discussed and commented on by Mr. Clemens. . . .

After the reporters had been introduced . . . there was a brief, uneasy moment's wait for somebody to break the ice. Colonel Higginson at once came to the rescue by suggesting that as Mr. Clemens was nearly 70 years of age a few reflections on old age from the dean of American humorists—and journalists—might be a proper beginning.

"I don't mind," said Mark, as he settled back in his chair, crossed his legs, and lighted a big cigar. "I'm ready to talk on anything. I never really knew what it was to be old until about five years ago. Now I believe I'm the oldest man in the world. . . .

When asked if he hadn't experienced any of the usual manifestations of old age up to his 65th year—the little pains and aches, the gray hairs, etc.—Mr. Clemens said: "No. As for the gray hairs, I had them when I was 50, and I might have had indigestions, but that is not a sign of age; it is a sign of indiscretion. No, I can't say that I began to feel old until I was past 60."

. . . [I]t might be well to give a few of his latest aphorisms. He said he had been writing aphorisms all his life—on occasion—and some day he hoped to publish a book of them. Here are the latest additions to his stock:

"Taking the pledge will not make bad liquor good but will improve it."

"It's not best to use our morals weekdays. It gets them out of repair for Sunday."

"Don't part with your illusions; when they are gone you may still exist, but you have ceased to live."

"It is noble to be good; it is still nobler to show others how to be good, and much less trouble."

"I like aphorisms," commented the humorist with a twinkle. . . .

The horrors of the Congo Free State, as told by missionaries, have brought down on the head of King Leopold of Belgium all the vials of Mark Twain's wrath and sarcasm. He has no use for King Leopold, and he has just published a little work entitled *King Leopold's Soliloquy*, which shows the monarch of Belgium, who is also monarch of the Congo Free State, in anything but a pleasant light.

He believes the report which has just been made by the committee which the king appointed to investigate conditions in the Congo is a farce and a lie. The missionaries and the photographs which the missionaries have taken give the lie to King Leopold's committee's report, he said.

"Leopold is too well known as a domestic person, as a family person," said Mark Twain, facetiously, "as a king and a pirate, to believe what he says. He sits at home and drinks blood. His testimony is no good. The missionaries are to be believed. I have seen photographs of the natives with their hands cut off because they did not bring in the required amount of rubber. If Leopold had only killed them outright it would not be so bad, but to cut off their hands and leave them helpless to die in misery—that is not forgivable.

"We're interested in all this because we were the first country to give recognition to Leopold's villainous Congo Free State in 1885."

Mr. Clemens commented on some of the brutalities perpetrated by other nations on the natives of Africa and cited the Matabele war, in which the English massacred so many thousands of the Matabeles.

Mr. Clemens apparently never had much use for Cecil Rhodes or the methods which he used in introducing civilization to South Africa. In 50 years he believes the mines in the Rand will be worked out and the country will revert once more to the Boers. . . .

"What do you think of the municipal reform wave and the municipal grafters?"

"The grafting seems to be all over the country, and I don't think much of the reforms."

"How about Philadelphia?" interposed Colonel Higginson.

"Well, of course in this country we have one great privilege which they don't have in other countries. When a thing gets to be absolutely unbearable the people can rise up and throw it off. That's the finest asset we've got—the ballot box, which has been exercised in Philadelphia. But graft seems to permeate everything in this country today."

When asked how he thought this new standard of ethics and morals in business had originated and if he thought Rockefeller's success had anything to do with it, Mr. Clemens said: "I suppose it has had something to do with it. It's a new thing. I believe, however, that it began with Jay Gould and Jim Fisk. The operations of these two men dazed people. Here were men who could make a million in a few minutes. This was all new.

"I remember being in the Lotus Club, I think it was in 1869, and hearing some prominent men discuss these things and I heard respectable men say: "'Well, give me the million and I'll take the odium.' The poison began to work then, you see. . . . We gave," said he, "to the world the spirit of liberty more than 100 years ago and now we are giving the world the spirit of graft. Look at the British army scandals during the Boer war. No British commissioned officer ever did such things before. The spirit of graft has spread."

Colonel Higginson said the sturdy old spirit of honesty still existed among many of the people in the New England towns and he cited one notable example of a man in Dublin, N. H., who did a little job for which he charged eight cents, and after being paid he tramped back in the rain a mile or more and said he had charged too much—the job was only worth six cents. He handed back two cents and returned to his home in the rain.

Mr. Clemens told a story of a burglar who had literary ideals—a New England burglar up at Dublin, N. H.—who when arrested was found deeply absorbed in a copy of *Innocents Abroad*.

# "Mark Twain Would Kill Bosses by Third Party"

*New York Herald,* 12 November 1905, II, 3–4

Mark Twain has suggested a remedy for bossism. . . . Mr. Clemens believes it is simple to bring about this state of political perfection. All that is required is the organization of a permanent third party, call it "mugwump," if you choose, which shall continually hold the balance of power in municipal, state, and national elections. It must be a party with no candidates and no political or personal interests to further, and its members may not even suggest the appointment of any of their friends to office. . . .

"It is a peculiar condition, but nonetheless true," said Mr. Clemens, "that the political liberty of which we are so proud is mainly responsible for the existence of the political boss. At any election the people, if they choose, may turn out the whole crowd. . . . We know that whenever we get tired of the domination of the bosses or those in office who represent them we have an unfailing remedy. We may apply it at any time, and for that reason we don't until some flagrant act causes an upheaval such as we have just seen in this city and in Philadelphia and in some other places.

"There is a way to escape from the thralldom of bossism, and that is by the organization of a third party, an independent party, made up of those who are generally called 'mugwumps'! I'm a 'mugwump.' I have never tied myself to any party, but have voted for the nominee who appealed to me as being the best man."

Mr. Clemens lighted his favorite pipe and blew a great cloud of smoke into which he gazed thoughtfully.

"What is party, anyway? That fog labeled 'democrat' or 'republican,' which means nothing to the average mind when it is analyzed. The democratic party shouts for free trade while the republican party shrieks for high tariff. Which is right? Why, there is no possible way of deciding which is right. If in the great party politic one-half believe high tariff is right and the other is certain free trade is the proper thing, who is there to settle the question?

"If you ask me what I suggest as a remedy for present conditions, I'll tell you that some one, a man of great executive ability, . . . will have to enlist all his energies in the formation of a permanent third party. It must be composed of men who are willing to give up all affiliations with either of the great parties. No man in it can have any political aspirations. He must not have any friends whom he wishes to push forward for political preferment. The sole reason for the existence of this new third party must be to elect the candidate of either the democratic or the republican party who is believed to be the best fitted for the office for which he is nominated.

"It is not the idea that this independent party is to consist of another fog of non-individualities to be swung in a mass for any candidate at any one's dictation. There would be nobody who could deliver that vote in a mass.

"It is a party made up of separate individualities, each holding and prizing the privilege of voting as he chooses, the rest to vote as they choose. And therefore you have this result, that if the candidate of one of the great parties is conspicuously a better man than the candidate of the other great party it is believable that the independent party would vote as a mass for that man.

"But if both are equally conspicuous for merit it is believable that this would split the independent vote in two with this final result, that, both of these candidates being excellent men, no one would care which was elected.

"If an independent party can obtain the nomination of excellent men on both sides this would certainly justify the organization of a third party."

"What if both the nominees are bad men?" Mr. Clemens was asked.

He turned upon the questioner a look of pity which there was no mistaking.

"Can't you see that if this third party has power to elect whomever it pleases, neither will select for its nominees any but the very best men? Don't you realize with what pains the names of the candidate would be considered before they were chosen for a place on the tickets? There could never be any question about their eligibility. All the 'mugwumps' would have to do would be to decide which man they liked best and vote for him. I admit it would be a mixed government, but that wouldn't matter.

"I have often wondered at the condition of things which set aside morality in politics and make possible the election of men whose unfitness is apparent. A mother will teach her boy at her knee to tell the truth, to be kind, to avoid all that is immoral. She will painstakingly guide his thoughts and actions so that he may grow up possessed of all the manly virtues, and the father of that boy will, when it comes time for his son to cast his first vote, take him aside and advise him to vote for a bad man who is on the democratic ticket because he has always adhered to democratic principles. Could anything be more absurd? . . .

"I cannot understand the philosophy of the man who, looked up to as a model citizen, loses sight of the morality of politics when it comes to casting his ballot. Why, it's nothing but a question of morality. And I know lots of men who will throw aside all considerations of morality when they go to the polls and will vote for the man nominated by his party irrespective of his personal fitness for the place. Prejudice influences him. He won't heed the dictates of his conscience.

"This question of prejudice is very important. There are lots of people who don't believe that a slice of ripe watermelon will cure dysentery. It cures my personal friends every time, but I'll bet if I tried to teach the gospel of ripe watermelon to a hospital full of dysentery patients and would sell watermelons for three cents a dozen they'd put me out of the institution."

## "Mark Twain / A Humorist's Confession"

A. E. Thomas, *New York Times* first magazine section,
26 November 1905, pp. 1, 5

Mark Twain will be 70 years old on Thanksgiving Day, and he has never done a day's work in his life. He told me so himself. . . .

"No, sir, not a day's work in all my life. What I have done I have done, because it has been play. If it had been work I shouldn't have done it.

"Who was it who said, 'Blessed is the man who has found his work'? Whoever it was he had the right idea in his mind. Mark you, he says his work—not somebody else's work. The work that is really a man's own work is play and not work at all. Cursed is the man who has found some other man's work and cannot lose it. When we talk about the great workers of the world we really mean the great players of the world. The fellows who groan and sweat under the weary load of toil that they bear never can hope to do anything great. How can they when their souls are in a ferment of revolt against the employment of their hands and brains? The product of slavery, intellectual or physical, can never be great.". . .

"Well, Mr. Clemens," I said, "what you say about work and play may be true, but a good many people would think that the immense amount of labor you went through to pay the debts of the publishing house of C. L. Webster & Co., after that firm went to smash, was entitled to be called by the name of hard work."

"Not at all. All I had to do was write a certain number of books and deliver a few hundred lectures. As for traveling about the country from one place to another for years—the nuisances of getting about and bad hotels and so on—those things are merely the incidents that every one expects to meet in life. The people who had to publish my books, the agents who had to arrange my lecture tours, the lawyers who had to draw up the contracts and other legal documents—they were the men who did the real work. My part was merely play. If it had been work I shouldn't have done it. I was never intended for work—never could do it—can't do it now—don't see any use in it."

It occurred to me to ask Mr. Clemens to tell the secret of the vital hold he has had for years upon the most intelligent people of the English-speaking world—a grip upon the public mind such as no mere humorist has ever held or ever could hold.

"Well," he answered, "I know it is a difficult thing for a man who has acquired a reputation as a funny man *to* have a serious thought and put it into words and be listened to respectfully, but I thoroughly believe that any man who's got anything worth while to say will be heard if he only says it often enough. Of course, what I have to say may not be worth saying. I can't tell about that, but if I honestly believe I have an idea worth the attention of thinking people it's my business to say it with all the sincerity I can muster. They'll listen to it if it really is worth while and I say it often enough. If it isn't worth while it doesn't matter whether I'm heard or not.

"Suppose a man makes a name as a humorist—he may make it at a stroke, as Bret Harte did, when he wrote those verses about the 'Heathen Chinee.' That may not be the expression of the real genius of the man at all. He may have a genuine message for the world. Then let him say it and say it again and then repeat it and let him soak it in sincerity. People will warn him at first that he's getting a bit out of his line, but they'll listen to him at last, if he's really got a message just as they finally listened to Bret Harte.

"Dickens had his troubles when he tried to stop jesting. The *Sketches by Boz* introduced him as a funny man, but when Boz began to take himself seriously people began to shake their heads and say: 'That fellow Boz isn't as funny as he was, is he?' But Boz and his creator kept right on being in earnest, and they listened after a time, just as they always will listen to anybody worth hearing.

"I tell you, life is a serious thing, and, try as a man may, he can't make a joke of it. People forget that no man is all humor, just as they fail to remember that every man is a humorist. . . .

"My advice to the humorist who has been a slave to his reputation is never to be discouraged. I know it is painful to make an earnest statement of a heartfelt conviction and then observe the puzzled expression of the fatuous soul who is conscientiously searching his brain to see how he can possibly have failed to get the point of the joke. But say it again and maybe he'll understand you. No man need be a humorist all his life. As the patent medicine man says, there is hope for all. . . .

"The quality of humor," Mr. Clemens went on hurriedly—for him—"is the commonest thing in the world. I mean the perceptive quality of humor. In this sense every man in the world is a humorist. The creative quality of humor—the ability to throw a humorous cast over a set of circumstances that before had seemed colorless is, of course, a different thing. But every man in the world is a perceptive humorist. Everybody lives in a glass house. Why should anybody shy bricks at a poor humorist or advise him to stick to his trade when he tries to say a sensible thing?"

"Even the English?" I suggested.

"The English don't deserve their reputation. They are as humorous a nation as any in the world. Only humor, to be comprehensible to anybody, must be built upon a foundation with which he is familiar. If he can't see the foundation the superstructure is to him merely a freak—like the Flat-iron building without any visible means of support—something that ought to be arrested.

"You couldn't, for example, understand an English joke, yet they have their jokes—plenty of them. There's a passage in Parkman that tells of the home life of the Indian—describes him sitting at home in his wigwam with his squaw and papooses—not the stoical, icy Indian with whom we are familiar, who wouldn't make a jest for his life or notice one that anybody else made, but the real Indian that few white men ever saw—simply rocking with mirth at some tribal witticism that probably wouldn't have commended itself in the least to Parkman.

"And, so you see, the quality of humor is not a personal or a national monopoly. It's as free as salvation, and, I am afraid, far more widely distributed. But it has its value, I think. The hard and sordid things of life are too hard and too sordid and too cruel for us to know and touch them year after year without some mitigating influence, some kindly veil to draw over them, from time to time, to blur the craggy outlines, and make the thorns less sharp and the cruelties less malignant."

Mr. Clemens doesn't mind being seventy years old, but he isn't especially gay about it.

"When our anniversaries roll up too high a total," he said, "we don't feel in a particularly celebratory mood. We often celebrate the wrong anniversaries and lament the ones we ought to celebrate."

## "What I am Thankful For"

W. O. Inglis, New York *Sunday World Magazine,*
26 November 1905, p. 1

"We have much to be thankful for: most of all, (politically), that America's first-born son, sole & only son, love-child of her trusting innocence and her virgin bed, King Leopold of the undertakers, has been spared to us another year, & that his (& our) Cemetery Trust in the Congo is now doing a larger business in a single week that it used to do in a month fifteen years ago. Mark Twain."

This remarkable sentiment was given to me by Mr. Clemens at the end of an interview. His seventieth birthday will be celebrated next Thursday, and, because his life is an additional reason why the American people should feel grateful, he was asked by the *Sunday World Magazine* to say why we should all be thankful at this particular season. . . .

"How do you keep so well?" was the question that inevitably suggested itself at the beginning.

"That's only a recent phase," Mr. Clemens replied. "I was until lately subject to the annoyance of attacks of acute indigestion. Never could tell when the miserable, nagging thing was going to pounce upon me and torture me. Midday or 3 o'clock in the morning was all the same to it. I can see now the trouble was due to my habit, of thirty years' standing, of eating only one meal a day." . . .

"How about your exercise?" I asked.

"No exercise at all," said Mr. Clemens. "For weeks at a time I did not leave my home up in the mountains. Often I lay in bed all day and wrote. It's a great luxury to arrange your desk in bed and write as long as you like. I've spent whole weeks that way. You see, I'm in no hurry for publication. It pleases me to do a certain amount of work every day. I keep some of the manuscript for years. If after lying unread for three, four, or five years, it comes up to the standard I have set, then I publish it; if not, it drops into the wastebasket. I write to please myself. No editor is so hard to satisfy as one's own standard."

"But don't you feel the lack of exercise?" I persisted.

"No," replied Mr. Clemens. "Perhaps I am exceptionally lucky. I may not need it. I never fail to run upstairs. That is exercise enough. . . .

"What a mistake we make in setting up two arbitrary definitions of effort and calling one work and the other play. You can't measure effort that way. ". . .

Mr. Clemens was walking up and down the long library, smoking a black cigar. In his earnest talk he kept forgetting the cigar and every little while he had to stop and relight it. So each match he struck marked the beginning of a paragraph.

"They apply the same cast-iron conventional rule to everything," he went on. "For years they have regarded me as a trifler, one who is always ready with a joke on any subject. I tell you, there never lived in this world a more serious man than I."

Now, here was a remarkable confession from one who has long been regarded as the greatest humorist in the world. . . .

"What is it that strikes a spark of humor from a man?" Mr. Clemens continued. "It is the effort to throw off, to fight back the burden of grief that is laid on each one of us. In youth we don't feel it, but as we grow to manhood we find the burden on our shoulders. Humor? It is nature's effort to harmonize conditions. The further the pendulum swings out over woe the further it is bound to swing back over mirth.

"I will not give you," he said, suddenly becoming grave, "any humorous trifling for this great and solemn day, for I am anxious not to hurt the feelings of any one to whom this day, with its deep and serious memories, appeals. But I will say this"—and here Mr. Clemens read the denunciation of Leopold. . . .

"I hope," said Mr. Clemens, "that the American people will bring retribution to this unclean, lying murderer who is taking lives day by day in order that he may clutch more and more of the tainted money he wastes. I hope that this Thanksgiving sentiment of mine will sink into the minds of *The World's* readers, make them think, make them act. In giving it to you I am trying not to do something that will please one, but to do something that will damage that wholesale murderer, that greedy, grasping, avaricious, cynical, bloodthirsty old goat!"

## "Congress Admires Mark Twain's Hair"
### New York *World*, 30 January 1906, p. 3

Mark Twain and Congress saw one another today. Before they separated each knew the other fairly well. Mr. Clemens did not shy at Congress, but Congress did shy a little at Mark.

Mark Twain's hair was the first thing that attracted the attention of Congress. From the floor and the galleries he looked like Chief Justice Fuller. After watching the hair for a time the Senate decided to get better acquainted, and Col. George B. Harvey and Mr. Clemens were invited to come down and see the Vice-President. Mr. Fairbanks tried to be cordial. He shook hands with Col. Harvey first. Then he warmed up and gave Mr. Clemens' hand a little squeeze—the kind that is known in Indiana as the "ice tongs." Then Mr. Fairbanks glanced at Mr. Clemens's hair and looked as though he would like to know him better so that he might ask what tonic he used. Thinking it over, Mr. Fairbanks carefully brushed four hairs over his bald spot.

The Vice-President was about to present his visitors with his autographed photographs when other Senators came romping in and insisted that Mr. Clemens and Col. Harvey take luncheon with them in the Senate restaurant.

"We lunched and lied together," Mr. Clemens said in describing the luncheon. "We would take a bite of pie and then indulge in a few flights of the imagination. Oh, n-o-o-o-o, the Senators did not eat pie with their knives, at least none of them that I saw; but of course, you know, I was pretty busy myself and couldn't watch all of them. I was really impressed by those Senators." ...

"What were the flights of imagination?" said Mark Twain in answer to a question. "Oh, they were said in open session, and nothing ever said by a Senator in open session amounts to much. Had they been said in executive session I would have made notes on my cuff or have written them on the back of an envelope, but before going to the Senate I was warned that nobody, at least no real weighty Senator, ever said anything in open session. I guess that's true. We had a most delightful time, though, and a good luncheon."

After being shown over the Senate part of the building, Mark Twain and Colonel Harvey went over to the House and were shown into the Speaker's room. "We called on my old friend, the Speaker," Mr. Clemens said. "I say he is my old friend because I met him on Saturday night. Any man who meets another on Saturday night has a right to refer to him as an 'old friend.' We got pretty well acquainted, too. I sat next to Speaker Cannon at the Gridiron Club dinner, and I think if the dinner had lasted half an hour longer I would have been calling him 'Joe' and he would have referred to me as 'Sam.' Members of the House came in and there were flights of imagination, but the Speaker and I stuck pretty close to the truth, except in a few instances the Speaker may have stretched a point or two."

## "Mark Twain in 'Uncle Joe's' Lair,"
### *New York Herald*, 30 January 1906, p. 5

Mark Twain and "Uncle Joe" Cannon have developed a mutual admiration society. For two days they have been much in each other's company, "swapping lies," according to "Uncle Joe." It started at the Gridiron dinner Saturday night when they sat side by side.

Mark Twain today spent an hour in the Speaker's room at the Capitol, where there was a "gabfest," in the language of the Speaker, and a conversazione, according to Mr. Clemens, that would live in history could everything that was said be told. . . .

Twain told his story of the boys caught playing cards in the preacher's room. They hid the cards in the sleeve of the minister's robe. A few days later when the preacher was engaged in baptizing a convert by the immersion method, a full hand floated out upon the waters.

"I've heard that before," said "Uncle Joe."

"I reckon you have," said Twain. "I invented that story forty years ago and the newspapers stole it. Why, about ten years later I was lecturing in England and stopping at a country house. What do you think I had to do? Sit by quietly and hear one dude tell that story to another as a personal experience. About twenty years later I was down in Australia on a lecture tour. I told that story and my English experience with it. A big strapping fellow from the brush got up and corroborated me in every detail. He was the dude who had told the story as his own."

## "Mark Twain Too Lazy for a U. S. Senator"
### *New York Herald*, 11 March 1906, 1, 5

Suggestions having come from various sources that in the event of retirement from Congress of either of the New York Senators Samuel L. Clemens (Mark Twain) would be named as successor, a reporter for the *Herald* called on the humorist yesterday at his home in Fifth avenue to get his expressions on the subject.

Mr. Clemens said: "If such an offer as that were made to me it would be the most gigantic compliment I ever received. I would not consider myself, however, a worthy successor to Dr. Depew or Mr. Platt, as I am in no way qualified for the post. A Senator needs to know the political history of the country, past and present, as well as its commercial, industrial, and financial affairs. Of these things I am blissfully ignorant. Even if I were qualified, the duties of a Senator would be distasteful to me: My own particular work is the greatest source of pleasure I have, and for that reason I do not consider it as work at all. I regard myself as the most lazy human being on earth. I have absolutely no industry in me whatever, and to 'make good' as a Senator one must be in love with the job and be industrious. If a man is to succeed in any occupation the work to him must be a labor of love. It has always been so with me and my work, and I think I can justly say, without vanity, that my career has been, to a fair degree, a success.

"For five days every week I am busy writing or dictating, and I'm in a modified paradise all the while. Saturdays and Sundays I take off, and during these two holidays, as I call them, I'm in a modified hades."

When reminded that the Senate, as a body, is sadly lacking in humor and needs livening up, Mr. Twain said smilingly: "Well, as 'Falstaff to the Senate' I guess I could fill the bill and earn my salary. But as a 'representative of the people' I would be certain to prove dead timber."

"But can't humorists be serious as well as other mortals, Mr. Twain?"

"Most assuredly. There is no man alive—not even excepting a Scotch Presbyterian minister—who can be more serious than I am. But as a Senator the people would refuse to take me any more seriously than they do in my natural capacity as a humorist, and I would score a failure if I attempted to convince them that I was in earnest. I don't care to make an unattractive exhibition of myself. It's a humorist's business to laugh at other folks, not inspire other folks to laugh at him."

## "Gorky Evicted Twice in a Day from Hotels"
### New York *World*, 15 April 1906, pp. 1–2

Maxim Gorky's time yesterday was completely taken up by events arising from the announcement that the woman whom he brought to this country as his wife was not Mme. Gorky, but Andreeva, a Russian actress. . . . The admirers of the Russian, with a few faithful exceptions, stayed away from him yesterday, apparently not having quite made up their minds how to regard the matter.

Mark Twain was authority for the information that the grand dinner which was to be given two weeks hence "by purely literary folks" in homage to Gorky's eminence in the world of literature had been called off. . . .

The humorist is a member of the American committee whose object is to make the Russian revolution succeed. He talked at some length last night on Gorky's case as he saw it.

"Now I'm a revolutionist," he said, "by birth, breeding, principle, and everything else. I love all revolutions no matter where or when they start.

"I sympathize with these Russian revolutionists, and, in common with some other people, I hope that they will succeed. So when the committee asked me to become a member, I did. I told them, as I am constantly telling other people, that I am always glad to lend my name if they won't give me anything to do. I love to be an ornament and a figurehead. I'd like to be an ornament and a figurehead all over town.

"Well, when Mr. Gorky came here, it seemed to us that he was going to be a prodigious power in getting the American people interested. I don't think it had ever occurred to him that any objection like this would be raised. The people in Russia had always made him feel that his acts were just as they should be.

"But every country has its laws of conduct. It is right that it should, and when anyone arrives from a foreign land he ought to conform to those laws.

"It seems to me that Mr. Gorky has seriously impaired—I was about to say destroyed—his efficiency as a persuader. He is disabled, and the propaganda by so much loses the help of his great genius and tremendous personality.

"I don't know what the committee will do. I can tell better after I have had a chance to speak to some of the members. Meanwhile, I believe in sticking by the flag until the last minute."

## "Twain Awes Capitol"
*Washington Herald*, 8 December 1906, pp. 1, 7

"I belong to the ancient and honorable society of perfection and purity. I am the president, secretary, and treasurer. I am the only member. In fact," drawled Mark Twain, stretched out in an easy chair in the press gallery, with his toes turned up to the crackling fire on the grate, "I am the only person in the United States who is eligible." . . .

"Honest," said Mark Twain, "I can't get over the abomination of the American clothes. The garments the average man wears are a fright; but I have reached that age of discretion which gives to years the right of individuality in dress. I wear my white serge not as clothes. No, it's my uniform.

"I have seen but one man dressed the way I would like to dress— dressed in the best way to dress. He was a Sandwich Islander, and he wore—let me see, it was a special occasion—a pair of spectacles. You may talk about clothes, but, after all, the human skin is the best thing in that line I have ever struck.

"Now, there's the plug hat. Whenever I see a man in a plug hat I begin to suspect him of something. Time was when a man couldn't be dressed in the United States unless he wore a plug hat. Now a man can't be dressed if he does wear one. I don't like to see men in black.

"Oh, now, I don't care for the gaudy effects. Something with color in it, though, catches my fancy. I love the women. They know how to get themselves up to capture the heart and eye, and I don't see why, as the ladies are constantly borrowing ideas in clothes from men—whenever they get any good ones—the men shouldn't borrow from the ladies.

"Were there ever any styles like the peek-a-boo waist, the low-cut gown, the short sleeves? Wouldn't man look gorgeous in that kind of a rig? Why not? Of course, I believe in it. For men? Certainly. I like to look over the theaters, the opera houses; but do you think I care about the men? Not by a considerable sight. They speck the landscape like a lot of crows. But with the women, it's different. There is something gay, and festive, and full of life and color, and warm and pleasing and artistic about a woman. They don't get themselves up like delegates to an undertaker's convention, with no more atmospheric fitness about them than a ham. No, sir; a woman knows how to blend herself with the scenery, and if there happens to be an aurora borealis or a rainbow around, it doesn't give her any chills. She comes right up smiling with the goods, and she sails in and makes the aurora borealis look sick. But with a man, it's different, and he couldn't shake off a waiter's coat unless—unless he should have attained the age of seventy-one, as I have."...

"The ideal dress doesn't exist now," he drawled. "You've got to go back to the Middle Ages for that. Now, I don't mean the tinned-goods era. I mean the doublet and hose period, the silk-and-velvet age, when the men decorated their heads with hats like the swinging garden of Babylon and drooping plumes. There weren't any anesthetic buttons in those days, and a man laced his pants on. It must have taken 'em some time to dress—and—I—guess—proved—embarrassing—when—the—house—caught—fire."

"But, Mr. Clemens, "said one of the correspondents, "what made you dress your Yankee at King Arthur's Court in armor and a silk hat?"

"Because when I wrote that book the plug hat was all the rage in America. I did it to cater to popular clamor. Now, there's William Dean Howells. He knows better, and his own taste tells him not to wear a plug hat. But he listens to what other people say. Why, when we came over from New York to attend this copyright hearing, Howells wore a plug hat. It was the only one on the ferry-boat. He looked like an ass. But, then, I didn't have to see him in a plug hat. I know that, anyhow.

"These are just some of the reasons why I wear white clothes in midwinter; I've got my real clothes underneath. It suits me, and I'm getting to be an old man now. So is Howells; he's seventy, and he ought to know better, but he never seems to learn."...

Somebody asked the venerable humorist his opinion about the public library board of Worcester, Mass., that barred his book, Eve's Diary. He smiled contentedly and drawled: "The whole episode has rather amused me. I have no feeling of vindictiveness over the stand of the librarians there—I am only amused. You see they did not object to my book; they objected to Lester Ralph's pictures. I wrote the book; I did not make the pictures. I admire the pictures, and I heartily approve them, but I did not make them.

"It seems curious to me—some of the incidents in this case. It appears that the pictures in Eve's Diary were first discovered by a lady librarian. When she made the dreadful find, being very careful, she jumped at no

Line drawings by Lester Ralph from *Eve's Diary* (NY: Harper & Bros., 1906).

hasty conclusions—not she—she examined the horrid things in detail. It took her some time to examine them all, but she did her hateful duty! I don't blame her for this careful examination; the time she spent was, I am sure, enjoyable, for I found considerable fascination in them myself.

"Then she took the book to another librarian, a male this time, and he, also, took a long time to examine the unclothed ladies. He must have found something of the same sort of fascination in them that I found. Now, if the pictures were so good as to occupy their attention so long, it seems to me that they were a little selfish not to permit the rest of the city a chance instead of shutting the volume out.

"Seriously, the pictures in the book are graceful and beautiful; they show fine and delicate feeling. So far from being immodest, I thought them chaste and in good taste. To the library that barred them it would, no doubt, have been satisfactory had the ladies in Eden been garbed with a fig-leaf each, but to my mind that sort of thing is only advertising immodesty."

Mr. Clemens was asked if he had any opinion as to the theory of Mrs. Parsons, promulgated in her book, advocating short-term marriages.

"It is no new thing," he said; "but as I have no idea of marrying, I guess I shan't be required to try it.

"That sort of a trial marriage was a common thing in Scotland 300 years ago—I wasn't there then, but I've heard so. A couple would unite for a year, and if at the end of that time they did not agree, they separated, without prejudice to either. I have never heard how the plan worked. At any rate, it did not continue, so there may have been something wrong with it. We should have to know all about how the project affected things in Scotland before we could venture to try it here." . . .

Then Mr. Clemens got down to the copyright bill that brought him to Washington. He said: "We want to have this copyright bill dissected— divided. The musical fellows should drop out, and there should be a law for authors of books only, and another one for the musical piano players. We want the copyright during the author's life, and for fifty years after. A few years ago I remember that in one year only two books were re-copyrighted, for the additional fourteen years allowed—only two books, which were to go on for a full forty-two years. One of these was *Innocents Abroad* and the other was Mrs. Eddy's Christian Science book. There have been 250,000 books published in this country since the establishment of the government, and not more than 1,000 books have been re-copyrighted. Out of the thousands of books published every year, ten will live, and the copyright law we want is aimed to protect the writers of those ten books that live. To remove the copyright doesn't give the people cheaper books, but it gives more money to the publishers. . . .

"The trouble is, Congress is composed of lawyers and agriculturists. No authors or publishers. That's why it's hard to get a good law passed. When the present international copyright bill was up in the House it looked as though it would fail. I went to Sunset Cox and told him I wanted the privilege of going on the floor.

"'Why, that's impossible,' replied Cox. 'Have you ever received the thanks of Congress?'

"'No,' said I, 'but I hope to.'

"'If you are caught by the Speaker and sentenced to Siberia, will you go quietly?'

"'I will,' said I."

## "Heard at the Capitol"
*Washington Post*, 12 December 1906, p. 4

Samuel L. Clemens (Mark Twain) was at the Capitol yesterday and took an informal leave of Speaker Cannon and Vice President Fairbanks and other prominent members of the national legislature. He told "Uncle Joe" that he was sorry to depart without receiving the thanks of Congress he had requested, as he needed it in his business; but it had been intimated to him that, if he would get out of town and leave Congress alone, the deferred thanks might be forthcoming at once. If the surmise should prove true, Uncle Joe, it is understood, will forward the 'thanks' to the noted humorist by special delivery letter. . . .

"I have found out several things since I have been in Washington," said Mr. Clemens yesterday. "I could write a book on my discoveries and not enumerate all of them. I have learned among other things that legislation is a much more complicated proposition than I ever dreamed it to be. It looked very simple and easy at a distance, but a closer view has given me quite a different impression.

"The mistake the authors made was to permit those mechanical fellows—the makers of musical instruments, phonographs, &c.—to break into our game. There appears to be no opposition in Congress to extending the copyright on books to one hundred years, and if the proposition stood alone it would go through both Houses, I think, by a practically unanimous vote. But I learn that there is serious opposition to granting such a long copyright to mechanical devices, phonographs, photographs, and other things of that character. Whether anything will be done at this session toward amending the copyright laws is doubtful. I was opposed to letting the mechanical fellows join hands with us at the time we held our copyright congress in New York, but my advice was disregarded. We now know what a dangerous thing it is to ignore my advice!"

## "Twain and the Telephone"
### *New York Times*, 23 December 1906, p. 2

"The trouble with these beautiful, novel things is that they interfere so with one's arrangements. Every time I see or hear a new wonder like this I leave to postpone my death right off. I couldn't possibly leave the world until I have heard this again and again."

Mark said this as he lounged on the keyboard dais in the telharmonium music room in upper Broadway. . . .

"Of course, I know that it is intended to deliver music all over the town through the telephone, but that hardly appeals as much as it might to a man who for years, because of his addiction to strong language, has tried to conceal his telephone number, just like a chauffeur running away after an accident.

"When I lived up in Hartford, I was the very first man, in that part of New England at least, to put in a telephone, but it was constantly getting me into trouble because of the things I said carelessly. And the family were all so thoughtless. One day when I was in the garden, fifty feet from the house, somebody on the long distance wire who was publishing a story of mine, wanted to get the title.

"Well, the title was the first sentence, 'Tell him to go to hell.' Before my daughter got it through the wire and through him there was a perfect eruption of profanity in that region. All New England seemed to be listening in, and each time my daughter repeated it she did so with rising emphasis. It was awful. I broke into a cold perspiration, and while the neighborhood rang with it, rushed in and implored her to desist. But she would have the last word, and it was 'hell,' sure enough, every time.

"Soon after I moved to New York; perhaps that had something to do with my moving. When I got there and asked for a fire-proof telephone the company sent up a man to me. I opened up all my troubles to him, but he laughed and said it was all right in New York. There was a clause in their contract, he said, allowing every subscriber to talk in his native tongue, and of course they would not make an exception against me. That clause has been a godsend in my case."

## "Mark Twain in White Greets 1907"
### *New York Tribune*, 1 January 1907, p. 2

Mark Twain (Samuel Clemens) celebrated the birth of the new year last night with a few friends in his home. . . .

"This is the famous suit I wore when I went to interview the copyright committee of Congress in Washington," said the humorist to several newspaper men during the festivities. "Yes, I insist that white is the best color for men's clothes. If men were not so near insane they would appreciate the fact."

A three-act entertainment called "Champagne" was the feature of the evening. It closed with a temperance lecture by Mr. Clemens. The first act was a satire on grand opera, in which a man and woman with cracked voices screeched as they sang the high notes from various operatic selections. This was the "sham." The second act, which represented the "pain," had as its only characters a nurse holding a screeching baby. In the last act Mr. Clemens appeared bound with a red ribbon to another man, and they were labeled the "Siamese Twins."

While Mr. Clemens was lecturing and decrying the evils of drink and begging his friends with tears in his eyes not to touch, taste, nor handle strong drink, his twin was drinking bottle after bottle of champagne. The liquor imbibed by Mark Twain's twin entered his system and the lecture ended with a "Hic, hic."

## "Mark Twain's Wanderings at an End"

*New York Times*, 31 March 1907, p. 3

Mark Twain is at last to have a home of his own building. He has wandered around the world for fifty years. Some of the time he had no home at all. . . . "Most of your admirers when they think of the Buffalo house," said the reporter, "will recall a favorite story about your life there. Mrs. Clemens, so the anecdote goes, urged you to pay a neighborly call on a family living across the street. You put it off from day to day. Finally you strolled across the street to visit them. It was summer, and several of the family were sitting on the front veranda. They rose to welcome you. 'We're so glad you called,' one of them said. Then you replied: 'I should have come before. I've dropped over now to say your house is on fire.'"

"It didn't happen in exactly that way," Mr. Clemens replied. "I certainly did tell them their house was on fire. Perhaps I did stroll across the street. Nowadays I would probably run. Age makes a lot of difference when you're telling your neighbors about a fire." . . .

The Hartford home is the one most closely identified with his name. So is a story of Mark Twain and Mrs. Harriet Beecher Stowe, one of his neighbors. Mr. Clemens' version of this anecdote exploded the popular conception of the yarn. It also gave an insight into a humorist's idea of humor.

"The version I've heard," said the reporter, "is that you called on Mrs. Stowe one day to find on your return that you had neither a collar nor a necktie on. Then, it is said, you wrapped a collar and a necktie in paper and sent it to Mrs. Stowe with the message that 'here is the rest of me.'"

"The incident was not like that," replied Mr. Clemens. "Mrs. Stowe and my family were neighbors and friends. We lived close to each other, and there were no fences between. I had a collar on when I made the call, but found when I got back that I had forgotten my necktie. I sent a servant to Mrs. Stowe with the necktie on a silver salver. The note I sent with it was ceremonious. It contained a formal apology for the necktie. I'm sorry now I didn't keep a copy of that letter. It had to be ceremonious. Anything flippant on such an occasion and between such close friends would have been merely silly."

## "Mark Twain is Going to be a Buccaneer"
*New York American*, 23 April 1907, p. 5

"Yes, I'm going to be a buccaneer," said the humorist, with only the faintest twinkle of his eye. "No pirate of finance, but just a carefree ocean searcher for havens of pleasure aboard the yacht of a friend of mine.

"And I'm a young buck, too," Mr. Clemens continued. "I never felt better in my life, and I'd have you know that I'm over seventy-one years young at that.

"The bucks and buccaneers on this cruise to the Spanish Main will be the guests of Henry H. Rogers, aboard his yacht *Kanawha*. We expect to have a bully time, and our first port of entry will be Jamestown, where we go to see the naval review."

Mr. Clemens became grave a moment after this last remark when he was asked if attending a naval review almost immediately after the termination of the Peace Conference did not smack of warlike leanings.

"You see, it's this way," he said solemnly. "I don't know a thing about peace, so how can I attempt to either extol or decry the efforts of those estimable persons who fought their way into the convention at Carnegie Hall.

"Of course, people always love to get up and shout about things they don't really know anything about. That's human nature, and as long as there are people on the earth there are always going to be esoteric discussions about the beauties of peace.

"But I am afraid that I will have to attend that naval review. There's something inspiring about seeing a lot of big warships that seem to say: 'Now, be good and there won't be any trouble, but if you aren't good and peaceful, then look out.'

"And I tell you," said Mr. Clemens, as he paused and lifted his right arm, "human nature hasn't changed in the past five thousand years. Mankind hasn't changed a whole lot, and the millennium of universal peace isn't very much nearer than a year or so ago, when the Russians and Japs were at each other's throats. Even opera-bouffe revolutions, where a few hundreds are shot down in Central America, give an intimation of what all this talk about peace really amounts to. I guess the people that attend the peace conventions haven't been in such positions yet.

"It seems to me the nations are a good deal like the little boy who knocked the chip off the other little boy's shoulder—somebody was very apt to get hurt. Of course, it all depends, though, upon whether the little boy with the chip on his shoulder really wants to fight. But he has the desire to hit the other little boy, even if he doesn't do it for matters of policy.

"As far as I'm concerned, I don't know whether I'm a man of peace or not. Certainly I could get up and shout for peace, whatever that means, just as well as any of the rest of us. Then I might get mad afterward and do just what I had been declaring, with the utmost positiveness, that I wouldn't and oughtn't to do.

"But peace conventions are a good thing for the world. They set a shining example of what people think they will do before the occasion arises that might precipitate the unleashing of the martial canines.

"Meanwhile, I guess it's a might good thing to have a whacking big navy. In times of peace prepare to have peace continued. Anyway, this old buccaneer is going down to Jamestown to see the naval review and I wouldn't be a bit surprised if some of the peace delegates are there, too, thinking after all that Uncle Sam can lick all creation."

## "Twain Hesitates to Admit He's Dead"
*New York American*, 5 May 1907, 1, 6

Mark Twain yesterday puffed at a big, black cigar and genially talked of how he wasn't lost at sea. *The Times* had printed a dispatch from

Virginia stating that Mr. Clemens, who was on H. H. Rogers's yacht *Kanawha*, probably had been drowned, it being supposed—according to the paper—that the *Kanawha* had been wrecked.

The venerable humorist gravely strode to a mirror, looked at himself, pinched himself, found his name in the directory, and then, just as gravely, turned to the reporter and said: "You may tell those friends of mine who are quaking and preparing to write my obituary that, in my opinion, the rumor of my having been lost at sea is somewhat overdrawn. I do not honestly believe that I was drowned, but I shall inaugurate a most rigorous investigation to determine whether I am alive or dead, or if I have been lost or stolen.

"To the best of my knowledge and belief, I arrived Wednesday night from Norfolk on the yacht. Should I find that I have been killed or have strayed away, I assure you that I shall at once inform the public.

"It is my sincere hope that I am not dead or lost."

## "Mark Twain Tells Literary Secret and Many Other Things"
### *Baltimore News*, 10 May 1907, p. 13

Samuel L. Clemens . . . came into Baltimore on the train arriving at 2:47 o'clock yesterday afternoon, accompanied by Miss Lyon, his secretary. On the platform were Governor Warfield and Colonel E. T. Woodside to escort him to Annapolis on the 3:30 train. . . . The famous man had hardly set foot on the platform when Colonel Woodside grasped his hand, and then Governor Warfield came up and beamed. The Governor introduced the newspapermen. . . .

"Mr. Clemens"—from a ubiquitous journalist—"is it true that you were lost at sea on H. H. Rogers' yacht, after leaving Norfolk?"

"Well, that is a matter of some conjecture, but I am looking into it. There was a very peculiar coincidence about that. I was lost, I believe, on May 2, and the news of the disaster reached New York the next day. While I was battling with the waves in my study I read all about it in the dispatches. On the same day I had cabled an acceptance to Whitelaw Reid, in response to a cabled offer of the degree of bachelor of letters in Oxford—an honor which, I believe, is a rare one extended to any man on this side of the waters—and I have no doubt that over in the Embassy at London they received my cablegram after having the news of my disappearance, which must have puzzled them. They may be figuring yet how the drowning man managed to cable. Perhaps I struck a merman station down below and tapped the cable. Anyhow, that would have been a very ingenious expedient."...

I have made my last long land journey. I never expect to go farther than from New York to Washington by rail. I may have said that I would never take another sea trip, but if I ever did I'll make an exception of this Oxford journey. I don't like the trains. They wobble. I intend to leave on June 8 for Europe, to take my Oxford degree on June 26, and I shall go in a cattle boat because it is the most comfortable. The cattle down below naturally sway their bodies against the motion of the boat, keeping it steady. Yes, I shall go on a cattle boat, and I shall travel on the main deck."

The train was ready to move. The Governor piled aboard; Mark Twain piled aboard; the newspapermen piled aboard. . . . He was asked if it was true that he had given up writing forever.

"I shall never write with the pen again," he said. "I am dictating my autobiography, and that is not literature; that is narrative. You can't write literature with your mouth. And in my autobiography I have invented what William Dean Howells says is the most unique thing in the history of recent letters by combining autobiography and diary, without any reference to chronological placing of events. It makes me sick to pick up a narrative that works you all up to the highest pitch and then runs into a paragraph: 'But of this we shall speak further in its proper place!' There you've got your reader worked up to that very incident, looking for what is going to happen next, and then you throw a pitcher of ice water down his back! I am jumping from 1847 to 1902, back to 1864 and then into the time of the Pilgrim fathers, to take a dip into the future about 2000, and them come back home again. That is the natural form of narrative. Here in our hour's chat we will jump all over the country and the century, which simply proves the point. I have to see the interest from my reader's standpoint. What interests me will interest him."...

Then Mark Twain told a secret. "Everything I have ever written," he said, "has had a serious philosophy or truth as its basis. I would not write a humorous work merely to be funny. In *Yankee in King Arthur's Court,* for instance, the fun is all natural to the situations, but the underlying purpose is a satire on the divine right of kings. My *Joan of Arc,* published in 1892, was the first of the historical novels, and it was not a pretense of history; it was real history; and after it came the school of historical novel writers, with their deluge of historical tales. But *Joan of Arc* started it all."...

Mr. Clemens referred to the collapse of the Webster publishing house, his publishers, and his eyes filled with tears as he recounted the famous struggle which ended only when he, by his personal efforts, involving a lecture tour of the world, paid penny for penny more than $100,000 of liabilities.

"The payment of that debt," he said, "was the happiest incident of my life. I value its memory more than all my work; more than all my royalties; more than fame, name, or anything material. When the publishing house failed letters began to pour in upon me from people I had never heard of, and, although I was already broke, it kept me broke again paying postage on checks which I returned to the generous senders. The first day after the failure I received two checks of $1000 each from men I did not know. Then creditors came to me and offered to settle at a discount, but I had to refuse them. Our home—I thought we could save that; my daughter was born there"—and his lip trembled as the tears started afresh—"but it went, too. Everything went. But it all came right in the end."

Incidental to the general talk, the subjugation of the Hereros in

South Africa by the German Government was introduced by a casual reference to Lord Calvert's former estates made by Governor Warfield.

"It makes my blood boil," said the humorist, "to think of the titled robbers of Europe who could give a man a piece of paper granting him vast estates not yet stolen from their real owners, but just about to be stolen. Think of Calvert in Maryland, Penn in Pennsylvania, and the rest—freebooters of the worst type—coming into a country, with no right but the right of superior force, and daring to claim possession of whole States! The German thieves, directed by the sceptred thief of all, go into South Africa with a force of 30,000 men and drive a handful of the Hereros from their possessions simply because they want the territory. The Hereros made a bold and brilliant fight, considering their numbers, but they were nothing to the murderers sent by a scoundrel in ermine to cut their throats and pick their pockets. We claim to be a democratic people—a square-dealing people—but we have bought our way into the Society of Sceptred Thieves by paying $20,000,000 to a country that didn't own it for an island group that we had no right to purchase. It was the stupendous joke of the century when the United States, after conquering Spain and acquiring the islands by right of conquest, gave Spain $20,000,000. What for? For the islands? Spain didn't own them. Then, what for? Why, just for this: An American goes abroad and sells his daughter to a title and buys his way into noble circles. Uncle Sam paid that $20,000,000 for his entrance fee into society—the Society of Sceptred Thieves. We are now on a par with the rest of them. We dare to turn what should be a benevolent protectorate into an autocratic monarchy!"

"And you think—"

"I think that if a man has anything any government wants he might as well give up. England stole, by thievery, plunder, murder, arson, and rapine, the diamond fields of Africa, and the same brave system of government would make short work of an individual who would steal a single precious stone from a jewelry store window."

## "As Mark Twain Watched Drill"

*Baltimore American*, 11 May 1907, p. 15

. . . "And why do you object to being interviewed?" was the plaintive query.

"Because . . . it is impossible for any reporter to get my exact language, my exact expression or my exact thoughts. I have often been quoted, but never, unless I have written out the interview myself, have I been quoted accurately. I do not know how it is with other writers, but my English is perfect, not through any merit of my own, but because I am a writer, and to speak and write perfect English is my profession or trade. I never use slang nor bad constructions, yet you will find that, with the exception of a very few persons who know me very well, and know what I have stated to be a fact, no one will believe this because there have been published articles which purport to be interviews from me that seem proof to the contrary. So, if I desire to give an opinion upon any subject in which I am interested, and I feel that I cannot wait a couple months until it can be published in magazine form, I write it myself and get it out." . . .

After he had talked for a little time Mr. Clemens wanted to smoke. Twice during his exploration of the Naval Academy grounds in the morning had he been admonished not to smoke, and he was sorely tempted to break the rule.

"I will fill the world with crime if I don't smoke," he announced, and Governor Warfield, perhaps awed at this terrible threat, said he would take unto himself the whole blame of Mr. Clemens' misdeeds. . . .

"Can I smoke there?" asked Mr. Clemens, and, upon being answered in the affirmative, eagerly made for the portico.

"Yes, I have smoked practically all my life," he announced, when placidly puffing a cigar, "and it has never done me any harm. I suppose I was only about 10 or 12 years old when I was commenced. It all depends upon a man's constitution what he can do."

Mr. Clemens likes automobiles, they are "so comfortable," he says, but he will never be arrested for exceeding the speed laws—he likes them to go about eight miles an hour.

"But you'd never get anywhere," was objected.

"Then I'd never go," he announced decidedly.

And he does not use a typewriter, he uses a pen for all the work he does, and dictates his autobiography. "I am accustomed to the pen, and am too old to try a typewriter now," he explained.

Mr. Clemens has a great deal of trouble because he looks like his photograph. In answer to a remark to that effect he told a story of a young girl whom we met at an evening reception. "Oh, Mr. Clemens," remarked this charmingly ingenuous demoiselle, "did anyone ever tell you how much you look like Mark Twain?" And then, there was the gentlemen on the railroad train who, after gazing admiringly at the author, came up to him and said: "I feel as if I must tell you that you are enough like the pictures of Mark Twain to be his brother."

"Is that so? How interesting," was Mr. Clemens' polite rejoinder.

## "Mighty Mark Twain Overawes Marines"

*New York Times*, 12 May 1907, p. 4

"Yes," said Mark Twain, with an air of conscious importance, "I have been arrested. I was arrested twice, so that there could be no doubt about it. I have lived many years in the sight of my country an apparently uncaught and blameless life, a model for the young, an inspiring example for the hoary-headed. But at last the law has laid its hand upon me.

"Mine was no ordinary offense. When I affront the law I choose to do so in no obscure, insignificant, trivial manner. Mine was a crime against nothing less than the Federal Government. The officers who arrested me were no common, or garden, policemen, they were clothed with the authority of the Federal Constitution. I was charged with smoking a cigar within a Government reservation. In fact, I was caught red-handed. I came near setting a stone pile on fire.

"It is true that the arrest was not made effective. One of the party whispered to the marines what Governor Warfield was going to say, and did say, in introducing me to the audience at my lecture—that I was one of the greatest men in the world. I don't know who proposed to tell that to the marines, but it worked like a charm. The minions of the law faltered; hesitated, quailed, and today I am a free man. Twice they laid hands upon me; twice were overcome by my deserved reputation.

"Perhaps I ought not to say myself that it is deserved. But who am I to contradict the Governor of Maryland? Worm that I am, by what right should I traverse the declared opinion of that man of wisdom and judgment whom I have learned to admire and trust?

"I never admired him more than I did when he told my audience that they had with them the greatest man in the world. I believe that was his expression. I don't wish to undertake his sentiments, but I will go no further than that—at present. Why, it fairly warmed my heart. It almost made me glad to be there myself. I like good company.

"Speaking of greatness, it is curious how many grounds there are for great reputations—how many different phases, that is to say, greatness may take on. There was Bishop Potter. He was arrested a few months ago for a crime similar to mine, though he lacked the imagination to select United States Government property as the scene of his guilty deed. Now, Bishop Potter is a great man. I am sure he is, because a street car motorman told me so. A motorman is not a Governor of Maryland, but then Bishop Potter is not a humorist. He could hardly expect a certificate like mine.

"I rode with the motorman one day on the front seat of his car. There was a blockade before we got very far, and the motorman, having nothing to do, became talkative. 'Oh, yes,' he said, 'I have a good many distinguished men on this trip. Bishop Potter often rides with me. He likes the front seat. Now there's a great man for you, Bishop Potter.'

"'It is true,' I responded. 'Dr. Potter is indeed a mighty man of God, an erudite theologian, a wide administrator of his great diocese, an exegete of—'

"'Yes,' broke in the motorman, his face beaming with pleasure as he recognized the justice of my tribute and hastened to add one of his own. 'Yes, and he's the only man who rides with me who can spit in the slot every time.'

"That's a good story, isn't it? I like a good story well told. That is the reason I am sometimes forced to tell them myself. Here is one of which I was reminded yesterday as I was investigating the Naval Academy. I was much impressed with the Naval Academy. I was all over it, and now it is all over me. I am full of the navy. I wanted to march with them on patrol, but they didn't think to ask me; curious inattention on their part, and I just ashore after a celebrated cruise. While I was observing the navy on land," said Mr. Clemens, "I thought of the navy at sea and of this story, so pathetic, so sweet, so really touching. This is one of my pet stories. Something in its delicacy, refinement, and the elusiveness of its humor fits my own quiet tastes.

"The time is 2 a.m., after a lively night at the club. The scene is in front of his house. The house is swaying and lurching to and fro. He has succeeded in navigating from the club, but how is he going to get aboard this rolling, tossing thing? He watches the steps go back and forth, up and down. Then he makes a desperate resolve, braces himself, and as the steps come around he jumps, clutches the handrail, gets aboard, and pulls himself safely up on the piazza. With a like manœuvre he gets through the door. Watching his chance, he gains the lowest step of the inside staircase, and painfully makes his way up the swaying and uncertain structure. He has almost reached the top when in a sudden lurch he catches his toe and falls back, rolling to the bottom. At this moment his wife, rushing out into the upper hall, hears coming up from the darkness below, from the discomfited figure sprawled on the floor with his arms around the newel post, this fervent, appropriate, and pious ejaculation, 'God help the poor sailors out at sea.' . . .

"I trust this matter of my arrest will not cause my friends to turn from me. It is true that, no matter what may be said of American public morals, the private morals of Americans as a whole are exceptionally good. I do not mean to say that in their private lives all Americans are faultless. . . . I am not perfect myself. I confess it. I would have confessed it before the lamentable event of yesterday. For that was not the first time I ever did wrong. No; I have done several things which fill my soul now with regret and contrition.

"I remember, I remember, it so well. I remember it as if it were yesterday, the first time I ever stole a watermelon. Yes, the first time.

"At least I think it was the first time, or along about there. It was, it was, must have been, about 1848, when I was 13 or 14 years old. I remember that watermelon well. I can almost taste it now.

"Yes, I stole it. Yet why use so harsh a word? It was the biggest of the load on a farmer's wagon standing in the gutter in the old town of Hannibal, Missouri. While the farmer was busy with another—another customer, I withdrew this melon. Yes, 'I stole' is too strong. I extracted it. I retired it from circulation. And I myself retired with it.

"The place to which the watermelon and I retired was a lumber yard. I knew a nice, quiet alley between the sweet-smelling planks and to that sequestered spot I carried the melon. Indulging a few moments' contemplation of its freckled rind, I broke it open with a stone, a rock, a dornick, in boy's language.

"It was green—impossibly, hopelessly green. I do not know why this circumstance should have affected me, but it did. It affected me deeply. It altered for me the moral values of the universe. It wrought in me a moral revolution. I began to reflect. Now, reflection is the beginning of reform. There can be no reform without reflection—

"I asked myself what course of conduct I should pursue. What would conscience dictate? What should a high-minded young man do after retiring a green watermelon? What would George Washington do? Now was the time for all the lessons inculcated at Sunday School to act.

"And they did act. The word that came to me was 'restitution.' Obviously, there lay the path of duty. I reasoned with myself. I labored. At last I was fully resolved. 'I'll do it,' said I. 'I'll take him back his old melon.' Not many boys would have been heroic, would so clearly have seen the right and so sternly have resolved to do it. The moment I reached that resolution I felt a strange uplift. One always feels an uplift when he turns from wrong to righteousness. I arose, spiritually strengthened, renewed and refreshed, and in the strength of that refreshment carried back the watermelon—that is, I carried back what was left of it—and made him give me a ripe one.

"But I had a duty toward that farmer, as well as to myself. I was as severe on him as the circumstances deserved: I did not spare him: I told him he ought to be ashamed of himself giving his—his customers green melons. And he was ashamed. He said he was. He said he felt as badly about it as I did. In this he was mistaken. He hadn't eaten any of the melon. I told him that the one instance was bad enough, but asked him to consider what would become of him if this should become a habit with him. I pictured his future. And I saved him. He thanked me and promised to do better.

"We should always labor thus with those who have taken the wrong road. Very likely this was the farmer's first false step. He had not gone far, but he had put his foot on the downward incline. Happily, at this moment a friend appeared—a friend who stretched out a helping hand and held him back. Others might have hesitated, have shrunk from speaking to him of his error. I did not hesitate nor shrink. And it is one of the gratifications of my life that I can look back on what I did for that man in his hour of need.

"The blessing came. He went home with a bright face to his rejoicing wife and I—I got a ripe melon. I trust it was with him as it was with me. Reform with me was no transient emotion, no passing episode, no Philadelphia uprising. It was permanent. Since that day I have never stolen a water—never stolen a green watermelon."

## "Mark Twain's Departs"
### *Baltimore Sun*, 12 May 1907, p. 20

Mr Samuel L. Clemens . . . left for New York yesterday. . . . The last place visited, save for a brief stop at the Governor's office, was to the Sun Building. The surroundings seemed to awake a flood of memories, and he grew eloquent in contrasting the most modern of newspaper establishments with those he had known.

"My, what an evolution!" he exclaimed. "Just think of the old *New York Tribune* editorial compartments in contrast with this! Peanut-stand

editorial accommodations were the idea in those days, it seems to me—
the least possible comfort in the least possible space, with the utmost
amount of dirt and confusion."

Of the editorial rooms and library he said: "This is a sanctuary, not
a sanctum. Beautiful! fine! I even believe I could even write something
good in here myself!"

Passing through the spacious business office and up the marble
stairway, Mr. Clemens had expressed his admiration at almost every
step. . . . Mr. Clemens' eye was attracted by an oil painting in which a
slice of watermelon almost gleams in its crispness.

"Let me see that first," he exclaimed. "Doesn't it look lifelike and
luscious! You cannot get any watermelon fit to eat north of Mason
and Dixon's line. Anywhere else it is either spoiled by ripening after
being plucked immaturely or by the effects of exportation after ripening
properly on the vine. Once in India I one time ate a piece of fairly good
melon. But the Southern watermelon on its native heath is the only real
thing in that line."

Just then the visitor seemed to miss something necessary to his
comfort. Those about him remembered that smoking is his favorite
diversion and the one almost unchangeable rule in the Sun Building. "No
Smoking Permitted" was suspended. Among all the thousands of guests
who have visited the new building—Governors, Senators, the Cardinal,
prelates, and citizens—no one had smoked in the main portion of the
building. By proclamation of Governor Warfield, who was personally
escorting him, the law was waived in favor of Mr. Clemens. With a
word of thanks for the unusual privilege, and a smile, he produced a long
cigar and was soon blowing out wreathes of smoke, christening the new
Sun Building with the incense of St. Nicotine.

Laying off his gray overcoat, he threw his leg over a desk, and seated
upon the flat top, breathed the balm of contentment. He was enjoying
himself. He wasn't being bored or wearied or lionized. . . .

"I guess I am beyond dispute the oldest journalist in the country,
for ever since the time I first began the business with my little paper
at Hannibal, Missouri, I have been in newspaper work, with scarcely

any interval whatever, in one form or another—if not actively writing or making material for the press, then figuring in interviews or as the subject of newspaper comment."

"I was reared on Tom Sawyer and Huckleberry Finn," said one of those present. "Were they real boys of your own boyhood acquaintance?"

. . .

"I never deliberately sat down and 'created' a character in my life. I begin to write incidents out of real life. One of the persons I write about begins to talk this way and one another, and pretty soon I find that these creatures of the imagination have developed into characters, and have for me a distinct personality. These are not 'made.' They just grow naturally out of the subject. That was the way Tom Sawyer, Huck Finn, and other characters come to exist. I couldn't to save my life deliberately sit down and plan out a character according to diagram. In fact, every book I ever wrote just wrote itself. I am really too lazy to sit down and plan and fret to 'create' a 'character.' If anybody wants any character 'creating,' they will have to go somewhere else for it. I'm not in the market for that. It's too much like industry."

Turning to Miss Isabel Lyon, his secretary, one of the group remarked: "I expect he doesn't mean half of that, does he? He is industrious enough when he has to be, isn't he?"

"Oh, I wish you could see him," she replied, "and see the tremendous pile of manuscript he has produced. It is simply marvelous.

"But there do come times when he winds a thing up that he is working on; won't go any further; just simply stops and puts it by. I remember when he was dictating the manuscript of 'Eve's Diary' we found one day that he had apparently concluded it 'Oh, don't stop,' I exclaimed. 'Do let her say some more.' 'No, no,' he responded, with a wave of his hand. 'That is all of it.' I persisted, and then he said he would see how matters were in the morning. The next morning he came in from the porch after smoking a cigar and I started at him, with pencil and notebook in hand ready for action, only to be met with another wave of his hand, this time in all positiveness, and the exclamation, 'No, no more! Eve hasn't spoken.'"

# Oxford

## June 9 1907–July 23 1907

The greatest honor Mark Twain received during his life was his receipt of an honorary Litt.D. conferred by Oxford University on 26 June 1907. He sailed from New York on June 8, and while in England he played well the part of literary lion. A gaggle of reporters met him literally on the gangplank upon his return to New York on July 22.

### "Mark Twain Sails; Shiest Man Aboard"
*New York American*, 9 June 1907, 1, 3

Mark Twain sailed on the Atlantic Transport Liner *Minneapolis* yesterday for what he said was probably the last trip he would make to London from this sphere. . . .

As soon as Mr. Clemens went on deck he took a cigar from his overcoat pocket and carefully peeled off its several wrappers. There was a smile of anticipation on his face, until he found the crowd had broken it.

"There," he said. "Just for that I will not smoke a cigar on the whole voyage."

Two minutes later he slipped away from his friends and searched out the deck steward.

"Get me the blackest cigar you have," he said.

As the ship slipped from the dock he was seen lighting it and his

Mark Twain and British reporters aboard the *Minneapolis* after docking at
Tilbury, London, 18 June 1907.
Courtesy of the Mark Twain House, Hartford, Connecticut.

smile returned and expanded with each puff.

"I am going to Oxford University to receive the degree of Doctor
of Literature on June 26, and shall spend two days in London before I
return," he said. "I am booked to come back on this same ship on June
29, that is, I expect to return then. But you never can tell. I lived eight
years in London and the boys there may tempt me to stay longer. I do
not know what they will do with me.

"However, I shall do my part. I am always ready to take my proper
share of dissipation to teach other people how to be better than I am
myself.

"I have given up all work, you know. I did so on my seventieth
birthday and that was so long ago I have almost forgotten it. Now my
idleness consists in dictating two hours a day for five days a week. I am
writing my autobiography, and it is not to be published until I am well
and thoroughly dead.

"It has in it all the caustic and fiendish and devilish things I want to say. It will be many volumes, I cannot say how many, because that depends on how long I live.

"It is not to appear until the people in it are dead and their children and their grandchildren also. I would hate so to hurt anybody's feelings. In fact, it will not appear in print until I am canonized."

## "Mark Twain on the Secrets of Youth"
### London *Leader*, 19 June 1907, p. 1

. . . Mark Twain . . . delivered himself body and soul to the *Morning Leader* representative and the other interviewers, and, resting his back on the iron bulwarks of the boat, he chatted to the group of them in a playful fashion—hardly ever serious for a moment. . . .

Before he had finished greeting the journalists a donkey-engine, not half a dozen yards away, set up a fearful clatter. The humorist's eye twinkled as he noticed the interviewers straining their ears to catch his words amid the roar and rattle, and he poked a little fun at them.

"Do you object to being placed with the *other* donkey-engines?" asked Mark, in tones of simulated sympathy. The journalists laughed at their own expense, and persuaded the humorist to lead them to a quieter corner of the boat.

With the inevitable cigar in his mouth, he confided (in a hushed whisper) that this visit is only a "preliminary vacation necessary before my funeral."

"Funeral!" gasped one of the audience, horror-stricken.

"Yes, funeral," replied Mark Twain, with mock gravity. "I'm making arrangements for my funeral now. I'm inviting hosts of people—it's a friendly sort of thing to do, don't you think?"

The palmists and fortune-tellers, he explained, told him recently that he was to die. "And as it's going to be a nice, large, showy funeral, one that will attract attention in the newspapers, I've got to hurry up and arrange for it. A little early, you think? Well, all the better. We shall be able to have a rehearsal."

Someone asked him to outline the program, and he boldly launched out on the task. "I hope the procession will be about five miles long! There'll be brass bands by the score—say, a brass band every 50 yards, and every one of 'em playing a different tune! It ought to be one of the greatest things ever seen!" Again he laughed at the prospect.

The Oxford Pageant, which Mr. Clemens is determined to attend—though it means lengthening his stay beyond his original intentions—is to supply him with some ideas for his funeral. "We haven't settled the time or the place of the funeral yet," he confessed to the disappointed interviewers, all athirst for hints; "but the American fortune-tellers say I'm going to die in a foreign land—it may be in New Jersey." . . .

The famous White Suit came out of the wardrobe on the voyage. "I wore it three days on the boat," confessed the humorist to the *Morning Leader* representative, "but I'm not intending to wear it in London. This white suit stands for a Purity Campaign," said he. "I am that Purity Campaign. I'm the only one in it—in fact, I'm the only one who's eligible!"

He is not fond of globe-trotting, he declared. Out of all his 37 voyages to different parts of the world, only two voyages has he taken from absolute free choice.

"Do you hope to come to England again?" asked the *Morning Leader* interviewer.

"Not unless I come over to take another degree," replied the humorist. "For such distinction one would be willing to walk two or three thousand miles."

At present busy with his autobiography, and having already written "The Diary of Adam and Eve," he is not contemplating at the moment the publication of more family history such as "The Diary of Cain and Abel."

"Cain is a delicate subject to handle," he said confidentially. "You see, Cain was one of my ancestors. You here may be descendants of the other branch, but we in the family never speak of that branch! Our side of the family began with murder and quiet assassination, and then descended into quiet theft and burglary, and things of that sort, but it got a bit too noticeable, and the family became noted for piety—which is always a characteristic of the family, even yet!"

Though a big reader (especially of books that he has read before and forgotten), he does not read novels; he does not like the phonograph, because it lacks expression, and because you can hear it "grating its teeth" when it talks; and he believes that he owes the fact that he feels only 14 years old, instead of 72, to his habit of taking plenty of rest and spending plenty of time in bed, even in the middle of the day.

"How many cigars do you smoke a day?" asked someone.

"As many as I can—one at a time as a rule," came the answer, almost before the question was finished.

## "Mark Twain in London"
### *Westminster Gazette*, 18 June 1907, p. 7

Mark Twain arrived in London this morning. . . . An incident of interest, but wholly accidental, occurred at the railway station. Among the few persons parading the platform was Mr. George Bernard Shaw, who was surprised to learn from a Pressman that, traveling in the train whose arrival he was awaiting, was Mark Twain. Mr. Shaw responded to an invitation to express an opinion on the great humorist. "He is by far the greatest American writer. America has two great literary assets—Edgar Allan Poe and Mark Twain. I understand Americans do not say much about Edgar Allan Poe. Mark Twain does not give you the chance of ignoring him." . . .

Mr. Clemens was immediately surrounded by a crowd of ladies on stepping on to the platform. He was dressed in a smart grey suit and bowler hat, and he chatted very cheerily.

Speaking to a Central News representative, he said he had come over for an Oxford degree. He would not say anything on the State subject of Anglo-American relations. "It is ancient; there is no vitality in it. The relations have been long established."

"Do you know that Mr. George Bernard Shaw is on the platform, Mr. Clemens?"

"Oh! Is he? I want to see him."

"Then you don't know him?"

"No, I have never met him," answered Mr. Clemens.

"Would you express an opinion on Mr. Shaw?"

"No," was the reply. "I never give an opinion unless I have studied the matter. I only give an opinion on my own deductions, and not somebody else's."

Mr. Clemens said he would stay in England for about a fortnight. He wanted to see the processions at Oxford.

"What do you think of these great pageants?"

"I have never seen one."

"But what do you think of the idea?"

"Oh! the idea is excellent."

"Don't you have them in America at all?"

"Why, yes," he replied. "In 1876, you know, they had a series at the 100th anniversary of the Declaration of Independence; and then, just as it happened here, any town or place that had some events in its history that connected it with the American Revolution all followed, one after the other. That was in our 100th year, but you are in your thousands. It is good, you know, to revive history and impress the people. It does not take us long, for there is not much of it; but you have got to concentrate in six days the history of a thousand years."

To a question whether he was at present engaged in another work, Mr. Clemens replied: "No; I have not written for two years; but I do dictate autobiography for one or two hours a day on five days a week, and that is sufficient to keep me alive and the blood circulating."

"When do you expect to finish that work?"

"Just when they send for the undertaker, and not sooner!"

"To judge from appearances, that time is a long way off," said the interviewer. "I don't know about that," replied the humorist, with a shake of the head; "all the palmists and clairvoyants tell me I am going to die, but they don't state any date."

At this point "G. B. S." came walking down the platform, and the distinguished pair were introduced. "Do you know," said Mr. Shaw, "these Pressmen were asking me before the train came in if I thought you were really serious in writing 'The Jumping Frog,'" and both laughed heartily.

"I answered for you," said "G. B. S.," "and I gave the correct answer."

## "Mark Twain Again Meets His Former Chum Edward"
### *New York American*, 23 June 1907, pp. 1–2

Mark Twain has renewed his acquaintance with King Edward.... Mark Twain wrote in a magazine a dozen years ago how he first met King Edward. "We were going down Piccadilly," he wrote; "the then Prince of Wales was riding in a State chariot at the head of a procession, going to some State function. I was on top of a bus. Our eyes met, and at that moment I felt that the Prince and I understood one another, that our souls were one."

Mark Twain said today that this incident is true, and he gave this very interesting sequel: "I really met the King for the first time at Homburg ten years ago. He was traveling incognito as the Duke of something or other. He was taking the baths, and an Englishman well up in the diplomatic circle who knew me asked me if I wouldn't be presented. I said 'Sure,' and he took me up to the Prince, who was sitting with one or two friends chatting and drinking at a café table.

"The Prince began to chat with me as glibly and familiarly as though he had known me for years. I was enjoying myself hugely, as you always do, you know, when you meet somebody that you can really treat as your equal. Presently the Prince asked me if I did not feel like taking a little stroll in the Park. 'Sure,' I said, and we strolled out and spent about half an hour in the park near the baths. I think he talked about every subject in the world except the most interesting one in the world—myself, and at parting he said, with a warm clasp of the hand, 'I am really delighted to have met you again.'...

I said to him, 'But your Royal Highness, I never had the pleasure of meeting you before. Your Highness has mistaken me for'—The Prince interrupted: 'I am afraid,' he said, 'that I have a better memory than you. Is it possible that you have forgotten our meeting in Piccadilly?'

"The Prince had read that old magazine article and had not forgotten it."

Mark Twain, who wore the regulation frock coat and silk hat, was the center of attraction at the garden party at Windsor this afternoon.... After tea, which was served on the lawns, Ambassador Reid presented Mark Twain to King Edward and Queen Alexandra, and the King and the humorist spent a quarter of an hour in conversation, the King laughing heartily at Twain's jokes. The Queen also joined in the conversation, and was much amused when Twain jokingly asked if he could buy the Windsor Castle grounds from Her Majesty....

After his interview with the Royal Party, Mark Twain said: "I think the Queen looks as young and beautiful as she did thirty-five years ago, when I saw her first. I didn't say this to her, because I learned long ago never to say an obvious thing. That she still looks to me as young and beautiful as she looked thirty-five years ago is good evidence that ten thousand people have noticed this and have mentioned it to her. I have kept the remark unuttered, and that has saved Her Majesty the vexation of hearing it for the ten thousandth and one time.

"All that report about my proposal to buy Windsor Castle and its grounds is a false rumor—I started it myself."

## "Mark Twain for Penny Post"
### New York *Sun*, 2 July 1907, p. 2

...Mr. Clemens is full of his Oxford experience. He relates one amusing mistaken impression which he obtained on the evening of his arrival at Oxford. His host said: "Come to Jesus?" Mark says: "I thought I was in

Cartoon showing Mark Twain in his bathrobe, from *New York American,*
22 June 1907, 6.

With Dorothy Quick at Tuxedo Park in early August 1907.
Courtesy of the Mark Twain Project, University of California, Berkeley.

for a revival meeting or something of that sort, but, being polite, I made no objections. Nevertheless, it was a great relief to find that my host meant Jesus College, where I had a mighty fine time."

## "Twain Home with English Jokes at 30 Cents a Word"
*New York American*, 23 July 1907, p. 5

. . . *The American* reporter who boarded the *Minnetonka* at Quarantine found the humorist in one of his famous white suits, sprawled on a steamer chair, gazing at the Staten Island shore.

"I was looking for the first mosquito," he pouted. "Not one to welcome me."

"What do you think of America?" was the first question.

"Ask my keeper," said Mark Twain, indicating little nine-year-old Dorothy Quick, of Plainfield, N.J., who adopted her distinguished fellow passenger the first afternoon out and guarded him closely during the voyage. She sat in his lap and leaned her head trustfully against his shoulder. "You can tell them," she consented, patting his cheek by way of encouragement.

"How do I like America?" repeated the humorist. "I don't know; I've been away six weeks. Now ask me what I think of the tall buildings."

"Suppose you tell us your latest joke instead," was suggested.

"I get thirty cents a word," he returned.

"Tell us one at night rates," was offered.

"No night rates on my jokes or cut rates either," said Mark Twain shrewdly. "It's thirty the word."...

"I met King Edward, all right," said Mr. Clemens. "He enjoyed it. But he wouldn't sell me Windsor! Fine place, that castle. Better than the bungalow I've been paying rent on out at Tuxedo. I'm going out there now, but I've been away so long I'll have to sit up nights to get even with the rent."...

"Have the British a sense of humor?" was one of the leading questions.

"They certainly have a humor," Dr. Twain answered promptly. . . . "King Edward told him a ripping joke, he said, a regular twister—but unfortunately he is saving it for thirty cents a word. It was a long joke, and he didn't think the reporters could buy it."...

"Don't you dread these reporter men?" asked little Miss Quick, who had stuck bravely to her post.

"No, my dear child," he smiled. "I've prepared myself for the next world."...

A long wicked looking scrape on the starboard side of the *Minnetonka,* a jagged hole and several bent plates told of her narrow escape in a fog by collision with an English bark. Mark Twain had reported the accident to *The American and Journal* by wireless. Asked why he turned reporter, he said: "The collision came at 6 in the morning. I had not left a call for that hour, but I went on deck. It turned out that I was too late for the collision, too late by several seconds. I wanted something to excuse my pink pajamas and bathrobe, so I turned reporter. "Do you know that, after hitting us that bark was different from any vessel I ever saw. It had the peculiarity that another ship wouldn't have. You couldn't tell her bow from her stern. You see, she had left us her bowsprit."

He was reminded that he had shocked London by crossing from his quarters in Brown's Hotel to the Bath Club in a bathrobe.

"Shocking! nothing," he said, shaking his shaggy white mane. "That was one of the privileges granted to one in his second childhood. Accumulated privileges form the chief advantage of old age. I'll be seventy-two in November. At 2 A.M. I feel every year of it, but at 8 in the morning, when I'm shaving, I feel twenty-five."

Mark Twain in his Oxford gown, c. 1907.
Courtesy of the Library of Congress.

# The Long Goodbye

## Oct 5 1907–May 1910

Lonely and depressed, Twain organized an "aquarium" of "angelfish," young girls with whom he regularly corresponded and who sometimes visited him. Twain moved into his last home, near Redding, Connecticut, in mid-1908. In a pique of anger and suspicion, he fired both his secretary, Isabel Lyon, and business manager, Ralph Ashcroft, in April 1909, persuaded by his daughter Clara that they had defrauded him in the construction of the house. Suffering from heart disease, Twain twice traveled to Bermuda in hopes of recovering his health.

### "A Prince of Humorists: Interview with 'Mark Twain'"
Isidore Harris, *Great Thoughts from Master Minds*,
5 October 1907, pp. 136–38

It is not easy at any time to secure an interview with Mark Twain. . . . He has denied himself to most interviewers ever since he reached the age of seventy. . . . All the same, the great humorist has not exactly retired. At the present time he is engaged in writing his autobiography. One of the most interesting chapters in this work will be the last, containing the experiences and impressions of his latest visit to England.

"Was your visit to England in 1897, on the occasion of the Diamond

Jubilee of the late Queen Victoria, the last time you visited this country?"
I asked.

"Not exactly. On that occasion I made a trip round the world, which occupied three years, and I returned to England. So I was here three years ago."

"And you have noted a good many changes that have come about in the appearance of things since that time?"

"Indeed I have. Seven years ago there were no motor-buses and motor-cars, and very few electric vehicles. Today people seem to ride nothing else. And, concurrently with this change, I have observed a noticeable absence of bicycles. When I was here before all sorts of people used bicycles. Even titled persons did not disdain them; but now, if they are used at all, it is only by the humbler classes. It has struck me also that London has been greatly altered and beautified in the meanwhile. The Strand, with the Kingsway thoroughfare, and the neighborhood of Pall Mall have been changed out of all recognition. New hotels and playhouses have sprung up, new thoroughfares and palatial public offices; vast series of flats have been erected, and, altogether, London is becoming a second Paris. Yesterday afternoon, being one of the few lovely days with which we have been favored of late, I drove out to Dollis Hill, which I used to know as the occasional summer residence of Mr. Gladstone. It has now become a public recreation-ground, but it struck me as being, if anything, more beautiful that it ever was. I have not had any occasion to go eastward into the City, so I am unable to say what changes have been made there."

"But you appear to have been almost everywhere?"

"I have done and seen a great deal. I have been to Windsor, where, as you know, I was received by the King and Queen. I have been to Oxford to receive my degree, by the right of which I am privileged to doctor the English literature as much as I please. "...

It will, probably, surprise many readers to learn that Mark Twain prefers to be considered as, before all things, a philosopher, and only secondarily as a humorist.... His polemic against Christian Science ... though humorously written, he regards as a serious piece of work. ...

Mark Twain does not even believe that *Science and Health* was written by Mrs. Eddy. "The known and undisputed products of her pen," he says, "are a formidable witness against her. I think she has been claiming as her own another person's book, and wearing, as her own property, laurels rightfully belonging to another person."

"Why has not that other person protested against such literary piracy?" I ask.

"Because her work was not exposed to print until after he was sagely dead." . . .

Speaking of *The Innocents Abroad*, Mark Twain assured me that this, one of his most humorous books, was taken so seriously by a prominent English journal when it first made its appearance that the review proved to be more deliciously funny than the book itself. The ingenious critic charged Mark Twain with displaying shocking ignorance and an utter disregard of truth. Now what the American writer had to say about his own country was both interesting and instructive, as, for instance, when he mentioned the quite new fact that in America the small farmers carry their farms away on wheelbarrows overnight to avoid paying the taxes! "I should think that was a new fact," said Mark Twain, "considering I made it up myself. And the reviewer took it for gospel truth, because it referred to America, which I was supposed to know all about.

"Nor was this writer alone in taking *The Innocents Abroad* seriously. The first time I visited England was in 1872. It was while I was riding up in the train from Liverpool to London, thoroughly enjoying the novel scenery, that I observed my fellow-passenger. He was so painfully absorbed in a book he was reading that he never once looked up. Curious to know what it was that could so take a man's attention to the exclusion of everything else, I looked over his shoulder and discovered that he was reading *The Innocents Abroad*. From that time I felt miserable. The man looked so solemn, and I had intended that book to make people laugh. Just as I wished that I was anywhere but sitting next to such a serious personage, the train slowed down. As we arrived at Crewe my fellow-passenger appeared to have reached the end of his volume. He put it in the rack and jumped out. Now, I thought, I should be able to resume the interrupted enjoyment of the scenery. But alas! presently he returned, reached into his handbag for the second volume, and all the way up to London he continued to read, but never smiled. Neither did I."

"Talking of humor," says Mark Twain, "there is no success in the literature of fun equal to what is attained by ignorant schoolchildren, without intention of being funny, in their heroic efforts to set forth hard facts and sober statistics. As, for instance, when a pupil sets forth the following meanings of words:—

*Amenable,* anything that is mean.
*Plagiarist,* a writer of plays.
*Equestrian,* one who asks questions.
*Mendacious,* what can be mended.
*Irrigate,* to make fun of.
*Emolument,* the headstone to a grave.
*Parasite,* a kind of umbrella.
*Tenacious,* ten acres of land.

"Or his knowledge of mathematics in this form:—

"A straight line is any distance between two places.
"Parallel lines are lines that can never meet until they run together.
"Things which are equal to each other are equal to anything else.
"A circle is a round straight line with a hole in the middle.

"Or his conceptions of geography thus:—

"The United States is quite a small country compared with some other countries, but is about as industrious.
"Russia is very cold and tyrannical.
"The two most famous volcanoes of Europe are Sodom and Gomorrah.
"Climate lasts all the time, and weather only a few days."

## "Mark Twain on the Scope of the Children's Theater"

Frederick Boyd Stevenson, *Brooklyn Eagle* news special,
24 November 1907, p. 1

"When I saw the performance of those children and heard the perfect rendition of the parts assigned to them," began Mark Twain, "one thing came uppermost in my mind: That was their perfect enunciation. . . .

"This fine enunciation of many of the young people of the East Side is due to the work of the Educational Alliance, and a great part of it is brought about by the training received at the Children's Theater, under the auspices of that organization. The work of this institution is one of the most remarkable educational developments in the country. Its influence has already spread throughout the lower East Side. I believe it will spread to all parts of the country and be universally adopted as an educational factor. . . .

"In this method of instruction you have the first incentive for obtaining knowledge—that is, personal interest. With that comes concentration and ambition to excel. It is not the theatrical idea that is aimed at. In fact, as Miss Herts, the manager of the theater, says, the idea of the theater as a profession is discouraged rather than encouraged. The scope of the movement is to interest these young people of the East Side in wholesome and classic dramas, to instill in them a love for good literature and a knowledge of the true motives of life. There is a great deal of the dramatic in the makeup of every human being. By the dramatic we can appeal to one's sympathies, to one's highest sentiments, to one's sense of justice and right and to one's ambition to progress. Not only are the mental attributes quickened by this method of instruction, but the esthetic attributes are developed also. . . . The improvement comes not only to the young people who take part in the plays, but extends to their families and friends. They rehearse their parts in the homes, and the plays become known to every one of the immediate family and acquaintances. So you see, this education is an education for all the people of the East Side.

"There is another point—perhaps it is the most important of all; yes, I am sure it is the most important," he continued slowly. "A point that we should all attend to—a point that America has good reason to attend to. . . . This chief point of importance," he said, "relates to citizenship."

Again he paused for just an instant. Then he said quickly, sharply: "Citizenship? We have none! In place of it we teach patriotism, which Samuel Johnson said a hundred and forty or a hundred and fifty years ago was the last refuge of the scoundrel—and I believe that he was right. I remember when I was a boy I heard repeated and repeated time and time again the phrase, 'My country, right or wrong, my country!' How absolutely absurd is such an idea. How absolutely absurd to teach this idea to the youth of the country."

He was speaking calmly and deliberately, but his voice showed the indignation that he felt.

"And this seems to be the sole idea of patriotism," he went on. "Not long ago I saw fifteen or more boys drilling. They assumed a military air, and went through the evolutions of trained soldiers. This was to teach them patriotism, but what incentive with our ideas of patriotism is there for the young man of today to shoulder his gun and fight for his country? I can imagine one situation—even under the present state of affairs—where a man could feel that he ought to fight for his country. That situation might be an invasion. In such a case a man should fight, but he should fight under protest, and for this reason: When a country is invaded it is because it has done some wrong to another country— some wrong like the United States did in taking the Philippines—a stain upon our flag that can never be effaced. Yet today in the public schools we teach our children to salute the flag, and this is our idea of instilling in them patriotism. And this so-called patriotism we mistake for citizenship; but if there is a stain on that flag it ought not to be honored, even if it is our flag. The true citizenship is to protect the flag from dishonor—to make it the emblem of a nation that is known to all nations as true and honest and honorable. And we should forever forget that old phase—'My country, right or wrong, my country.'" . . .

"It may be," he continued, "that we must learn our lessons of citizenship on the East Side in the Children's Theater. There the true principles of true life which mean true citizenship are being taught to those boys and girls who are to be the future citizens of America. First of all they are taught self-respect and confidence. They are taught that the true motives of life are to reach for the highest ideals. The dramas that they play have morals that tend toward this aim. And best of all, they are taught to act for themselves and to think for themselves. It is this self-thinking that goes to make up the true public opinion. We say we have public opinion in America. We have none. We only think second hand. How many of us are there today who know whether it is better for the country to have a tariff or free trade? The only opinions most of us have on this subject are the opinions derived second hand from certain men who seek to influence us to their way of thinking, and their way of thinking is generally in a direction that will subserve their own private ends or the ends of the party which they represent. So, you see, we have no citizenship, and our so-called patriotism is a patriotism that is employed for the benefit of political parties and is made a party cry.

"Now, then, is there a new cult forming on the East Side? Are we to learn what true citizenship means and what true patriotism means from this new cult? Is the beginning here to extend universally? For fourteen years Isidor Straus, the president of the Educational Alliance, has devoted himself to educating these future citizens. The Educational Alliance greets them at the steamship landing and from that time onward never loses track of them. Their morals are watched; they are educated in the practical things of life—the things that make for this very citizenship which we, as a nation, have lost. We have good reason to emulate these people of the East Side. They are reading our history and learning the great questions of America that we do not know and are not learning, and they are learning them first hand and are doing their own thinking." . . .

"Your life has been a busy one," I ventured. "The public owes much to you. But perhaps the most important work of your life is the work of helping this movement of the Children's Theater."

"It is the most important work of my life," he said emphatically.

## "Rival Jokesmiths Off for Bermuda"
New York *World*, 23 February 1908, p. 3

Mark Twain and his friend, H. H. Rogers, sailed on the *Bermudian* yesterday for Bermuda. Years ago Mark Twain warned "my young friend Harry Rogers to mend his ways" or he would "come to some bad end."

"I see we're discovered," said Mark Twain, when the reporters appeared. "That's what I get for being in bad company."

"You've got no edge on me," returned the Standard Oil's chief jester. "Some of my methods may be bad. The public says so, at least. But they're no worse than your jokes, Sam."

"Listen," said Mr. Twain. "I'll sell you a joke for a dollar and Rogers will sell you financial information for another dollar. I keep my jokes to sell, just as he keeps his knowledge on finance to sell."

"I'm going because Mark is paying my fare," said Mr. Rogers. "I'm broke again."

"Yes; I'm paying his fare, but I'm $2 shy," said the other. "I'm going to shake him down for that $2 when we get out to sea."

"That's one of his jokes," returned Mr. Rogers, "but it isn't worth $2, is it? My picture? I'll pose, but only on condition that Twain will promise not to pick the photographer's pocket when the cloth is over his head."

"I'm rather particular about who poses with me," drawled Mark Twain between puffs at his cigar. "Of course it will be a step down to pose with Rogers, but I suppose I'll have to take a couple of steps down like that before I die. Rogers usually has his picture taken up in Mulberry street, but—well, I'll submit."

"That kind of financiering is too high for me," said the author.

"I'm as near to you as I want to stand," remarked Mr. Rogers.

"I'm really going along to keep Rogers straight," said Mr. Twain in a stage whisper.

## "Mark Twain Faced 2 Perils"

*New York American*, 14 April 1908, p. 3

After an escape from being washed overboard while gallantly showing a young lady how a log works at the taffrail of the Quebec steamship *Bermudian*, Mark Twain with his friend H. H. Rogers, arrived from Bermuda yesterday. . . . Miss Dorothy Sturgis of Boston is the young woman who had the honor of being drenched with the world-famous humorist. . . . The ship was pitching heavily. Mr. Clemens and Miss Sturgis were watching the revolving of the little wheel that tells how fast the ship is going.

Suddenly and without warning a huge wave came up from behind the ship and the two were engulfed in it. The young lady was lightly dressed and Mark Twain had on his famous white suit. When the water receded and they could be seen again they looked as if they had been in swimming.

The humorist, in speaking of the incident yesterday, said: "Miss Sturgis, being from Boston, is always in the swim, but at my time of life I have lost interest in surprise parties. I prefer something more formal than a slap in the back, even from my old friend Neptune."

Continuing, Mr. Clemens said: "My other old friend, Rogers, has improved very much as a result of our trip. He is not any heavier, but he takes more interest in life and is rather steadier on his feet than when he went away. Financially he is just as bad as ever. I had to help him out repeatedly. At one time I was so careless as to offer to lend him $2. He did not take me up, so I am in $2, but it was a terrible risk.

"Yes, it is true I have joined the anti-noise society. Having made all the noise I could, and getting tired of it, I have decided that nobody else is to make any at all hereafter. I have given up the lecture platform and banquets, and now everybody else has got to be still. Mrs. Rice came to me just at the proper moment. The anti-noise society is an excellent thing. I am going to be quiet hereafter and so must everybody else."

## "Mark Twain Their Guest"
### Baltimore Sun, 11 June 1909, p. 13

His eyes twinkling, the inevitable long cigar clenched between his teeth and with a springy step that belied his 73½ years, Samuel L. Clemens, who likes to be called Mark Twain, jumped into an automobile yesterday morning in front of the Belvedere Hotel and went to see his "granddaughter," Miss Frances Nunnally of Atlanta, graduated at the commencement of St. Timothy's School at Catonsville. . . . Mr. Clemens made the long journey from his home in Redding, Conn., with Mr. Albert Bigelow Paine, a biographer and novelist and close friend of the great humorist, just to hand Miss Nunnally her diploma and incidentally tell the other five graduates some things they should avoid in after life. . . .

"I don't know what to tell you girls to do," said Mr. Clemens, "[but] I must give you some don'ts.

"There are three things that come to my mind, which I consider excellent advice. First, girls, don't smoke—to excess. I am 73½ years old and have been smoking 73 of them. But I never smoke to excess—that is, I smoke in moderation, only one cigar at a time. Also, never drink—to excess."

The third admonition—"don't marry—to excess"—created much amusement among the newly qualified alumnæ, the students, and the audience.

## "Mark Twain's Smokes"
### Danbury, Conn., Evening News, 3 August 1909, p. 6

Mark Twain, who has been known for years as an inveterate and incessant smoker, has had to reduce his smokes to four a day, by the order of his physician. This is one of the means by which he is with the aid of the physician combating a heart trouble with which he has been afflicted for two months or more, he told a reporter of *The News* who called upon him at his country home yesterday afternoon. . . .

He was seated in the loggia of his Redding home, reading one of the late magazines and enjoying what was probably a third smoke of the four smokes a day which he is allowed. . . .

"In fact I did quit entirely for a time," said Dr. Clemens, "but the doctor said that was not necessary. The object would be accomplished just as easily with not more than four smokes a day. And I am not sure but there is just as much pleasure to be derived from the four smokes as from forty, in the more complete enjoyment of the four and the delight of anticipating the approach of the time for one of the smokes."

Dr. Clemens said that he was not able to walk three hundred yards or to take a couple of extra smokes in a day without paying the penalty in a severe pain in his heart. The humorist spoke quite whimsically of the fact that he had lived almost seventy-four years in the belief that a man could smoke any time or all the time without any injury to his health, only to have that belief shattered at last by the condition in which he now found himself.

## "Mark Twain Feeling Blue"
### New York *Sun,* 21 December 1909, p. 5

Mark Twain, who has been a month in Bermuda, where he celebrated his seventy-fourth birthday on November 30, returned yesterday by the Quebec Line steamship *Bermudian* somewhat out of sorts physically and even disinclined to jest. . . .

"I have spent most of my time in Bermuda riding," said Mr. Clemens. "I am getting too old to play golf and tennis and I have not the inclination to do much work. When I got down to Bermuda that pain in the breast left me; now, on my return, I have got it again. I have five or six unfinished tasks, including my autobiography, and I do not know when I will finish them. I have done almost nothing in the last three years. I may take up my autobiography again in a few weeks. I have already published 100,000 words and expect to have 500,000 published, most after I am dead." . . .

He had this to say about woman suffrage: "I not only advocate it now, but have advocated it earnestly for the last fifty years. As to the militant suffragettes I have noted that many women believe in the militant methods. You might advocate one way of securing rights and I might advocate another, and they both might help to bring about the result desired. To win freedom always involves hard fighting. I believe in the women doing what they deem necessary to secure their rights."

Mr. Clemens said he had been invited to lecture on women suffrage by women's organizations. They knew where he stood on the matter. "I cannot oblige them," he said, putting his hand over his left breast; "I am troubled too much here. I would not have the strength to deliver a lecture. I won't lecture any more. My work is over in this life and this world."

## "Mark Twain Hastily Returns to Bermuda"
### New York *World*, 6 January 1910, p. 2

Mark Twain sailed again unexpectedly for Bermuda on the *Bermudian* yesterday for a four week's stay. . . .

On December 20 the humorist returned from Bermuda to celebrate Christmas with his daughter, Miss Jean Clemens, at his home in Redding, Conn. While preparing for the Christmas festivities Miss Clemens, who was subject to fainting spells, suddenly met her death, having been found on Christmas eve drowned in her bath.

It had not been Mark Twain's intention to go back to Bermuda before April, when his daughter was to have sailed with him. The pain in his left chest, he said yesterday, was still annoying, and he thought Bermuda was the best place for him.

"It is a digestive pain," said he, "and does not alarm me at all.

"Naturally I am not pessimistic; I certainly was not feeling pessimistic then, for I was returning to spend what I anticipated as a very merry Christmas. I had small idea of the blow which was soon to come.

"This is my only companion and solace," he added, holding up a long black cigar. "It is about all I care for now, and I have been warned about making it too constant a companion. I detest the idea of shaking him though, for he and myself have been companions such a long time."

## "Mark Twain at Bermuda"
### Mildred Champagne, *Human Life*, 11 (May 1910), 15–16

...I walked around to the side of the veranda and paused in astonishment before a glass door. Through it I peered into the room. A white iron bed stood within three feet of the door, and upon it, full length and face downward, lay a familiar figure in a white linen suit, with a band of black crepe around his arm. . . . It was Mark Twain.

I knocked at the door very gently. . . . He rose hastily from the bed and came toward the door. A beautiful smile lit up his face, which I noticed at once was scarlet, almost livid, against its shaggy frame of silvery hair. His face looked small and pinched and ill. His frame was bent and his walk unsteady. He opened the glass door and with both hands extended he gave me a joyous welcome. . . . He shook my hands cordially and said in his kindest, most joyous way, "I'm so glad to see you. How do you do? Come right in. Let me take you right through to the parlor, and then I'll call the family."

"Oh, please don't call the family," I begged. "I haven't come to see the family. I've come to see you—only you."

And then, oh, Horrors! Instead of being, like the rest of mankind, pleased at this frank bit of flattery from a petticoat, Mark Twain's smile faded into a look of reserve and sadness, with perhaps a shade of annoyance. And then he started to cough, a miserable, nerve-racking cough that shook the whole of his slight frame and left him nervous and trembling and a trifle irritated. He held his hand on his chest.

"I don't see anybody," he said. "Nobody, nobody. I'm not—er—

extravagantly well. I—er—I bark, bark, bark all the time. I can't talk to anybody. Now, mind you, I didn't get this cough in Bermuda. Somebody kindly imported it for me from the United States."

I expressed my sympathy. He was sweet again and mollified.

"Have you seen the crystal cave yet?" he asked. "Or the aquarium?"

I said, "No. I came to see you first."

A sparkle of humor was in his keen, blue eyes.

"Well, you shouldn't have seen me first," he said quickly. "I run an opposition show to the Crystal Cave and the Aquarium. . . . I'm going to charge an admission fee. It's a shilling a look." He coughed again that terrible, racking cough that left him weak and gasping after each onslaught. "The price is going up—up—all—the time—," he continued weakly. "Tomorrow it will be two shillings—the next day—three—"

He raised his head and squared his shoulders. There was a faraway look in his eye. I felt a lump in my throat and my heart ached.

He took my hand again and smiled into my face.

"What has impressed you most on the island, besides myself?" he asked jocosely. I answered with a will, "A certain Englishman, who said to me, 'George'—er—George—yes, that was it—my word, yes—George— er—Let me see—what was the chap's last name—'Washington'—er— was it not? Yes—er—I believe it was Washington—or something. By the way, who was this—er—George Washington?'"

Mark Twain laughed and seemed to enjoy himself. . . .

Just then Mrs. Allen, wife of the vice-consul, rushed in upon us. Mark Twain is her especial care. She looked anxiously at us. His smile reassured her and we were introduced.

"I'm very glad I saw you," said Mark Twain, shaking my hands cordially. "I'll leave you now to Mrs. Allen. Good-bye, good-bye. Remember the Englishman was selling you. Good-bye."

He kissed his hands to me repeatedly and then receded within his own chamber and softly closed the door, leaving us in the parlor.

Again and again I heard him cough, as Mrs. Allen chatted pleasantly about the various points of interest on the island and about their own house, which she assured me was over two hundred years old. But all

I heard was that pitiful cough in the next room, and all I saw was that dear, familiar old face in its shaggy frame of silvery hair. . . .

I saw Mark Twain again before I left Bermuda. His face was paler than when I had first seen him and he was more composed. I inquired solicitously after his health and he thanked me.

"I am much better," he replied. "I suppose I am as well as could be expected of a man of my age and circumstances. Fairly well—but not extravagantly well—you understand. Not—extravagantly—well—"

He smiled sadly and waved his hand to me as I left him.

# Index

112